GADAMER AND THE LEGACY OF GERMAN IDEALISM

The philosophy of Hans-Georg Gadamer interests a wide audience that spans the traditional distinction between European (Continental) and Anglo-American (analytic) philosophy. Yet one of the most important and complex aspects of his work – his engagement with German Idealism – has received comparatively little attention. In this book, Kristin Gjesdal shows that Gadamer's engagement with Kant, Hegel, and Schleiermacher is integral to his conception of hermeneutics. She argues that a failure to take this aspect of Gadamer's philosophy into account leads to a misunderstanding of the most pressing problem of post-Heideggerian hermeneutics: the tension between the commitment to the self-criticism of reason, on the one hand, and the turn towards the meaning-constituting authority of tradition, on the other. Her study offers an illuminating assessment of both the merits and the limitations of Gadamer's thought.

KRISTIN GJESDAL is Assistant Professor of Philosophy, Temple University.

MODERN EUROPEAN PHILOSOPHY

General Editor

Robert B. Pippin, *University of Chicago*

Advisory Board

Gary Gutting, *University of Notre Dame*
Rolf-Peter Horstmann, *Humboldt University, Berlin*

Some recent titles

Daniel W. Conway: *Nietzsche's Dangerous Game*
John P. McCormick: *Carl Schmitt's Critique of Liberalism*
Frederick A. Olafson: *Heidegger and the Ground of Ethics*
Günter Zöller: *Fichte's Transcendental Philosophy*
Warren Breckman: *Marx, the Young Hegelians, and the Origins
of Radical Social Theory*
William Blattner: *Heidegger's Temporal Idealism*
Charles Griswold: *Adam Smith and the Virtues of Enlightenment*
Gary Gutting: *Pragmatic Liberalism and the Critique of Modernity*
Allen Wood: *Kant's Ethical Thought*
Karl Ameriks: *Kant and the Fate of Autonomy*
Alfredo Ferrarin: *Hegel and Aristotle*
Cristina Lafont: *Heidegger, Language, and World-Disclosure*
Nicholas Wolsterstorff: *Thomas Reid and the Story of Epistemology*
Daniel Dahlstrom: *Heidegger's Concept of Truth*
Michelle Grier: *Kant's Doctrine of Transcendental Illusion*
Henry Allison: *Kant's Theory of Taste*
Allen Speight: *Hegel, Literature, and the Problem of Agency*
J. M. Bernstein: *Adorno*
Will Dudley: *Hegel, Nietzsche, and Philosophy*
Taylor Carman: *Heidegger's Analytic*
Douglas Moggach: *The Philosophy and Politics of Bruno Bauer*
Rüdiger Bubner: *The Innovations of Idealism*
Jon Stewart: *Kierkegaard's Relations to Hegel Reconsidered*
Michael Quante: *Hegel's Concept of Action*
Wolfgang Detel: *Foucault and Classical Antiquity*
Robert M. Wallace: *Hegel's Philosophy of Reality, Freedom, and God*
Johanna Oksala: *Foucault on Freedom*

Wayne M. Martin: *Theories of Judgement*
Béatrice Longuenesse: *Kant on the Human Standpoint*
Otfried Höffe: *Kant's Cosmopolitan Theory of Law and Practice*
Béatrice Longuenesse: *Hegel's Critique of Metaphysics*
Rachel Zuckert: *Kant on Beauty and Biology*
Andrew Bowie: *Music, Philosophy and Modernity*
Paul Redding: *Analytic Philosophy and the Return of Hegelian Thought*

GADAMER AND THE LEGACY OF GERMAN IDEALISM

KRISTIN GJESDAL
Temple University

CAMBRIDGE
UNIVERSITY PRESS

CAMBRIDGE UNIVERSITY PRESS
Cambridge, New York, Melbourne, Madrid, Cape Town,
Singapore, São Paulo, Delhi, Tokyo, Mexico City

Cambridge University Press
The Edinburgh Building, Cambridge CB2 8RU, UK

Published in the United States of America by Cambridge University Press, New York

www.cambridge.org
Information on this title: www.cambridge.org/9781107404335

First published 2009
First paperback edition 2011

A catalogue record for this publication is available from the British Library

Library of Congress Cataloguing in Publication Data
Gjesdal, Kristin.
Gadamer and the legacy of German idealism / Kristin Gjesdal.
p.   cm. – (Modern European philosophy)
Includes bibliographical references (p. 219) and index.
ISBN 978-0-521-50964-0 (hardback)
1. Gadamer, Hans-Georg, 1900–2002. Wahrheit und Methode.   2. Idealism,
German.   3. Hermeneutics.   4. Aesthetics.   I. Title.   II. Series.
B3248.G33W3435 2009
193–dc22
2009008466

ISBN 978-0-521-50964-0 Hardback
ISBN 978-1-107-40433-5 Paperback

"Using Heidegger's analysis, my starting point was a critique of German Idealism and its Romantic traditions."

HANS-GEORG GADAMER,
"Reflections on my Philosophical Journey," 27.

CONTENTS

PREFACE

Over the past decade, Hans-Georg Gadamer's *Truth and Method* (1960) has enjoyed a renaissance. With its concern for the question of validity in interpretation, the so-called Gadamer–Habermas debate has faded into the background. So has the discussion between Gadamer and Derrida over the relationship between hermeneutics and deconstruction. When philosophers such as Richard Rorty, John McDowell, and Robert Brandom turn to Gadamer, it is in order to find support for the notions of *Bildung,* historicity, and the linguistic nature of reason.

While it offers new perspectives on Gadamer's work, the recent Anglophone reception overlooks how philosophical hermeneutics develops in critical interaction with German Idealism and its legacy in modern aesthetics and philosophy of art. Through a critical investigation of *Truth and Method,* the present study argues that Gadamer's engagement with Kant, Fichte, Hegel, and Schleiermacher is integral to his understanding of hermeneutic reason and that a failure to engage with this aspect of Gadamer's philosophy leads to a misunderstanding of the most pressing problem of post-Heideggerian hermeneutics: the tension between the commitment to the self-criticism of reason, on the one hand, and the turn towards the meaning-constituting authority of tradition, on the other. Arguing that Gadamer fundamentally misconstrues the legacy of German Idealism, this book proposes that this tension can only be overcome by a return to early nineteenth-century hermeneutics as it develops in the wake of the Enlightenment and Kant's critical philosophy.

ACKNOWLEDGEMENTS

I would like to thank Michael Forster for his ongoing encouragement, countless discussions on hermeneutics and German Idealism, and for carefully commenting on substantial parts of the manuscript. Over the past three years, I have benefitted from conversations on German philosophy and aesthetics with Paul Guyer. At the University of Oslo, Bjørn Ramberg has been – and still is – a generous yet critical sounding-board. Rudolf Makkreel, Joseph Margolis, Andrew Bowie, John Gibson, and Shelley Wilcox all read through and offered helpful comments on various parts of the manuscript. I thank Richard Eldridge and Stephen Houlgate for valuable criticism and suggestions. Most of all, however, my love and gratitude go to my husband, Espen Hammer, whose combination of patience, generosity, and critical readership has made an enormous difference.

The University of Oslo, the Norwegian Research Council, and the Fulbright Foundation have offered financial support for this project. I would like to thank Temple University for a Summer Research Grant and a Research Incentive Award, and the Center for Humanities at Temple for a Faculty Fellowship during 2007/2008.

Finally, I thank the following journals for permission to use material from my previously published essays: "Between Enlightenment and Romanticism: Some Problems and Challenges in Gadamer's Hermeneutics," *Journal of the History of Philosophy*, vol. 46, no. 2, 2008, 285–306; "Reading Kant Hermeneutically? Gadamer and the *Critique of Judgment*," *Kant-Studien*, no. 3, 2007, 351–371; "Aesthetic and Political Humanism: Gadamer on Herder, Schleiermacher, and the Origins of Modern Hermeneutics," *History of Philosophy Quarterly*, vol. 24, no. 3, 2007, 275–296; "Hermeneutics and Philology: A Reconsideration of Gadamer's Critique of Schleiermacher," *British Journal for the History of*

Philosophy, vol. 14, no. 1, 2006, 133–156; "Against the Myth of Aesthetic Presence: A Defense of Gadamer's Critique of Aesthetic Consciousness," *Journal of the British Society for Phenomenology*, vol. 36, no. 4, 2005, 293–311; "The Hermeneutic Impact of Hegel's Phenomenology," *Hegel-Studien*, no. 43, 2008.

ABBREVIATIONS

Works by Hans-Georg Gadamer:

DD   *Dialogue and Dialectic: Eight Hermeneutical Studies of Plato.* Ed. and trans. P. Christopher Smith. New Haven: Yale University Press, 1980.

GW   *Gesammelte Werke.* Tübingen: J.C.B. Mohr, 1985–1995.

HD   *Hegel's Dialectic: Five Hermeneutical Studies,* trans. P. Christopher Smith. New Haven: Yale University Press, 1976.

HDi   *Hegels Dialektik. Sechs hermeneutische Studien.* Tübingen: J. C. B. Mohr, 1980.

HsW   *Heidegger's Ways.* Trans. John W. Stanley. Albany, N.Y.: SUNY Press, 1994.

HW   *Heideggers Wege.* Tübingen: J.C.B. Mohr, 1983.

PDE   *Plato's Dialectical Ethics.* Trans. Robert M. Wallace. New Haven: Yale University Press, 1991.

PdE   *Platos dialektische Ethik. GW,* vol. V, 3–164.

PH   *Philosophical Hermeneutics.* Ed. and trans. David E. Linge. Berkeley: University of California Press, 1976.

RAS   *Reason in the Age of Science.* Trans. Frederick G. Lawrence. Cambridge, Mass.: MIT Press, 1981.

RB   *The Relevance of the Beautiful and Other Essays.* Ed. Robert Bernasconi. Trans. Nicholas Walker. Cambridge: Cambridge University Press, 1986.

TM   *Truth and Method.* Trans. Joel Weinsheimer and Donald G. Marshall. New York: Continuum, 1994.

WM   *Wahrheit und Methode.* 2 vols. *GW,* vols. I and II. (Unless otherwise noted, *WM* refers to vol. I of this work.)

Works on Hans-Georg Gadamer:

LLP   *The Philosophy of Hans-Georg Gadamer.* The Library of
Living Philosophers. Vol. XXIV. Ed. Lewis E. Hahn.
Chicago: Open Court, 1997.

Works by G. W. F. Hegel:

EiGP   *Einleitung in die Geschichte der Philosophie.* Ed. Johannes
Hoffmeister. Hamburg: Felix Meiner, 1940.

ILHP   *Introduction to the Lectures on the History of Philosophy.*
Trans. T. M. Knox and A. V. Miller. Oxford: Clarendon
Press, 1995.

LFA   *Aesthetics: Lectures on Fine Art.* 2 vols. Trans. T. M. Knox.
Oxford: Clarendon Press, 1975.

PhG   *Phänomenologie des Geistes. Werke in 20 Bänden.* Ed. Eva
Moldenhauer and Karl Markus Michel. Vol. III.
Frankfurt am Main: Suhrkamp Verlag, 1986.

PS   *Phenomenology of Spirit.* Trans. A. V. Miller. Oxford:
Oxford University Press, 1977.

VsK   *Vorlesungen über die Ästhetik.* 3 vols. *Werke in 20 Bänden.*
Ed. Eva Moldenhauer and Karl Markus Michel. Vols.
XIII, XIV, and XV. Frankfurt am Main: Suhrkamp
Verlag, 1986.

Works by Martin Heidegger:

BT   *Being and Time.* Trans. John Macquarrie and Edward
Robinson. San Francisco: Harper, 1962.

GA   *Gesamtausgabe.* Frankfurt am Main: Vittorio
Klostermann, 1975–.

N   *Nietzsche.* Trans. David F. Krell. 2 vols. San Francisco:
Harper, 1991.

Ni   *Nietzsche. Der Wille zur Macht als Kunst. GA,* vol. XLIII.

OWA   *The Origin of the Work of Art.* Trans. Albert Hofstadter. In
Poetry, Language, Thought. San Francisco: Harper, 1975,
15–87.

SZ   *Sein und Zeit.* Tübingen: Max Niemeyer Verlag, 1993.

UdK   *Der Ursprung des Kunstwerkes.* Stuttgart: Reclam, 1960.

Works by Immanuel Kant:

CJ   *Critique of Judgment.* Trans. Werner S. Pluhar.
Indianapolis: Hackett Publishing Company, 1987.

CPR   *Critique of Pure Reason.* Trans. Norman Kemp Smith.
             London: Macmillan, 1986.
KdrV   *Kritik der reinen Vernunft. Gesammelte Schriften.* Vol. III.
             Preussische Akademie der Wissenschaften. Berlin:
             Georg Reimer, 1911.
KdU   *Kritik der Urteilskraft. Gesammelte Schriften.* Vol. V.
             Preussische Akademie der Wissenschaften. Berlin:
             Georg Reimer, 1913.
KdU, First   "Erste Einleitung." *Gesammelte Schriften.* Vol. XX.
Introduction Preussische Akademie der Wissenschaften. Berlin:
             Georg Reimer, 1942.

Works by Friedrich Schleiermacher:
Ä   *Ästhetik (1819/25). Über den Begriff der Kunst (1831/32).*
             Ed. Thomas Lehnerer. Hamburg: Felix Meiner, 1984.
D   *Dialektik (1811).* Ed. Andreas Arndt. Hamburg: Felix
             Meiner, 1986.
Di   *Dialectic or, the Art of Doing Philosophy: A Study Edition of the
             1811 Notes.* Ed. and trans. Terrence N. Tice. Atlanta:
             Scholars Press, 1996.
E   *Ethik (1812/1813) mit späteren Fassungen der Einleitung,
             Güterlehre und Pflichtenlehre.* Ed. Hans-Joachim Birkner.
             Hamburg: Felix Meiner, 1990.
GdaP   *Geschichte der alten Philosophie.* Ed. Heinrich Ritter.
             Sämmtliche Werke, Dritte Abtheilung. Zur Philosophie.
             Zweiten Bandes erste Abtheilung. Berlin: G. Reimer,
             1839.
HC   *Hermeneutics and Criticism.* Ed. and trans. Andrew Bowie.
             Cambridge: Cambridge University Press, 1998.
HKi   *Hermeneutik. Nach den Handschriften.* Ed. Heinz
             Kimmerle. Heidelberg: Carl Winter, 1974.
HK   *Hermeneutics: The Handwritten Manuscripts.* Ed. Heinz
             Kimmerle. Trans. James Duke and Jack Forstman.
             Missoula: Scholars Press, 1977.
HuK   *Hermeneutik und Kritik.* Ed. Manfred Frank. Frankfurt am
             Main: Suhrkamp Verlag, 1993.

HV   "Die allgemeine Hermeneutik" (1809–1810). Ed.
Wolfgang Virmond. *Schleiermacher-Archiv*, Band I,
Teilband 2. Ed. H. Fisher, H.-J. Birkner, G. Ebling,
H. Kimmerle, and K.-V. Selge. Berlin: Walter de Gruyter,
1985, 1271–1310.

OR   *On Religion: Speeches to its Cultured Despisers.* Trans.
Richard Crouter. Cambridge: Cambridge University
Press, 1988.

ÜR   *Über die Religion. Reden an die Gebildeten unter ihren
Verächtern* (1799), KGA, vol. II, *Schriften aus der Berliner
Zeit 1796–1799*, ed. Günther Meckenstock.

KGA   *Kritische Gesamtausgabe.* Ed. Hermann Fischer, Ulrich
Barth, Konrad Cramer, Günter Meckenstock, Kurt-
Victor Selge *et al.* Berlin: Walter de Gruyter, 1983–

LPE   *Lectures on Philosophical Ethics.* Ed. Robert B. Louden,
trans. Louise Adey Huish. Cambridge: Cambridge
University Press, 2002.

MdÜ   "Über die verschiedenen Methoden des Übersetzens,"
KGA, Erste Abteilung, Schriften und Entwürfe, vol. XI,
Akademievorträge. Ed. Martin Rössler and Lars
Emersleben, 67–93.

T   "On the Different Methods of Translating." Trans. Susan
Bernofsky. In Lawrence Venuti (ed.), *The Translation
Studies Reader.* London: Routledge, 2002, 43–64.

INTRODUCTION

Since its publication in 1960, Hans-Georg Gadamer's *Truth and Method* has come to redefine the meaning of hermeneutics. In Gadamer's work, hermeneutics is no longer a methodological tool for classicists, theologians, or legal scholars but a fully fledged philosophical account of truth, meaning, and rationality. The reception of *Truth and Method* traverses the traditional distinction between Anglo-American and European philosophy. Over the past forty years or so, *Truth and Method* has been critiqued, discussed, and adopted in the work of Jürgen Habermas, Karl-Otto Apel, Ernst Tugendhat, Jacques Derrida, Charles Taylor, Paul Ricoeur, Donald Davidson, Richard Rorty, John McDowell, and Robert Brandom. Yet, in the reception of Gadamer's work, diverse and wide-spanning as it is, one aspect of his thinking is systematically left out: the relationship between hermeneutics and German Idealism. There are, to be sure, a number of studies of Gadamer's relation to Socrates, Plato, and Aristotle. There is also no shortage of works that examine Gadamer's indebtedness to his teacher, Martin Heidegger, or even his relation to Habermas and critical theory. His reading of Kant, Fichte, Schleiermacher, the romantics, and Hegel, however, has for the most part been left unvisited.

The present study argues that Gadamer's critique of German Idealism is integral to his hermeneutics. At the center of this critique is the idea that reason ought reflectively to investigate the epistemic, moral, political, and aesthetic norms with which it identifies. While Gadamer takes over from German Idealism the emphasis on the self-reflection of reason, he also claims that its idea of self-reflection is guilty of overlooking the situatedness of reason in history. In spite of promising insights, German Idealism, in its Kantian, Fichtean, and

1

Hegelian permutations, ends up being locked into what Gadamer speaks of as a Cartesian model of absolute self-reflection.

Under the influence of Heidegger's ontological turn, Gadamer sets out to overcome the shortcomings of German Idealism by exploring the idea of understanding as a "truth-happening" or "an event of being." He wishes to correct the picture of an autonomous, self-reflective subjectivity by presenting the interpreter's relation to tradition in light of a play into which he or she is passively drawn, and by committing to a notion of understanding as the experience of a world-disclosive truth that is ontologically prior to the critical-reflective capacities of the individual interpreter. In Gadamer's work, hermeneutics is no longer about the objective reconstruction of the meaning of the works of the past; tradition is instead seen, at a normative as well as a descriptive level, as a process of taking over (*aneignen*) and understanding oneself in light of the truths and insights conveyed by eminent texts.

As such, Gadamer's hermeneutics is not, as it has been perceived, primarily a critique of Cartesian epistemology or an attempt to carve out a notion of normativity that steers clear of the equally problematic alternatives of foundationalism and relativism. At stake, rather, is an endeavor to overcome the drift, in modern philosophy, towards an ahistorical understanding of ourselves and our cultural-intellectual surroundings, the tendency to see ourselves as cut off from tradition and to view tradition as irrelevant to the concerns and self-understanding of the present. To the extent that his philosophy criticizes the idea, espoused in the tradition from Schleiermacher to Dilthey, of a method in the humanities, this is not in order to develop an alternative epistemology for the humanities, but to leave behind the narrow epistemological approaches to the past and win back the thick, experiential richness that he associates with a truthful historical existence. According to Gadamer, this involves rehabilitating the notion of *Bildung* and taking seriously the possibility of self-understanding opened up by the eminent texts of tradition. This is why he takes the experience of world-disclosive art to be paradigmatic for the hermeneutic experience as such, and why *Truth and Method* begins with a discussion of the subjectivization of taste in Kant's *Critique of Judgment* and ends with a plea, developed through a discussion of classical art and the play-like structure of the hermeneutic experience, for stepping beyond the framework of German Idealism and its legacy.

However, by viewing the experience of art as paradigmatic for the hermeneutic situation, Gadamer ends up espousing an aestheticizing model of understanding. Even though the reader of *Truth and Method* might well endorse Gadamer's emphasis on the historicity of understanding and his wish to critique a naïve, Cartesian model of self-reflection, it is problematic to assume, as he does, that the experience of eminent texts can serve as the basis for an account of what it means to engage with tradition. Furthermore, no matter how sympathetic one is to the overall cause of Gadamer's work, the reader of *Truth and Method* is left wondering whether his notion of a hermeneutic truth-happening, taking the form of a demand, captured in the words of Rilke's famous poem, that the interpreter must change his or her life, really allows for the reflective-dialogical model of rationality that Gadamer posits as an alternative to the idea of rationality ensuing from the tradition of German Idealism. Gadamer's *Bildungs*-oriented account underestimates, downplays, and sometimes even masks the fact that tradition is not only a background against which the interpreter questions his or her prejudices, deepens self-understanding, and expands his or her experiential horizon, but is also a field where unwanted prejudices are segmented and sometimes even reinforced. Although Gadamer would not deny that tradition may shelter illegitimate prejudices and beliefs, his over-generalizing critique of method and reflective standards in interpretation prevents him from developing an adequate notion of normative issues in hermeneutics. His wish to keep tradition alive as a process of continuous application of the insights of the great works of the past makes him overlook the philological and philosophical difficulties of dealing with expressions from culturally or temporally distant eras – works that may be expressive of a set of questions or concerns that fundamentally differ from those of the interpreter and hence do not trigger existential-ontological self-understanding along the lines of Gadamer's thinking. In order to engage with texts from historically or culturally distant communities, these works must be recognized in their potential otherness. This process of recognition cannot be vouched for by a model which, like Gadamer's, places the main emphasis on the self-transformation that happens in the moment of applying the insights of the past within the horizon of the present. As it develops in the wake of Heidegger's critique of modern philosophy, Gadamer's hermeneutics addresses one particular prejudice, the modern tendency to abstract from the fundamental historicity of human existence, at the cost of overlooking a larger specter of hermeneutic problems and issues, including those of critique, reflection, and normativity in understanding.

To mend this situation, I recommend a return to the early nineteenth-century theory of interpretation. Within this tradition, as it develops in relative continuity with the philosophy of the Enlightenment, the hermeneutic experience is not viewed as a truth-happening that initiates a more authentic existence, but deals with the epistemological, ethical, and political challenges of understanding and interpreting the symbolic expressions that derive from temporally or culturally distant communities. In the philosophies of Herder, Schleiermacher, the Schlegels, Hegel, and the von Humboldts, we find, for the first time, the systematic articulation of the idea that languages and cultures are expressive of forms of life, so that an expansion of the field of understanding and interpretation is at the same time an expansion of the field of thinking, action, and self-reflection. Within the scope of early nineteenth-century hermeneutics, however, this expansion of horizons is not seen as the result of a happening of truth (*Wahrheitsgeschehen*) into which the interpreter is drawn, but as a process that requires philological and historical labor, as well as critical reflection on the prejudices that limit the interpreter's outlook.

Among the many representatives of early nineteenth-century hermeneutics, I have chosen to focus on the work of Friedrich Schleiermacher, whose philosophy of interpretation is given considerable attention in *Truth and Method*. In its sensitivity to cultural diversity, the plurality of historical cultures, and the problem of the individuality of the text (its being a unique expression of a given, linguistically mediated life-form), Schleiermacher's philosophy points the way towards an intellectually sound and philologically responsible theory of understanding and interpretation. The rationale of his hermeneutics rests not with its appeal to an immediate, self-transforming truth-happening in the encounter with tradition, but with the effort to overcome the obstacles of historical and cultural distance through working out a sustainable notion of normativity in interpretation. However, in Schleiermacher's work, such a notion of validity in understanding is not perceived as contrary to but, rather, emerges as a condition of possibility for a sustainable notion of *Bildung* and the enhanced self-understanding of the interpreter, as expounded in his *Dialektik* as well as his practical philosophy. If

Schleiermacher distinguishes between interpretation and application, this is not because he overlooks the way in which an interpreter may learn from, reject, or understand him- or herself in terms of the past, but because he finds that in order for something to be accepted or rejected it should first be understood.

My discussion of Gadamer's critique of German Idealism is divided into six chapters. Chapter 1 examines Gadamer's reading of Kant, focusing in particular on the relation between the *Critique of Judgment* and the *Critique of Pure Reason*. Gadamer's reading of Kant is more complex than it is often assumed to be. In *Truth and Method*, he argues that Kant's notion of knowledge leads to a subjectivization of art and beauty. However, even though Gadamer is critical of the subjectivization of taste in the *Critique of Judgment*, he finds that Kant's turn from taste and reflective judgment to the relationship between art and morality evokes a promising notion of the experience of art as a dialogical, hermeneutic encounter. According to Gadamer, however, Kant is not primarily interested in art but in natural beauty, and natural beauty entails no hermeneutic experience of this kind. Hence he ends up leaving behind the promising hermeneutic insights that he had been hinting at in the beginning of the third Critique. However, Gadamer's critique of Kant misses its target. Because Gadamer approaches Kant's treatment of natural beauty through the lens of artistic beauty, he overlooks how Kant's notion of natural beauty is intrinsically related to his notion of knowledge and empirical research within the natural sciences.

Even if Gadamer misunderstands Kant's third Critique, his reading paves the way for an important criticism of the romantic appeal to immediacy and pure aesthetic presence – or aesthetic consciousness, as Gadamer calls it. This criticism, as it grows out of Gadamer's review of the treatment of epistemological skepticism in post-Cartesian philosophy, is the subject of Chapter 2. Gadamer views aesthetic consciousness as a failed attempt to overcome the scientific orientations of modern philosophy. Aesthetic consciousness, he claims, celebrates art and aesthetic expression as the domains of subjectivity proper but fails to ask, as Gadamer himself wishes to, whether it is right to reserve the notion of truth to the procedures of scientific reason in the first place. Gadamer's critique of aesthetic consciousness entails an apt analysis of a drift in post-Kantian philosophy towards a model of immediacy and pure aesthetic presence. Yet his objections to romantic aesthetics are too coarse and sweeping. In his eagerness to expel every orientation towards immediacy and pure aesthetic presence, Gadamer fails to acknowledge that the romantics, in drawing on (Kantian) notions such as autonomy, individuality, and feeling, respond to the situation of art in modernity rather than hypostatizing a set of ahistorical and faulty aesthetic ideals.

Leaving behind the critique of Kant and aesthetic consciousness, Chapter 3 turns to Gadamer's own, hermeneutic conception of art and the relationship between aesthetic experience and hermeneutic reason. I discuss Gadamer's attempt to criticize the tradition of modern epistemology by completing the notion of truth as correspondence with the idea of truth as world disclosure. Gadamer, however, goes too far in his universalizing of the world-disclosive truth that he ascribes to art in particular. This hampers the historical as well as the systematic relevance of his model. From a historical point of view, Gadamer's notion of the world-disclosive truth of art leaves him ill-equipped to deal with practical, interpretative challenges within the tradition of modern as well as of pre-modern art. From a systematic point of view, his notion of a truth that is prior to critical judgment and reflection, a sublime and sudden event of being, represents a return to the old paradigm of immediacy that he himself had criticized so aptly throughout his reading of aesthetic consciousness.

Chapter 4 addresses the ramifications of Gadamer's failure to overcome aesthetic consciousness by going over his relation to the Enlightenment. Gadamer worries that the enlightenment paradigm in philosophy represses the historicity of reason and understanding, and thus falls prey to a prejudice against prejudice. However, even though Gadamer is critical of the putative ahistoricity of enlightenment thinking, he does not want to let go of the commitment to self-reflection and self-understanding. Rather, he wishes to rescue a notion of reflection, albeit one that is historically mediated. He finds such a notion in the work of Hegel. Yet Gadamer's appropriation of Hegel is not without problems. Whereas Hegel identifies with the Enlightenment and its focus on norms and questions of legitimacy, Gadamer, with his entire Heideggerian luggage, fails to distinguish between an epistemic and an existentialist notion of self-understanding. Art is taken to be paradigmatic for the hermeneutic experience precisely because the experience of the great works of tradition, with their world-disclosive authority, is ascribed a self-transformative dimension. Hence the right question with regard to Gadamer's hermeneutics is not, as Habermas, Apel, and Tugendhat suggest, whether it ends up simply rejecting the enlightenment commitment to a critical use of reason. Rather, the real question is to what extent his commitment to critical reflection can be squared with the way in which he takes the sublime and existentially challenging experience of art to be expressive of hermeneutic truth as such.

In Chapter 5, I discuss how Gadamer's failure to distinguish between epistemic and existential self-understanding influences his own work on historical texts. I address this issue by looking at Gadamer's account of Schleiermacher's theory of interpretation. Gadamer focuses on Schleiermacher's notion of individuality and his appeal to a method in interpretation. He argues that Schleiermacher offers an early version of hermeneutic positivism combined with a problematic aesthetic turn in the theory of interpretation. However, in his critique of early nineteenth-century hermeneutics, Gadamer fails to acknowledge that the fundamental difference between Schleiermacher's theory and his own is not that Schleiermacher is a hermeneutic positivist and Gadamer is not, but that Schleiermacher takes hermeneutics to be all about correct understanding of the symbolic expressions of the past, whereas Gadamer, modeling understanding on the paradigmatic case of art, takes it to be about a self-transformative, world-disclosive truth in the encounter with the great works of the tradition.

Chapter 6 sketches an alternative reading of early nineteenth-century hermeneutics and advocates a retrieval of post-Kantian hermeneutics and its concern for critical-normative standards in interpretation. I argue that although Schleiermacher is attentive to the need for such standards, he does not abstract from the interpreter's situatedness within a given, historical context. Instead, it is precisely because the interpreter is historically situated that a dimension of normativity is called for. Furthermore, Schleiermacher's hermeneutics, in being closely related to his theory of translation as well as his practical philosophy, allows for a notion of *Bildung* as well as the idea of the interpreter engaging in an ongoing expansion of his or her horizon. And if Schleiermacher does not believe in the idea of a dialogue between work and interpreter, he nonetheless emphasizes, in his dialectics, the intersubjective dimension of understanding. Rather than the discussion of the world-disclosive and sublime happening of the classical work, this – the tradition of early nineteenth-century philosophy – is where we need to look for a hermeneutics that may give rise to a philosophically relevant humanism. With its effort to combine a notion of historicity with a notion of normativity in understanding, it is this tradition, rather than Gadamer's ontologically oriented appeal to understanding as truth-happening, that deserves a renaissance within contemporary philosophy, be it in a European or Anglo-American vein.

ART, DIALOGUE, AND HISTORICAL KNOWLEDGE: APPROPRIATING KANT'S *CRITIQUE OF JUDGMENT*

Any study of Gadamer's critique of German Idealism must begin with a discussion of his reading of Kant. The relationship between Gadamer's own tradition, that of twentieth-century phenomenology, and Kant's program for a transcendental philosophy is itself a complex issue. First there is Edmund Husserl, who was both attracted to and critical of Kant's first Critique.[1] Then there is Heidegger and his ambition to survey the entire field of the three Critiques. However, most important in this context is Heidegger's reading of the *Critique of Pure Reason* in *Kant and the Problem of Metaphysics* (1929).[2] Faithful to his notion of a salvaging destruction of the philosophical tradition,[3] Heidegger argues that the earliest version of the first Critique, the so-called A-deduction of pure reason, is radically different from the epistemological position that had been eagerly promoted by the neo-Kantians.[4] According to Heidegger, Kant was initially not interested in epistemology in the narrow meaning of the term. Rather, Kant was verging upon a genuine ontology of Being, but then felt forced to leave this path behind in order to pursue the transcendental conditions of knowledge. As for the second Critique, Heidegger approaches

---

1 See Iso Kern, *Husserl und Kant. Eine Untersuchung über Husserls Verhältnis zu Kant und zum Neukantianismus* (The Hague: Martinus Nijhoff, 1964) and Paul Ricoeur, "Kant and Husserl," in Rudolf Bernet, Donn Welton, and Gina Zavota (eds.), *Edmund Husserl: Critical Assessments* (London: Routledge, 2005), vol. I, 320–344.

2 *Kant and the Problem of Metaphysics*, trans. Richard Taft (Bloomington: Indiana University Press, 1990); *Kant und das Problem der Metaphysik* (Frankfurt am Main: Vittorio Klostermann, 1991).

3 I return to Heidegger's program for a phenomenological destruction of the works of the tradition in Chapter 5.

4 For a discussion of Heidegger's relation to the neo-Kantians, see Michael Friedman, *A Parting of the Ways: Carnap, Cassirer, and Heidegger* (Chicago: Open Court, 2000).

this work through a discussion of the Kantian notions of freedom and causality. What, then, of the third Critique, that is, Kant's aesthetics? There are scattered remarks about the *Critique of Judgment* throughout Heidegger's work from the early 1930s onward (especially in the late 1930s Nietzsche lectures, to which I return in Chapter 3). A lengthy, systematic account of the relevance of the third Critique, however, is lacking in the work of Heidegger. This leaves Gadamer fertile ground on which to carve out his own philosophical niche, which is precisely what he does in the first part of *Truth and Method*: He sets out to rescue the hermeneutically important insights of Kant's aesthetics from the dominant nineteenth- and twentieth-century reception of this work.

When Gadamer published *Truth and Method*, his work on Plato's *Philebus*, the *Habilitationsschrift* of 1931, was already well known in Germany. Arguing that Plato's dialogical form is not merely a stylistic or rhetorical device, but an intrinsic part of his conception of rationality – rationality rests with the dialogical activity itself – Gadamer worries that the Socratic–Platonic notion of philosophizing gets substantially weakened with Aristotle's more academic form and, even more so, with the development of post-Aristotelian philosophy. However, while turning to the *Critique of Judgment*, Gadamer discovers the traces of a dialogical spirit akin to the one in Plato's work, yet in Kant's case, it is not played out performatively. Strictly speaking, this dialogical spirit is not part of Kant's discussion of pure, aesthetic judgment, but occurs in his analysis of the relationship between art and morality in §§16 and 17 of the *Critique of Judgment*. Gadamer, in other words, traces the hermeneutic insights of the third Critique to the parts of the work where Kant deviates from his main objective of providing an a priori justification of the pure judgment of taste.[5] According to Gadamer, Kant, in these sections, suggests that art, while expressing the ideals of reason, must be ascribed a cognitive dimension, only that this dimension, being dialogically constituted, differs from the cognitive comportments of the physical sciences. In Gadamer's reading, this, rather than Kant's better-known doctrine of pure aesthetic judgment, is the place to look for the contemporary relevance of the third Critique. In this part of the Critique, Gadamer claims, Kant connects art with the

5 A more elaborate reading of the hermeneutic impact of Kant's third Critique, and in particular of the transcendental imagination, cannot be found in Gadamer's work. Rudolf Makkreel offers such a reading in *Imagination and Interpretation in Kant: The Hermeneutical Import of the "Critique of Judgment"* (Chicago: University of Chicago Press, 1990).

idea of a self-reflective encounter of human reason in the concrete, historical world.

Self-reflection, truth, and history – these are three unmistakably Hegelian topics. Yet in Gadamer's reading, Kant's aesthetics is brought in not only to strengthen, but also to modify a Hegelian understanding of art. For whereas Hegel famously claims that in modernity art, as a reflection of the absolute, gets surpassed by religion and, ultimately, philosophy, Kant insists that the experience of art can never be fully exhausted by conceptual (philosophical) means. Although Gadamer is not entirely faithful to Kant's text – I argue that he reads the third Critique in a far too Hegelian light – the interpretation of the *Critique of Judgment* proves important to his overall argument in *Truth and Method*. The encounter with the *Critique of Judgment* allows Gadamer to develop, on the basis of the experience of art, a modern notion of dialogical rationality.

This chapter begins by rehearsing the basic outlines of Gadamer's critique of Kant's subjectivization of taste and his discussion of Kant's aesthetic formalism. The next issues to be addressed are Gadamer's retrieval of the hermeneutic dimensions of Kant's conception of a self-encounter in the work of art and the Hegelian premises of this reading. I continue by suggesting that Gadamer's Hegelian (mis-)reading of Kant's aesthetics allows him to sustain a notion of dialogical rationality that is broad enough to embrace our relationship with art and tradition in general while at the same time criticizing Hegel's idea of great art having come to an end. Within Gadamer's intellectual environment, such a reading of Kant implies an indirect response to Heidegger's wholesale rejection of aesthetics as the element in which art dies. Nonetheless, Gadamer ultimately finds that Kant gives systematic priority to natural beauty, hence leaving behind the hermeneutic outlook that he himself had been hinting at in his discussion of the moral relevance of art. Kant, Gadamer claims, illegitimately determines natural beauty as the other of reason. Again, this kind of criticism follows the lead of Hegel's rejection of natural beauty. Hegel's argument, however, presupposes too sharp a distinction between natural and artistic beauty. Returning to the question of the hermeneutical potential of the third Critique, I propose that the problem with Gadamer's reading of Kant is not that he categorically dismisses the *Critique of Judgment*, but that he, like Hegel, ends up hypostatizing an artificial contrast between Kant's reflections on art and his reflections on natural beauty.

Taste and knowledge in the third Critique

For a philosopher whose ambition it is to explore the hermeneutic potential of Kant's *Critique of Judgment,* Gadamer, from the very outset, adopts an unexpectedly polemical tone. To expound on Kant's aesthetics is, for Gadamer, to address "the subjectivization of aesthetics through the Kantian Critique" (*TM*, 42; *WM*, 48). Thus any engagement with Gadamer's reading of the third Critique must discuss the claim that Kant's Critique represents a subjectivization of beauty and taste. How does Gadamer arrive at this notion? Is it not Kant's aim to show, against the relativism that he ascribes to Hume and the Scottish empiricists, that the validity of aesthetic judging rests on an a priori principle?

In the *Critique of Judgment* – at least the part of the work that Gadamer is interested in, namely the critique of aesthetic judgment (and not the teleology of nature) – Kant attempts to demonstrate that the judgment of taste may be granted an a priori principle of its own. This is why the *Critique of Judgment,* as the last of the three critiques, offers a novel approach to aesthetics.

The third Critique was published in 1790, nine years after the *Critique of Pure Reason.* Yet Kant had been interested in the problem of taste from the beginning of the 1760s. However, not until the late 1780s had he been able to see how the judgment of taste could be endowed with a transcendental principle.[6] As such, the *Critique of Judgment* not only aspires to a deduction of the pure judgment of taste, but also contains an argument for the conditions of possibility for providing such a deduction in the first place. According to Gadamer, the *Critique of Judgment* is therefore not a "critique of taste in the sense that taste is the object of critical judgment by an observer. It is a critique of critique; that is, it is concerned with the legitimacy of such a critique in matters of taste" (ibid.). If the possibility of a deduction of the validity of pure aesthetic judging depends upon the

---

6 In the first Critique, Kant rejects Alexander Baumgarten's "fruitless" endeavors to "bring the critical treatment of the beautiful under rational principles, and so to raise its rules to the rank of a science" (*CPR*; *KdrV*, A21/B35, footnote). This, however, changes throughout the second half of the 1780s. In 1787, Kant announces to Reinhold that he is now prepared to write a "Critique of Taste." That is, he has discovered that "there are three faculties of the mind: the faculty of cognition, the faculty of pleasure and displeasure, and the faculty of desire," and that each of these faculties can be ascribed a transcendental principle of its own. Kant's letter to Karl Leonhard Reinhold is quoted from John Zammito, *The Genesis of Kant's "Critique of Judgment"* (Chicago: University of Chicago Press, 1992), 46–47.

possibility of disclosing a transcendental principle for this type of judging, then it is the aim of the third Critique to answer the question of what a transcendental principle within the area of taste amounts to, as well as to demonstrate that such a principle can indeed be found. When he claims that Kant's work represents a subjectivization of taste, Gadamer does therefore not suggest that Kant is unaware of the normativity inherent in pure aesthetic judging. Rather, what troubles him is the very way in which normativity is grounded in Kant's account of taste.

Like most eighteenth-century aestheticians, Kant is interested in the beautiful, and not, like the later generations of romantic philosophers, in the ugly, the repulsive, or the abject. In accordance with the Copernican turn, Kant questions the view that beauty is an intrinsic quality of objects in themselves. Strictly speaking, Kant claims that a judgment of the kind "x is beautiful" is not a judgment regarding the properties of an object "x" at all. It is a judgment about the feeling that the contemplation of this object induces in us. The feeling that Kant has in mind is the pleasure elicited by the free play of the cognitive powers, the imagination ("die Einbildungskraft"), and the understanding ("der Verstand"). In our cognitive activities, these faculties cooperate by mutually curbing one another. The understanding is restricted in its application to what is given in intuition, while the imagination, on its side, must meet with the understanding's call for unity. In aesthetic experience, by contrast, the two faculties exist in a state of harmony, wherein the imagination spontaneously synthesizes the given sensuous manifold so that it matches the demands of the understanding.[7] This spontaneous cooperation – this free play of the faculties – induces a feeling of pleasure that differs from the sensuously pleasing, as well as from the pleasure we take in the morally good. As opposed to sensuous and moral pleasure, aesthetic pleasure is disinterested; that is, it is not engaged with the actual existence of the object.[8] This disinterested pleasure is the basis of the pure aesthetic judgment.

---

7 Dieter Henrich sums this up rather nicely by suggesting that "The harmonious agreement of the cognitive powers . . . is playful in a particular sense: the mutual agreement comes about without coercion, and the two activities concur automatically." Dieter Henrich, "Kant's Explanation of Aesthetic Judgment," in *Aesthetic Judgment and the Moral Image of the World* (Stanford: Stanford University Press, 1992), 52.

8 According to Kant, it applies that, in relation to the good, "what we like is not just the object but its existence as well. A judgment of taste, on the other hand, is merely *contemplative*, i.e., it is a judgment that is indifferent to the existence of the object: it

While investigating the transcendental conditions for validity in aesthetic judging, Kant takes as his point of departure the beauty of natural forms (which is not to say that he cuts himself off from discussions of artistic beauty). This focus on natural beauty is, in part, motivated by the overall structure of the critical project, and in particular by the potential tension between Kant's account of the causality of nature, in the *Critique of Pure Reason,* and his account of moral freedom, in the *Critique of Practical Reason.* Only the focus on natural beauty may help him bridge the gap between causality and freedom.

According to Kant, the experience of natural beauty typically directs us towards the idea of a higher purpose in nature. Yet we have no criterion by which to determine whether this is objectively the case. The anticipation of a higher purposiveness of nature occasions no cognitive claim. It remains subjective, but without this subjective status diminishing the importance of this kind of purposiveness. Instead, this is a purposiveness of a peculiar kind, one that serves no purpose save that of making human beings feel at home in the world. Kant speaks of this as a purposiveness without a purpose. The purposiveness without a purpose is the a priori principle of aesthetic judgment. And since Kant has already argued in the first Critique that the cognitive powers must be the same in all human beings,[9] he can ascribe to the judgment of taste a transcendental dimension of validity, thus explaining how we, in aesthetic judging, may legitimately demand the agreement of others, even if empirical experience confronts us with a variety of aesthetic preferences. Within the realm of taste, the demand for agreement cannot be based on an objective universality. What Kant has in mind, rather, is a subjective universality. This is a kind of universality that differs from objective (logical) universality in that it "does not connect the predicate of beauty with the concept of the *object,* considered in its entire logical sphere, yet it extends that predicate over the entire sphere of *judging persons*" (*CJ; KdU,* §8, 215). The notion of a subjective universality offers a basis against which

[considers] the character of the object only by holding it up to our feeling of pleasure and displeasure" (*CJ; KdU,* §5, 209).

9 In the third Critique, Kant claims with regard to the aesthetic power of judgment that "in all people the subjective conditions of this power are the same as concerns the relation required for cognition as such between the cognitive powers that are activated in the power of judgment." This must be true, Kant continues, "for otherwise people could not communicate their presentations to one another, indeed they could not even communicate cognition" (*CJ; KdU,* §38, 290, footnote).

Gadamer's criticism of Kant's subjectivization of taste may be further expounded. Kant's conception of aesthetic judgment, Gadamer claims, represents a subjectivization in two related, yet slightly different, meanings of the term. First, the Kantian Critique represents a subjectivization in that the normativity of aesthetic judgment is traced back to the free play of the cognitive faculties. Pure aesthetic judgment relates to a subjective feeling, and not to objective features in the world. Second, the subjective universality of aesthetic judgment deprives it of every cognitive claim. By grounding the validity of taste in the feeling induced by the free play of the cognitive faculties, Kant, in Gadamer's view, "denies taste any *significance as knowledge*" (*TM*, 43; *WM*, 49).

Deeming Kant's account of aesthetic normativity a subjectivization of judgment, Gadamer is primarily concerned with taste's relation to knowledge. According to Kant, the judgment of taste is a reflective, as opposed to a determinative, kind of judging. Determinative judging proceeds by subsuming the particular under a general rule, principle, or law. Reflective judging, by contrast, moves from the particular to the universal, but without a universal at hand by which to make that move. As Kant puts it in the introduction to the *Critique of Judgment*, "[i]f the universal (the rule, principle, law) is given, then judgment, which subsumes the particular under it, is *determinative* . . . But if only the particular is given and judgment has to find the universal for it, then this power is merely *reflective*" (*Cf, KdU*, Introduction, IV, 179).

The distinction between a judgment that issues from a universal rule and one that issues from the particular has an unmistakably Aristotelian flair. In the *Nicomachean Ethics*, a work to which Gadamer regularly refers, the employment of the reflective type of judgment is closely related to the logic of practical reasoning. It is, in fact, *the* distinguishing mark of practical knowledge (*phronesis*). As Gadamer puts it, practical knowledge is expressed in a kind of judging that "is delimited against any technical rationality" because here "the 'universal' . . . derives its determinacy by means of the singular."[10] In Aristotle, however, the idea of a reflective judging is never pushed in the direction of a philosophy of taste. To develop a notion of taste, in the modern sense of the term, was simply not an option within the ancient Greek mindset. This, however, changes as centuries pass. With the early modern humanists, the notion of reflective judgment is moved right into the center of the philosophy

---

10 "What is Practice?" *RAS*, 81; "Was ist Praxis?" *Vernunft im Zeitalter der Wissenschaft* (Frankfurt am Main: Suhrkamp Verlag, 1976), 70.

of taste and culture. Indeed, within this tradition, taste emerges as the realm of practical judgment *per se*. This becomes particularly clear in the work of the seventeenth-century Spanish Jesuit, Baltasar Gracián.

Gadamer's reading of Gracián is heavily indebted to a now largely forgotten study, *Baltasar Gracián und die Hoflitteratur in Deutschland* (1894). The author, Karl Borinski, argues that, as a representative of the early modern spirit, Gracián seeks to articulate "a moral anatomy of mankind," hence also working out a new ideal of cultural formation (*Bildungsideal*).[11] According to Borinski, taste holds a special place within this ideal. It is not an aspect of culture, but is the root of it as such.[12] In Borinski's view, however, Gracián's notion of taste as the root of culture is intrinsically connected to the rise of a capitalist economy. Because it is based on education and know-how, rather than old, inherited privileges, the exercise of taste and *sensus communis* reflects the principles of modern economy within the field of culture.[13] Gadamer does not consider the sociological depth and critical spirit of Borinski's account. Rather, what interests Gadamer is how Gracián and the early modern humanists took taste to be a mark of practical wisdom, that is, more than a merely aesthetic phenomenon. In this era, Gadamer argues, taste emerges as "more a *moral* than an *aesthetic* idea" (*TM*, 35; *WM*, 40, emphasis added). This co-determination of taste and morality, Gadamer continues, is anchored in a particular conception of the validity of the judgment of taste. The validity of the judgment of taste is not, as in Kant, based on the appeal to a transcendental principle, but rests with the capacity of the judgment to gain recognition from the members of the community within which it is passed. Indeed, taste and historical sociality are taken to be intrinsically connected. For as Gracián puts it, even though man "is born a barbarian ... Culture turns us into true persons."[14] An individual who has developed a cultured personality is recognized for his or her sound judgment. That judgment

11 Karl Borinski, *Baltasar Gracián und die Hoflitteratur in Deutschland* (Halle: Max Niemeyer, 1894), 24f.
12 "Als ein allgemeines Kulturelement, und zwar als kein nebensächliches, sondern als die Wurzel aller, ja als die treibende Kraft der gesamten Kultur sehen wir also den Geschmack hingestellt" (ibid., 43).
13 It is "ganz einfach der unentbehrliche, stets geforderte Maßstab des Käufers und Verkäufers für ihr Objekt, für die Ware" (ibid., 40).
14 Baltasar Gracián, *The Art of Worldly Wisdom: A Pocket Oracle*, trans. Christopher Maurer (New York: Doubleday, 1992), 49.

articulates the reflective or pre-reflective self-understanding pre-vailing within the community. As retrieved by Gadamer, this implies that in its essential nature ("seinem eigensten Wesen nach") taste is "not private but a social [*gesellschaftliches*] phenomenon of the first order" (*TM*, 36; *WM*, 41).

In Gadamer's reading, Gracián and the early modern humanists are brought in so as to provide an intellectual backdrop against which the implications of Kant's subjectivization of judgment may be critically assessed.[15] As a social phenomenon, taste cannot be restricted, as in Kant, to the evaluation of the beautiful and the sublime. According to Gadamer, "[o]ne cannot even say, with Kant, that the productivity of judgment is to be found 'chiefly' in this area" (*TM*, 38; *WM*, 44). Rather, "*all* moral [*sittlichen*] decisions require taste – which does not mean that this most individual balancing of decision is the *only* thing that governs them, but it is an *indispensable* element" (*TM*, 39; *WM*, 45, emphasis added). In early modern humanism, morality is not under-stood in a narrow sense (as in the *Critique of Practical Reason*), but is connected to culture, tradition, and community (as in Hegel's notion of *Sittlichkeit*). Furthermore, taste is not, as Kant would have it, dis-tinguished from practical knowledge, but emerges, as Gadamer puts it, as "the supreme consummation of moral judgment ['sittlichen Urteils']" (*TM*, 40; *WM*, 45).

I return to the limitations of Gadamer's appropriation of Gracián in Chapter 3. Maintaining the focus on Kant and aesthetic judging, we need, at this point, only to ask why Kant, in Gadamer's reading, so categorically breaks with Gracián and the humanist tradition in dis-tinguishing between taste and practical knowledge. According to Gadamer, Kant's understanding of reason and morality must be traced back to his conception of epistemic validity. This also applies to his notion of taste. In the *Critique of Pure Reason*, Kant had reserved the notions of truth and cognitive relevance for the subsumption of par-ticulars under general laws, concepts, or rules – that is, for deter-minative (as opposed to reflective) judging. But is it, Gadamer polemically asks, really right to reserve "the concept of truth for conceptual knowledge" (*TM*, 41; *WM*, 47)?

Gadamer responds to this question with a firm denial. As a faculty of practical consideration, taste constitutes "a special way of knowing"

---

15 Gadamer does not pay sufficient attention to Kant's notion of *sensus communis*, but treats it only as part of the larger complex of taste.

(*TM*, 38; *WM*, 43). Likewise, all (practical) knowing and judging involves a reflective dimension. At stake is not so much a "knowing that" as a "knowing how." As such, the phenomenon of taste challenges the idea that knowledge, by definition, is subsumptive and law-oriented. The limitation of reflective judgment to the realm of pure aesthetic feeling must therefore be overcome by a theory that offers a more comprehensive notion of rationality and knowledge than Kant is ever willing to consider. This is the ambition of Gadamer's philosophical hermeneutics: To provide such a theory of rationality and knowledge.

I will get back to Gadamer's understanding of rationality and knowledge, and to the role that art plays in his hermeneutic re-articulation of these notions, in Chapter 3. However, before we get that far, it is necessary to explore in more detail the implications of Gadamer's engagement with Kant's *Critique of Judgment*, and in particular his discussion of art and the ideal of beauty.

Art and morality

The call for a move beyond the subjectivization of taste has made a number of commentators conclude that Gadamer fails to acknowledge the hermeneutic relevance of the third Critique. Peter Bürger, for one, argues that Gadamer can only develop his position by abstractly negating Kant and the Kantian tradition. This, Bürger claims, betrays a major inconsistency in Gadamer's philosophy. By failing to appreciate the hermeneutic dimension of Kant's *Critique of Judgment*, Gadamer not only misreads Kant, but he also strains against his own idea of a continuous effective history.[16] Bürger polemically suggests that Gadamer can only develop his notion of the continuity of tradition by breaking with tradition itself, thus performatively contradicting the gist of his own argument. However, Bürger jumps too hastily to his conclusion. Gadamer's reading of the third Critique is not limited to the discussion of taste and judgment, but encompasses a thorough engagement with Kant's understanding of art. Due, perhaps, to the widespread interest in the hermeneutic conception of practical knowledge and normativity – an interest

---

16 Bürger claims that Gadamer "seine eigene Konzeption einer 'Ontologie des Kunstwerks' nur im Bruch mit der Tradition der Ästhetik seit Kant einführen kann." Peter Bürger, *Zur Kritik der idealistischen Ästhetik* (Frankfurt am Main: Suhrkamp Verlag, 1983), 15.

fueled by the so-called Gadamer–Habermas debate (to which I return in Chapter 4) – this aspect of Gadamer's discussion has not received the attention it deserves.[17] Hence one may easily overlook how Gadamer, having first criticized the subjectivization of taste in Kant's *Critique of Judgment*, modifies his critique by arguing that hermeneutics not only should distinguish itself from Kant's account of pure, aesthetic judging, but also understand itself as heavily indebted to his notion of art and artistic beauty.

In the *Critique of Judgment*, Kant distinguishes between four different aspects or moments of taste. Gadamer begins his discussion of Kant's notion of art by carefully examining a few excerpts from the third moment, that is, Kant's analysis of the judgment of taste according to its relation.[18] Here Kant argues that the possibility of offering a deduction of the (subjective) universality of taste depends on the possibility of distinguishing the pure judgment of taste from the type of judging that is based on a conceptual determination of the object considered. Kant addresses this question through a discussion of the difference between free and adherent beauty in §16. Free beauty presupposes no concept. Adherent beauty, by contrast, does. Only when judging free beauty can the judgment of taste be pure (*CJ; KdU*, §16, 229).

Natural beauty, Kant continues, provides the ultimate example of free beauty. We do not have to know what an object of nature is or represents in order to appreciate it aesthetically. No concept is required in order to take pleasure in the contemplation of its form. When encountering free beauties such as, for instance, flowers,

17 A significant exception is Joel Weinsheimer's discussion of Gadamer's understanding of modern aesthetics. See Joel C. Weinsheimer, *Gadamer's Hermeneutics* (New Haven: Yale University Press, 1985), 98ff.

18 Gadamer's investigation into Kant's understanding of art is limited to Kant's account of the aesthetic judgment of beauty. The analytic of the sublime, a part of Kant's work that has exercised an enormous influence on modern as well as post-modern conceptions of art, is not a subject of Gadamer's attention in *Truth and Method*. However, in a later essay, Gadamer addresses the aesthetically sublime and emphasizes the necessity of "incorporat[ing] the aesthetic of the sublime into the theory of art, in a way Kant did not fully accomplish himself" ("Intuition and Vividness," *RB*, 167; "Anschauung und Anschaulichkeit," *GW*, vol. VIII, 199). Such an incorporation of the sublime into the theory of art, Gadamer argues, would prepare us for the elevation of mind to its supernatural vocation. And "since we thus experience a satisfaction that elevates us beyond the unpleasant experience of our insignificance and powerlessness," he concludes that the experience of the sublime is dependent on "an intellectual interest." Hence, on Gadamer's reading, an incorporation of the sublime into our conception of art does not integrate "that aspect of formlessness and immeasurability offered by the sublime in nature" (*RB*, 168; *GW*, vol. VIII, 199).

"[h]ardly anyone apart from the botanist knows what sort of thing a flower is [meant] to be; and even he, while recognizing it as the reproductive organ of a plant, pays no attention to this natural purpose when he judges the flower by taste" (ibid.). Here, the imagination synthesizes the sensuous manifold without being limited by a notion of objective purposiveness, i.e., by the question as to what a thing, such as a flower, "is [meant] to be" and how it lives up to this determination.

Entering the world of human practice, however, the notion of free beauty becomes increasingly problematic. As opposed to natural beauty, "the beauty of a human being . . . or the beauty of a horse or of a building (such as a church, palace, armory, or summer-house) does presuppose the concept of the purpose that determines what the thing is [meant] to be" (*CJ; KdU*, §16, 230). Domesticated animals, people, and buildings appear within the realm of human ends and intentions. Thus, it seems, we can hardly judge (a representation of) these objects without considering their place within the field of human practice, that is, without considering their purpose. However, this purpose is not a purposiveness without purpose, one that only serves the subjective aim of generating aesthetic pleasure. Hence we risk contaminating the aesthetic judgment with a determinative (objective) purpose. Informed by such a criterion as perfection, the aesthetic judgment instantly loses its purity. Baumgarten, Kant argues, did not see this. By appealing to the criterion of perfection, Baumgarten had been opting for a didactic model according to which beauty is appreciated only to the extent that it prepares for a conceptual grasp of the contemplated object. But reduced to a mere means, Kant remarks, beauty is worth no more than the honey with which one bribes a young child to do something that is experienced as unpleasant or scary.[19]

A beauty that is conceived along the lines of such pragmatic considerations – a beauty that, rather than being an end in itself, is reduced to a means – is not free but "obscured and limited" (*TM*, 45; *WM*, 51). This claim of Kant's might initially seem uncontroversial. Yet Gadamer questions this part of the third Critique. What worries him is not Kant's rejection of the criterion of perfection within the sphere of

---

19 "Die Ästhetik ist nur ein Mittel, Leute von gar zu großer Zärtlichkeit an die Strenge der Beweise und Erklärungen zu gewöhnen. So wie man Kindern den Rand des Gefäßes mit Honig beschmieret." Kant, *Akademie Ausgabe*, vol. XVI, 102 (no. 1753). Quoted in Manfred Frank, *Einführung in die frühromantische Ästhetik* (Frankfurt am Main: Suhrkamp Verlag, 1989), 40.

pure aesthetic judgment. Gadamer takes no interest in rehabilitating an aesthetic model that is geared towards the perfection of the aesthetic object. The problem, rather, is the extension ascribed to this area by Kant. For within it Kant includes "the whole realm of poetry, of the plastic arts and of architecture" (ibid.). To the extent that we follow Gadamer's reading, most art ends up being barred from Kant's definition of free beauty, and thus also from the pale of pure aesthetic judging. In this interpretation, Kant's conception of aesthetic judgment seems unfit to accommodate any kind of art, save the arabesque or other merely ornamental expressions.

According to Gadamer, the only way to avoid this conclusion would be to regard taste as a mere pre-condition (*Vorbedingung*) for aesthetic experience. Along the lines of such a reading, pure aesthetic judgment would emerge as a preparatory and incomplete condition that, upon encountering the artistically beautiful, would stand in need of further elaboration. Such an elaboration could then be given by reference, say, to the idea of artistic genius. However, even if a vague and preliminary notion of genius might be found at this stage of Kant's discussion (§16), it is, Gadamer points out, not yet granted a systematic place or explanation within the third Critique. Such an explanation is only offered in §46. In §16, the standpoint of taste appears to provide an exhaustive account of aesthetic judgment, protecting it from any appeal to intellectual standards of evaluation. Accordingly, it seems that Kant is simply claiming that "True beauty is that of flowers and of ornament, which in our world, dominated by ends, present themselves as beauties immediately and of themselves, and hence do not require that any concept or purpose be consciously disregarded" (*TM*, 45; *WM*, 51).

If we for a moment leave behind the hermeneutic framework of Gadamer's discussion, there is, in fact, a way to get round this problem. This is the route suggested by the American art critic Clement Greenberg. According to Greenberg, the aesthetic implications of Kant's philosophy do not rest with his discussion of art in particular, but are connected to the general direction of his critical turn. By bringing reason to the stage of self-criticism, Kant anticipates the driving impulse of modernist art. Indeed, on Greenberg's interpretation, aesthetic modernism represents "the intensification, almost exacerbation, of [the] self-critical tendency that began with the philosopher Kant."[20]

20 Clement Greenberg, "Modernist Painting," in *The Collected Essays and Criticism*, ed. John O'Brian (Chicago: Chicago University Press, 1993), vol. IV, 85.

Within the realm of painting, which is what Greenberg is most interested in, modernism takes the shape of an investigation into the medium of the painterly itself. "Realistic, naturalistic art had dissembled the medium, using art to conceal art; Modernism used art to call attention to art," as he puts it.[21]

However, from a Gadamerian point of view, such a formalist approach does not do justice to the *Critique of Judgment*. Kant's account of art does not culminate in the exclusion of art from the realm of beauty proper. Instead, Kant goes on to investigate the wider hermeneutic relevance of symbolic beauty.

At this point, Gadamer takes a step back, singling out and highlighting the part of §16 that deals with the decoration of sacred buildings and the human body. With regard to the ornamental decoration of a church or the human body, Kant emphasizes that in spite of its formal capacity to induce the free play of our cognitive faculties (thereby evoking a feeling of aesthetic pleasure), this kind of beauty is unwanted, and that this is due to *moral* considerations. What happens here – and Gadamer finds this to be of the utmost importance – is that Kant brings into his discussion of the judgment of taste an extra-aesthetic premise, that of reason and morality. As Gadamer reads this section of the Critique, Kant's point is not really to warn against the ornamentation of the sacred space or the human body, but to suggest that symbolic beauty may gain from a reference to reason and morality even if this means that the purity of the aesthetic judgment is sacrificed. Hence there is indeed a way to save a Kantian philosophy of art without resorting, as Greenberg does, to a formalist notion of aesthetic modernism.

According to Gadamer, §16 aims to clarify the distinction between two different ways in which the judgment of symbolic beauty relates to concepts: with regard to the perfection of the aesthetic object or with regard to its moral reference. This distinction allows Kant to reject the kind of conceptual reference that presupposes the idea of the object's perfection (according to its empirical concept), while at the same time maintaining the relationship between taste and morality (rational

---

21 "Modernist Painting," 86. Greenberg's understanding of Kant is put into critical perspective by Ingrid Stadler in "The Idea of Art and of its Criticism: A Rational Reconstruction of a Kantian Doctrine," in Ted Cohen and Paul Guyer (eds.), *Essays in Kant's Aesthetics* (Chicago: University of Chicago Press, 1982), 195–218. For an alternative discussion of Greenberg's Kantianism, see Thierry de Duve, *Clement Greenberg between the Lines*, trans. Brian Holmes (Paris: Éditions Dis Voir, 1996), chapter 3.

concepts). As Gadamer puts it, taste's relation to empirical concepts is rejected because it restricts the freedom of the imagination, while its relation to rational concepts is endorsed because here our "'looking to a concept' does not abrogate [*aufheben*] the freedom of the imagination" (*TM*, 46; *WM*, 52). Kant does, in other words, grant that there are cases in which we should allow aesthetic judgment to be guided by an intellectual concern, even at the cost of such a judgment losing its purity. The imagination, Gadamer explains, is simply "not richest where it is merely free . . . as in the convolutions of the arabesque, but rather in a field of play where the understanding's desire for unity does not so much confine it as suggest incitements to play" (ibid.).

This is a conclusion that anticipates the point brought forth in the next section, §17, where Kant continues his examination of the relation between the judgment of taste and the possibility of an intellectualized aesthetic liking.

The self-encounter of spirit in the work of art

The relation between taste and reason (rational concepts) makes it possible for Kant to argue that whenever a disagreement about a matter of taste arises, two judges with opposing opinions may in theory lay equal claims to validity. One may be right according to the intellectualized (moral) interest she takes in the object; the other according to a pure aesthetic liking. Yet such conflicts are not the rule. On the contrary, Kant remarks that surprisingly often these two approaches to beauty exist side by side. This leads him to address the possibility of there being a deeper, common ground behind our judgments on art and beauty.

If such a ground exists, then it cannot be of a conceptual nature, since there is, Kant argues, no objective rule of taste. Reflective judgment is an aesthetic judgment; it is based on a subjective feeling induced by the disinterested contemplation of a beautiful form and not on a concept of the object itself. The search for a conceptual criterion of taste is therefore in vain. Hence Kant continues to address the possibility of there being something like an archetype of taste. Such an archetype would, he claims, have to be "a mere idea, an idea which everyone must generate within himself and by which he must judge any object of taste, any example of someone's judging by taste, and even the taste of everyone [else]" (*CJ*, *KdU*, §17, 232). An idea properly, Kant explains, means a rational concept. When a rational concept is given a concrete expression, it appears as an ideal of beauty. Rooted in "reason's indeterminate idea of a maximum," the ideal of beauty cannot "be presented . . . through concepts but only in an individual exhibition" (ibid.). As such, it is an ideal of the imagination.

Given Kant's distinction between free and adherent beauty (and his tendency to identify art with adherent beauty), one must ask what kind of beauty could possibly be susceptible to such an ideal of the imagination. Although such beauty could not be determined by a concept, it would have to be partly fixed by it. It would have to belong to an aesthetic judgment that is, in Kant's phrasing, "partly intellectual" (ibid.). Thus we can a priori exclude from the ideal of beauty the non-conceptual beauty of flowers or a beautiful view (Kant's own examples). How, then, about the kind of beauty that has a specific purpose, the beauty pertaining to objects that belong to the realm of human practice (the realm of means and ends)? In these cases, Kant argues, the purpose of the object is not "sufficiently determined." This kind of beauty is therefore "nearly as free as is the case of *vague* beauty [that is, beauty which is not fixed by a concept]" (*CJ, KdU*, §17, 233). The question is thus whether Kant, given the resources of the third Critique, is able to uncover a kind of beauty that has a conceptual reference, without thereby being externally determined by it.

If we follow Kant's argument, such beauty would have to be related to the presentation of a being whose purpose is an inherent part of its own existence. According to Kant, only human beings meet such a requirement. Only "[m]an can himself determine his purposes by reason," as he puts it (ibid.). Through the faculty of reason, human beings give themselves their own purpose. The purpose of a human being is intrinsic to humanity as such. This is why a human being, as we know from Kant's moral philosophy, should never be reduced to a mere means. Humanity is an aim in itself. Of all beings in the world, only humans would be susceptible to an ideal of beauty.

As much as he initially began by criticizing Kant's subjectivization of taste and judgment power, the ideal of beauty is a notion of which Gadamer approves. According to Gadamer, there is "an ideal of beauty only of the human form precisely because it alone is capable of a beauty fixed by a concept of end" (*TM*, 47; *WM*, 53). Between vague, conceptually underdetermined beauty, on the one hand, and conceptually

overdetermined beauty, on the other, Kant uncovers a third alternative: a kind of beauty that has an intellectual reference, yet
remains undetermined by external constraints (concepts or purposes). While contemplating the beautiful presentation of humanity,
the intellectual pleasure that we take in this presentation does not,
in Gadamer's words, "distract us from the aesthetic pleasure but is
rather one with it" (*TM*, 48; *WM*, 54).

However, as Gadamer points out, the artistic presentation of natural objects may also lend voice to moral predicates or ideals. Yet
when we ascribe to nature (or aesthetic representations of nature) a
set of moral predicates, these are borrowed from one context and
projected onto another. When attributed to a human being, by contrast, moral predicates are no longer derived from an external context
but are intrinsically related to the being of this being as such.[22] When
human beings are regarded in terms of a moral (*sittliches*) ideal, there
is no gap between the ideal and its area of application: The ideal of
humanity is extracted from humanity's own being.

According to Gadamer, Kant's discussion of the ideal of beauty is
the place to look for the hermeneutic potentials of the third Critique.
It is a discussion, he finds, that shows "clearly how little a formal
aesthetics of taste ... corresponds to the Kantian idea" (*TM*, 47;
WM, 53). More importantly, Kant's discussion of the ideal of beauty
leads to an insight that is even more significant, namely that our
interest in the artistically beautiful is related to the possibility of a
particular kind of self-encounter. In the experience of art, humanity
faces itself. At stake is a dialogical relation in which the parties are at
the same time one (in that they take part in the realm of human
meaning and expression) and divided (into work and recipient). Only
through the development of such a dialogical concept, Gadamer
argues, "can '*art*' become an *autonomous phenomenon* ['einer autono-
men Erscheinung']" (*TM*, 49; *WM*, 55, emphasis added). What
Gadamer proposes here is nothing less than that in Kant's discussion
of the ideal of beauty, autonomy is not conceived of in terms of the

---

22 As expounded by Gadamer, "[a] tree that is stunted because of unfavorable conditions
of growth may seem wretched to us, but the tree does not feel wretched or express this
wretchedness, and from the point of view of the ideal of the tree, being stunted is not
'wretchedness.' The wretched man is wretched, however, as measured by *the human
moral ideal itself* (and not only because we demand that he submit to a human ideal
that is simply not valid for him, measured by which he would express wretchedness for
us without being wretched)" (*TM*, 48f.; *WM*, 54, emphasis added).

aesthetic judgment's claim to validity (subjective universality), but in terms of the idea, to be developed further by Hegel, of art as an expression of self-reflecting spirit.[23] This kind of self-reflection – or self-understanding, one might even say – implies a dimension of knowledge. Connecting art and reason, Kant thus moves beyond the idea, decisive for his notion of the pure judgment of taste, that our engagement with beauty is void of cognitive interest. He realizes, as Gadamer puts it, that "something must be more than merely tastefully pleasant in order to please as a work of art" (*TM*, 47; *WM*, 53), hence also that "The very recognition of the non-conceptuality of taste leads *beyond* an aesthetics of mere taste" (*TM*, 49; *WM*, 55, emphasis added).

In Gadamer's reading, Kant's third Critique not only subjectivizes taste but paves the way for a wider, hermeneutically relevant response to the relationship between art and knowledge. Contrary to what one would expect if judging from the brazen tone of Gadamer's initial discussion of the *Critique of Judgment*, he suggests that it is Kant himself who plots a route beyond the narrow notion of pure aesthetic judging. He does this, first, by showing (without appealing to the criterion of perfection or to empirical concepts) that our experience of art benefits from the reference to rational concepts, and, second, by hinting at a dimension of knowledge that transcends the realm of science proper: the notion of knowledge as self-knowledge.

In order to overcome Kant's subjectivization of taste, one may well have to go beyond the scope of Kant's account of pure, aesthetic judging, but not beyond the intellectual framework of his philosophy as such. This – and not an abstract, unmediated negation – is the gist of Gadamer's encounter with Kant's philosophy of art.

Art and hermeneutic reason

It is one thing to argue, as Gadamer has so far been doing, that Kant's notion of the ideal of beauty transcends the restrictions of pure aesthetic judging. It is something else, however, to suggest that Kant, while doing so, at the same time anticipates a hermeneutic

---

23 According to Hegel, "art and works of art, by springing from and being created by the spirit, are themselves of a spiritual kind, even if their presentation assumes an appearance of sensuousness and pervades the sensuous with the spirit. In this respect art already lies nearer to the spirit and its thinking than purely external spiritless nature does. In the products of art, the spirit has to do solely with its own" (*LFA*, vol. I, 12; *VsK*, vol. I, 27).

conception of art and experience. Yet this is precisely what Gadamer proposes.

At this point we have not yet discussed Gadamer's own (hermeneutic) understanding of art. However, we do know that Gadamer recommends a return to Gracián and pre-Kantian humanism, with its notion of a practical, context-sensitive knowledge that is sourced in concrete intersubjectivity. This kind of knowledge does not aim at abstract and universal concepts but grows in richness and concreteness as time and history pass. As we will see, the idea of such knowledge is a crucial part of Gadamer's own account of art.

To show how Kant's notion of the ideal of beauty aspires to a hermeneutic account of art, Gadamer must bring into his interpretation an additional premise. Not only will he have to argue that Kant's notion of the ideal of beauty makes it possible to conceive of aesthetic experience as a self-encounter of spirit, but he must also claim that the ideal of beauty allows us to cast this encounter in concrete, historical terms. At the end of his interpretation of the *Critique of Judgment*, §17, Gadamer thus claims that Kant's conception of the moral relevance of art guides us towards the idea of art's ability to "enable man to encounter himself in nature and in the human, historical world" (ibid.).

This claim finds little backing in the *Critique of Judgment*. In §17, Kant argues that the moral relevance of art consists in its capacity to exhibit a wide range of abstract moral deeds. What Kant has in mind is the work's ability to voice the universal ideals of reason – "everything that our reason links with the morally good: goodness of soul, or purity, or fortitude, or serenity, etc." (*CJ*; *KdU*, §17, 235) – not its ability to express the ethical-political horizon of a given, historical community. According to Kant, the work of art that tends to evoke our full interest is the one that presents us with a set of ideals for which reason inevitably strives, but for whose actual realization in this world it can only hope.

Gadamer's argument is confusing because it ascribes to Kant a good deal more than can actually be justified with reference to §17. Moreover, it undermines his own critique of Kantian morality. For while calling for a return to the early humanist notion of the co-presence of taste and morality, Gadamer, as we have seen, claims that with Kant, the concept of morality is reduced to an abstractly universal imperative, the exercising of the stern law of pure practical reason (*TM*, 33; *WM*, 38). This, however, is a conception of reason that differs substantially from a dialogical reason expressing itself through a "human, historical world." In order to sustain the coherence of his argument, Gadamer must moderate one of his two claims. He must *either* grant to Kant a more comprehensive notion of moral life in the first place *or* make it clear that Kant, while developing the idea of a self-encounter in the work of art, does not determine this self-encounter in terms of a concrete, historical world. The fact that Gadamer fails to realize this weakens substantially his reading of the *Critique of Judgment.*

If Gadamer, in his interpretation of §§16 and 17, reads into Kant's third Critique an empirical-historical notion of morality, he is by no means the first to do so. Hegel also argued that Kant's brief elaboration on art reflects the ethical and historical relevance of the work.[24] Yet in Hegel's mind this conception of art is brought to maturity only through his own understanding of the artwork as "the sensuous presentation of the Absolute" (*LFA*, vol. I, 70; *VsK*, vol. I, 100). Gadamer explicitly acknowledges this. Even though Kant, in Gadamer's view, uncovers the affinity between art and ethical life, it is only Hegel's lectures on aesthetics that fully explore this relation. As he puts it, it is in Hegel's aesthetics that "the truth that lies in every artistic experience is recognized and at the same time mediated with historical consciousness" (*TM*, 98; *WM*, 103). Only here does the work of art emerge as a substantial part of reason's search for self-understanding and knowledge (*TM*, 97; *WM*, 102).

However, if Gadamer, first, maneuvers himself into a position in which he reads Kant's understanding of art (in §§16 and 17) in a way that threatens to undermine the force of his own critique of Kantian morality, and if, second, he admits that it is only Hegel who fully redeems the moral-historical aspect of art, then a question arises. Why does Gadamer bother to discuss the *Critique of Judgment* in the first place? Why does he not turn straight to Hegel's lectures on aesthetics? The reason is that Gadamer, while heavily influenced by Hegel's aesthetics, remains troubled by some of its most fundamental assumptions.

According to Gadamer, Hegel was "able to recognize the truth of art only by subordinating it to philosophy's comprehensive

---

24 Paul Guyer expounds on this aspect of Hegel's reading of the *Critique of Judgment* in "Hegel on Kant's Aesthetics: Necessity and Contingency in Beauty and Art," in Hans-Friedrich Fulda and Rolf-Peter Horstmann (eds.), *Hegel und die "Kritik der Urteilskraft"* (Stuttgart: Klett-Cotta, 1990), 81–99.

knowledge" (*TM*, 98; *WM*, 104). In Hegel's view, the sensuous appearance of the idea fails – not contingently but necessarily so – to express the self-understanding of the modern spirit. The sensuousness that defines art makes it incapable of expressing the highest form of truth: truth as conceptual understanding. Hence the truth of art is sublated into the reflectively more advanced stages of religion and, finally, conceptual knowledge (philosophy). Art is bound to transcend itself; it is bound to forsake "the element of a reconciled embodiment of the spirit in sensuous form and pass . . . over from the poetry of the imagination to the prose of thought" (*LFA*, vol. I, 89; *VsK*, vol. I, 123). This is a view that Gadamer does not share.[25] Any account of art, he argues, must, from the very outset, acknowledge that the truth of art cannot be rendered in terms of definitive knowledge ("abschließenden Erkenntnis"). There is, Gadamer claims, "no absolute progress and no final exhaustion of what lies in a work of art" (*TM*, 100; *WM*, 105). Kant, he argues, recognized this. It is the achievement of the third Critique "to dissolve the *subordination* of art to conceptual knowledge without at the same time eliminating the *significant relation* of art to conceptual understanding."[26] In Kant's discussion of the ideal of beauty, art is granted a capacity to elicit self-understanding – be it, strictly speaking, moral (as in the Kantian meaning of the term) or more generally ethical-political (as in the Hegel–Gadamer interpretation) – without this threatening the autonomy of aesthetic expression vis-à-vis conceptual reason. Art is granted a cognitive dimension, yet its truth cannot be exhausted by conceptual reason itself. Against what he takes to be Hegel's tendency to hypostatize conceptual knowledge, Gadamer seeks to justify "art as a way of truth in its own right" (*TM*, 98; *WM*, 104). This is why Gadamer, in working out the premises of a hermeneutic philosophy of art, turns to Kant's *Critique of Judgment*, and not just to Hegel's "admirable lectures on aesthetics" (*TM*, 98; *WM*, 103) – and it is why

25 Even though Gadamer is critical of Hegel's end-of-art thesis, he does not endorse the more reductive interpretations of this idea. According to Gadamer, Hegel's formulation of the end of art points to something essential ("sie trifft etwas Wesentliches"). The end-of-art thesis does not imply that art is deprived of a future, but that it, in its essence, is always past: "Hegels Lehre von dem Vergangenheitscharakter der Kunst [meint] nicht in erster Linie, daß die Kunst keine Zukunft mehr habe, sondern daß sie in ihrem Wesen immer schon vergangen ist, wenn sie auch fortblühen mag, bis in welche Zukunft immer." "Ende der Kunst?" (1985), *GW*, vol. VIII, 208.

26 "Intuition and Vividness," *RB*, 164; "Anschauung und Anschaulichkeit," *GW*, vol. VIII, 196, emphasis added.

he does so in spite of the obvious philological and interpretative problems generated by such a move.

Observing how Gadamer reads into Kant's notion of the ideal of beauty a hermeneutical awareness of the self-encounter in the work of art while at the same time maintaining a versatile notion of the work's autonomy vis-à-vis conceptual reason, one cannot help asking how this reading is brought to bear on his overall approach to hermeneutic truth and rationality. For as part of an attempt to defend the criticism launched by, among others, Bürger – i.e., that Gadamer can only develop his own position by rejecting that of the third Critique – the contours of an objection emerge. Although one may argue that Gadamer's interpretation of the third Critique influences his concept of art, it could still be irrelevant to his understanding of knowledge, truth, and rationality. However, such a worry proves groundless. Gadamer repeatedly accentuates how philosophy and art are intertwined in his hermeneutics. Expressing his affiliation with the Stefan George circle,[27] Gadamer claims that it simply was not possible for him to "ignore the fact that the experience of art had something to do with philosophy" and that "the price that the university philosophy of the post-Hegelian era had to pay for its failure to recognize this truth – was barrenness."[28]

Even more important is the fact that Gadamer's engagement with the third Critique – at least as spelled out in his reading of §§16 and 17 – is fueled by the hope that Kant here hints at a conception that neither reduces art to a question of pure aesthetic feeling nor takes it to be solely a matter of conceptualized ideas or knowledge. Kant, he claims, draws up the contours of a third alternative: a conception of truth that embraces our relation to art but which nonetheless reflects that the truth of art cannot be given a final, conceptual explanation. Hence Gadamer's engagement with the third Critique is no mere prolegomenon to his discussion of reason and knowledge, but an entirely essential part of it. However, if Gadamer's interpretation of the *Critique of Judgment* proves essential to his discussion of reason and knowledge, one ought to ask in what way his reading of the third Critique colors his

---

27 For a study of the George circle and its aesthetics, see Robert E. Norton, *Secret Germany: Stefan George and his Circle* (Ithaca: Cornell University Press, 2002). Gadamer, who himself was associated with the George circle in Marburg (Friedrich Wolters, Hans Anton, and Max Kommerell), criticizes the George readings of Plato in "The Origins of Philosophical Hermeneutics," *Philosophical Apprenticeships*, trans. Robert S. Sullivan (Cambridge, Mass.: MIT Press, 1985), 185; "Selbstdarstellung," *WM*, vol. II, 501.

28 "Reflections on my Philosophical Journey" (1996), trans. Richard E. Palmer, *LLP*, 6.

hermeneutic philosophy. Again, this can only be explained by taking into account his critique of Hegel's understanding of the dialectical sublation of the truth of art into religion and, ultimately, philosophy.

Although Gadamer claims that only Hegel succeeds in spelling out the full, hermeneutic potential of the third Critique, he still blames him for sacrificing the autonomy of aesthetic experience in favor of a monolithic notion of philosophical reason. If Hegel ascribes to art a dimension of cognitive validity, he also deems its truth subordinate to conceptual thinking. For Gadamer, Hegel fails to appreciate how art can be granted the capacity to question the sovereignty of conceptual reason. Gadamer, by contrast, wants to pursue this aspect of art. Hence he introduces into the discussion of art and knowledge an explicitly non-Hegelian premise, namely that the work of art, due to its non-discursive qualities, may challenge the way in which our ideas of conceptual reason, truth, and knowledge have come to monopolize our understanding of reason, truth, and knowledge as such (I return to this point in Chapter 4).

In discussing Kant's conception of the ideal of beauty, Gadamer takes the experience of art to be dialogical: it is an experience in which spirit meets itself, one in which self-reflection, knowledge, and truth are at stake. Yet, as realized in the work of art – as concretized in a sensuous (symbolic) form – truth (that towards which we are directed in the dialogical encounter) cannot be exhausted by conceptual interpretation alone. As symbolic, the truth of art transcends the resources of conceptual thinking; it "distinguishes itself in that one never completely understands it."[29] The (self-)knowledge obtained through the encounter with the work therefore cannot be final. It is not a knowledge that may be summarized in the form of a propositional judgment or doctrine, but one that is, essentially, inconclusive and provisional.

This, however, is an insight that challenges Hegel's understanding of knowledge. Although knowledge, for Hegel, is historically developed, history is perceived in terms of the unity of spirit, whose journey through history culminates in the transparency of speculative logic. As we will see in Chapter 4, Gadamer does not accept this transition from history to logic. This is what the example of art shows us. With regard to art, we cannot think of knowledge as a final result or achievement. As far as art is concerned, knowledge emerges as a

---

29 "Zwischen Phänomenologie und Dialektik. Versuch einer Selbstkritik" (1985), WM, vol. II, 7; an English version of this essay is included as part of Gadamer's "Reflections on my Philosophical Journey," LLP, 43.

process that reflects the constitutive finitude pertaining to our understanding of the world and of ourselves.

Dialogue and the self-encounter of reason in the work of art

The notion of dialogical reason first appears in Gadamer's study of
Plato's *Philebus*. In this work, Gadamer extracts from Plato's dialogue a
process-oriented understanding of reason.[30] Critically alluding to Paul
Natorp's interpretation of the Platonic forms as scientific hypotheses,
Gadamer claims that Plato is "no Platonist."[31] Plato offers no doctrines;
his philosophy is open-ended and dialogical – it is, in short, Socratic.
The Socratic–Platonic way of philosophizing is therefore not something
that exists, as it were, along with or independent of Plato's philosophical position. On the contrary, the dialogical aspect of Plato's
writing is essentially tied up with his conception of truth, rationality,
and knowledge. As Gadamer puts it, "Plato's philosophy is a dialectic
not only because in conceiving and comprehending ['im Begreifen'] it
keeps itself on the way to the concept ['zum Begriff'] but also because,
as a philosophy that conceives and comprehends in that way, it knows
man as a creature that is thus 'on the way' and 'in between.'" (*PDE*, 3f.;
PdE, 6).[32] The understanding of knowledge as a dialogical practice is
more or less buried at the moment of its being preserved in the form of
Platonic dialogue. From Aristotle onwards, "philosophizing is no longer
the carrying out of a shared philosophical process" (*PDE*, 5; *PdE*, 8). In
Gadamer's formulation, it is Aristotle's questionable honor to be "the
first theoretician" (ibid.). Furthermore, he claims that as academic
(theoretical), all post-Platonic philosophy is "Aristotelian." All scientific

---

30 For further discussion of Gadamer's return to ancient Greek philosophy, see Giuseppe
Cambiano, *Le retour des Anciens*, trans. Silvia Milanezi (Paris: Éditions Belin, 1994),
chapter 2; Pierre Fruchon, *L'Herméneutique de Gadamer. Platonisme et modernité* (Paris:
Les Éditions du Cerf, 1994); Jean Grondin, *Hermeneutische Wahrheit?* (Königstein:
Forum Academicum, 1982), chapter 1; Brice R. Wachterhauser, *Beyond Being* (Evanston: Northwestern University Press, 1999); as well as Francis J. Ambrosio, "The Figure
of Socrates in Gadamer's Philosophical Hermeneutics"; Donald Davidson, "Gadamer
and Plato's *Philebus*"; and Robert J. Dostal, "Gadamer's Continuous Challenge:
Heidegger's Plato Interpretation," all in *LLP* (259–273, 421–432, and 289–307).

31 "On the Origins of Philosophical Hermeneutics" (1977), *Philosophical Apprenticeships*, 193.

32 Donald Davidson offers a sympathetic elaboration of this aspect of Gadamer's reading
of Plato in "Gadamer and Plato's *Philebus*."

philosophy "is Aristotelianism insofar as it is conceptual work" (*PDE*, 8; *PdE*, 10).

It is only when encountering this predicament, aporetic as it may seem, that it becomes clear why the experience of art figures so prominently in Gadamer's hermeneutics. Resisting conceptual exhaustion – and offering, instead, a kind of self-understanding that is processual and non-conclusive – art reminds us of what philosophy sacrificed in turning from dialogue to a more academic form. However, in order to do so, art must be granted a relative autonomy vis-à-vis conceptual thought. It cannot, as Gadamer takes Hegel to be suggesting, appear as a less mature stage of reason itself. What Hegel took to be the particular limitation of artistic truth – namely that it, as the sensuous expression of the idea, allows for no conclusive, conceptual knowledge – proves, on Gadamer's analysis, to be its particular strength, a strength that is given its first articulation in Kant's discussion of the ideal of beauty in the *Critique of Judgment*.

Gadamer, Heidegger, and the aesthetic tradition

As mentioned at the beginning of this chapter, there was a wider phenomenological engagement with Kant throughout the 1920s and 1930s. Husserl, for one, had shown a strong interest in Kantian epistemology, and Heidegger, shortly after the publication of *Being and Time*, threw himself into the book-length study of the first Critique that, although it was initially intended as a second volume of *Being and Time*, would culminate in *Kant and the Problem of Metaphysics*. When it comes to the third Critique, however, we are left without a systematic study of this sort. This does not imply that Heidegger took no interest in art and beauty or that he considered Kant's aesthetics irrelevant. The 1930s, when Gadamer starts working on the first part of *Truth and Method*, is also the period in which Heidegger lectures on the development of aesthetics, in the first version of *The Origin of the Work of Art*,[33] and in his

---

33 Heidegger's reflections on the origin of the work of art are available in three different editions. A first version of the text was presented in Freiburg in November 1935, a second version of this lecture was offered in Zurich the year after, entitled "Vom Ursprung des Kunstwerkes," and finally the last version, the artwork essay as we now know it, was read in Frankfurt and published as part of the *Holzwege* in 1945. For an overview of the genesis of Heidegger's *The Origin of the Work of Art*, see Jacques Taminiaux, "The Origin of 'The Origin of the Work of Art'," in *Poetics, Speculation, and Judgment*, ed. and trans. Michael Gendre (Albany, N.Y.: SUNY Press, 1993), 153–169.

1936–37 seminar on Nietzsche, "The Will to Power as Art." Heidegger's analysis is bleak. Modern *Dasein* is surrounded by artworks, he claims, yet it no longer knows what art is. Aesthetics has destroyed its relation to art. As Heidegger emphatically puts it, aesthetics is "the element in which art dies" (*OWA*, 79; *UdK*, 83).

Right from his early work towards the end of the 1920s, Gadamer has an ambivalent relation to Heidegger.[34] Although Gadamer is definitively influenced by Heidegger's critique of aesthetics, he is not prepared to follow his teacher blindly. The same applies to his appropriation of Heidegger's ontology. While he adopts Heidegger's ontological turn in hermeneutics and his insistence on the temporality of *Dasein*'s being, Gadamer worries that Heidegger's way of doing philosophy "made it easy to raise the charge of mythological thinking against him."[35] Consequently, Gadamer's first philosophical work on Plato, written when he was still a student of Heidegger, was, as he himself puts it, driven by the wish to "emancipate" himself "from the style of Heidegger."[36] But Gadamer does not only want to liberate himself from Heidegger's style of philosophizing. More importantly, he sets out, in this early study, to rehabilitate a thinker whom Heidegger had already rejected as one of the figures who had had a significant impact on the subsequent development of Western philosophy, ushering it in a problematic metaphysical direction.[37] In Gadamer's view, Plato is not a metaphysical thinker in Heidegger's meaning of the term. Rather, it is Plato's achievement to question the (metaphysical) idea of knowledge as a final result, that is, as something we have or possess. Plato relates knowledge to the dialectical self-questioning that is indexed to the to-and-fro movement of the dialogical interaction. Hence if Gadamer's inquiry into Plato's dialogical concept of

---

See also Heidegger, *The Origin of the Work of* Art, trans. Albert Hofstadter, in *Poetry, Language, Thought* (San Francisco: Harper, 1975), 15–87; *Der Ursprung des Kunstwerkes* (Stuttgart: Reclam, 1960).

34 Gadamer's indebtedness to (and criticisms of) Heidegger is discussed in Ingrid Scheibler, *Gadamer: Between Heidegger and Habermas* (Lanham: Rowman & Littlefield, 2000), chapters 4 and 5, and in Grondin, *Hermeneutische Wahrheit?*, chapter 3.

35 "Historicism and Romanticism," in Hans-Georg Gadamer, *Hans-Georg Gadamer on Education, Poetry, and History*, ed. Dieter Misgeld and Graeme Nicholson, trans. Lawrence Schmidt and Monica Reuss (Albany, N.Y.: SUNY Press, 1992), 128.

36 "Writing and the Living Voice," in ibid., 66.

37 This is the standard retrieval of Heidegger's reading of Plato. For a more balanced interpretation of Heidegger's studies of Plato, see Stephen Mulhall, *Inheritance and Originality: Wittgenstein, Heidegger, Kierkegaard* (Oxford: Clarendon Press, 2001), 185ff.

knowledge is indebted to Heidegger – for example, to his critique of scientific objectivism and his wish to rescue the philosophy of the past by staging a radical and novel reading of the texts of the tradition (two points to which I return in Chapter 5) – he nonetheless develops the phenomenological project in his own, original way.[38] This also applies to his reading of Kant and the beginning of modern aesthetics. By turning to the *Critique of Judgment*, and by reading into this work a set of distinctly hermeneutic premises, Gadamer marks a clear distance from the monolithic nature of Heidegger's critique of the history of modern aesthetics. In Gadamer's reading of Kant's third Critique, modern aesthetics is not simply "the element in which art dies." It is also, at least if read "destructively," that is, critically and against the grain, a tradition that offers some very powerful philosophical resources.[39]

One would have wished, perhaps, that Gadamer's engagement with Kant had ended on this positive note. Yet having spelled out the hermeneutic implications of the *Critique of Judgment*, Gadamer returns to the alleged non-hermeneutical aspects of Kant's work. The rationale of this move is partly historical. According to Gadamer, it is not the promising insights into the dialogical meaning of art that will be of interest to the post-Kantian thinkers who were soon to adopt the aesthetic philosophy of the third Critique. Instead, they used the *Critique of Judgment* to back up a much more problematic turn to artistic genius and the immediacy of aesthetic experience. This is possible because the post-Kantian philosophers focused on Kant's notion of natural beauty, rather than his account of the fine arts.

38 In this context, I would like to revise the standard picture of the relationship between Gadamer and Heidegger, which portrays Gadamer as a thinker who, in Habermas's words, "urbanizes the Heideggerian province." The idea of philosophy as a process, and the claim that this process – the move from philosophy to philosophizing – involves an aspect of self-reflection or self-understanding, is, perhaps, absent in the later Heidegger. However, it is not absent from Heidegger's work in the period leading up to and around the publication of *Being and Time*. What is new with Gadamer, rather, is that he sees this process as inherently dialogical. See Heidegger's 1921–22 lectures *Phenomenological Interpretations of Aristotle: Initiation into Phenomenological Research*, trans. Richard Rojcewicz (Bloomington: Indiana University Press, 2001); *Phänomenologische Interpretationen zu Aristoteles. Einführung in die phänomenologische Forschung*, ed. Walter Bröcker and Käte Bröcker-Oltmanns, *GA*, vol. LXI, part II, in particular. For Habermas's reading of Gadamer, see Jürgen Habermas, "Hans-Georg Gadamer: Urbanizing the Heideggerian Province" (1979), trans. Frederick G. Lawrence, *Philosophical-Political Profiles* (Cambridge, Mass.: MIT Press, 1983), 189–197; "Hans-Georg Gadamer. Urbanisierung der Heideggerschen Provinz," in *Philosophisch-politische Profile* (Frankfurt am Main: Suhrkamp Verlag, 1981), 392–401.

39 In Chapter 3, we will see how this modified position is, to some extent, anticipated by Heidegger's Nietzsche lectures.

In Gadamer's view, Kant's notion of natural beauty completely bypasses the idea of a dialogical self-encounter that he had been hinting at in his discussion of the ideal of beauty. Instead, nature is perceived as the other of human culture. But, Gadamer argues, when nature is seen as such an other, the encounter with beauty remains problematically undetermined. Beauty is reduced to a blank screen, ready for each and every subjective projection. According to Gadamer, this un-hermeneutic conception of beauty is the ultimate result of Kant's tendency to purge his philosophy of every notion of truth and knowledge that fails to meet the standards of validity inherent to the natural sciences.

Natural and artistic beauty

While addressing the (allegedly) non-hermeneutical aspects of Kant's understanding of beauty, Gadamer turns from the "Analytic of the Beautiful" to a later part of the Critique, the Deduction of Pure Aesthetic Judgments (§§41–45). At the close of the deduction, Kant claims to have demonstrated the subjective universality of the pure judgment of taste. We have already seen that a pure judgment of taste is focused on free beauty. It is a judgment on an object that does not presuppose intellectual apprehension or determination. Kant finds the beautiful forms of nature to be the best examples of such beauty. Art, by contrast, qualifies as adherent beauty. Yet as long as the concept by which this beauty is determined (or in terms of which it is dependent) is morally indexed – as long as it is determined in light of a rational concept, rather than an empirical one – the judgment of taste may gain from this relation, even if a judgment that is based on moral interest would no longer qualify as a pure judgment of taste. Kant, it seems, has thereby completed his account of artistic beauty. He has granted art a significant place within the space of human practice, but without jeopardizing the purity of aesthetic judgment. Why, then, is the problem of art once again brought into Kant's discussion? This question guides Gadamer's reading of the Deduction.

In moving on to Kant's discussion of art in §41, one cannot help noticing how this section bears every mark of a new beginning.[40]

---

40 For a more detailed discussion of this point, see Zammito, *The Genesis of Kant's "Critique of Judgment,"* 130f. See also Henry E. Allison, *Kant's Theory of Taste: A Reading of the "Critique of Aesthetic Judgment"* (Cambridge: Cambridge University Press, 2001), 271ff.

Hence Gadamer first seems justified in suspecting that this part of the Critique may shelter an alternative – less hermeneutic – conception of art. Yet the fact that this discussion appears to mark a fresh beginning does not imply that Kant has lost interest in the relation of the beautiful to morality. Kant continues to investigate this relation, although at this point it is approached from a different angle. At the center of Kant's attention is now the pure and non-intellectual beauty of nature.

Kant's interest in the beauty of nature is present from the very beginning of the third Critique. It is, moreover, an interest that is motivated by the architectonic of the critical system. The architectonic purpose of the *Critique of Judgment*, Kant explains, is to bridge the idea of a causally determined nature under laws (developed in the first Critique) and the idea of freedom (central to the second Critique). For, as he puts it, even if:

> an immense gulf is fixed between the domain of the concept of nature, the sensible, and the domain of the concept of freedom, the super-sensible, so that no transition from the sensible to the supersensible (and hence by means of the theoretical use of reason) is possible, just as if they were two different worlds, the first of which cannot have an influence on the second; and yet the second *is* [*soll*] to have an influence on the first, i.e., the concept of freedom is to actualize in the world of sense the purpose enjoined by its laws. (*CJ, KdU*, Introduction, II, 176)

In the first Critique, Kant shows that no formal contradiction exists between the standpoint of necessity and the standpoint of freedom. While resolving the third antinomy of reason, he claims that freedom:

> is here being treated only as a transcendental idea whereby reason is led to think that it can begin the series of conditions in the [field of] appearance by means of the sensibly unconditioned, and so becomes involved in an antinomy with those very laws which it itself prescribes to the empirical employment of the understanding. What we have alone been able to show, and what we have alone been concerned to show, is that this antinomy rests on a sheer illusion, and that causality through freedom is at least *not incompatible with* nature. (*CPR, KdrV*, A 558/B 586)

A demonstration of the *reality* of freedom within a causally determined nature was still not part of the critical agenda. However, to provide such a demonstration is precisely the task assigned to the *Critique of Practical Reason*. By introducing the distinction between an agent's

empirical and intelligible character, Kant not only claims that freedom must be allocated a "logical space,"[41] but also that the moral
agent is ascribed freedom at the noumenal level. At this point Kant
leaves no room for the possibility of freedom's appearance within the
phenomenal sphere of experience.

The third Critique carries this problem a significant step further.
In this work, Kant accepts the (subjective) presumption that nature,
even if causally determined, may also leave room for the realization
of freedom.[42] In the *Critique of Judgment*, he is therefore not concerned with the definition of fine art in particular, but rather asks
what status we may ascribe to the feeling, induced by the experience
of the forms of nature appearing as if they were designed to ease
the operations of the cognitive faculties, of there being a higher
meaning behind the causally determined order of nature. Natural
beauty is granted what Gadamer describes as a methodological
priority over the artistically beautiful, for "[n]atural beauty alone,
not art, can assist in legitimating the concept of purpose in judging
nature" (*TM*, 55; *WM*, 60).

However, in the sections that follow immediately after the deduction of the pure judgment of taste, Kant not only defends the methodological priority of natural beauty, but ascribes to natural beauty a
priority of content (*Inhalt*) (*TM*, 50; *WM*, 56). On Gadamer's interpretation, this strains at Kant's hermeneutic idea that in order to do
justice to art, philosophy must surrender the purity of aesthetics. For
in Kant's discussion of the ideal of beauty, we were presented with the
"advantage of *art* over natural beauty: the advantage of [art] being a
more direct expression of the moral" (ibid., emphasis added). Two
questions thus arise. First, how does Kant arrive at the idea of the
priority of natural over artistic beauty (in terms of its content)? Second, what does this priority tell us about Kant's overall approach to art

41 The expression is borrowed from Henry Allison's discussion of the third antinomy in
    Kant's Theory of Freedom (Cambridge: Cambridge University Press, 1990), 25.
42 "The effect [at which we are to aim] according to the concept of freedom is the final
    purpose which (or the appearance of which in the world of sense) ought to exist;
    and we [must] presuppose the condition under which it is possible [to achieve] this
    final purpose in nature (in the nature of the subject as a being of sense, namely, as a
    human being). It is judgment that presupposes this condition a priori, and without
    regard to the practical [so that] this power provides us with the concept that
    mediates between the concepts of nature and the concept of freedom" (*CJ*; *KdU*,
    Introduction, IX, 195f.).

and aesthetic experience? Gadamer answers these questions by way of a closer study of §§41 and 42.

The immediacy of natural beauty

In §41, Kant examines our empirical interest in beauty. This interest does not, as in a judgment that is based on the ideal of beauty, serve as a determining ground for the judgment (such a determining ground would undermine the purity of the aesthetic). What is being pursued in this context is the possibility of an empirical interest that may be combined with pure aesthetic judgment. The empirical interest in the beautiful exists, Kant argues, but only in a society (*Gesellschaft*) (*CJ, KdU*, §41, 297). A person who is isolated from society, who is, say, abandoned alone on a desolate island, would not, Kant claims, "adorn either his hut or himself; nor would he look for flowers, let alone grow them, to adorn himself with them" (ibid.). "Only in society," he continues, does it occur to a human being "to be, not merely a human being, but one who is also refined in his own way" (ibid.).

Given Gadamer's insistence on the sociability of taste, one would perhaps expect him to find in these remarks a promising echo of a pre-Kantian, humanist notion of taste. However, although Kant uncovers a strong link between sociality and our empirical interest in taste, he maintains, against the humanist conception, that this connection does not speak to taste's advantage. Motivated by a deep distrust of everything refined, cultured, and artificial, Kant suggests that taste's relation to society "can provide only a very ambiguous transition from the agreeable to the good" (*CJ, KdU*, §41, 298). Virtuosi of taste, he explains, are "not just occasionally but apparently as a rule . . . vain, obstinate, and given to ruinous passions" (*CJ, KdU*, §42, 298). Hence they "can perhaps even less than other people claim the distinction of being attached to moral principles" (ibid.). True to the Rousseauian spirit of this section, Kant is quick to add that the kind of taste he has in mind only relates to artistic beauty, under which he includes "the artistic use of natural beauties for our adornment, and hence for vanity's sake" (ibid.). On encountering the beauty of natural forms, however, the situation is reconsidered. As opposed to the interest in man-made beauty, the interest in natural beauty "is *always* a mark of a good soul" (ibid., emphasis added). Thus, according to the Kantian scheme, we may assume that it takes a particularly moral sensitivity to appreciate the beautiful forms of nature. This sensitivity, we may further assume, bears no analogy within the realm of artistic beauty.

Our interest in the artistically beautiful, Kant claims, is mediated "through our inclination to society" (*CJ, KdU,* §41, 297). As such, it is an indirect interest (ibid.). The interest in natural beauty, by contrast, is direct. Kant is not concerned with our empirical, direct interest in natural beauty, but rather with the a priori, intellectual interest we take in their formal qualities. Consequently, Kant refers approvingly to the genuine lover of natural beauty. This person, he claims, would be someone:

> who is all by himself (and has no intention of communicating his observations to others) and who contemplates the beautiful shape of a wild flower, a bird, an insect, etc., out of admiration and love for them, and would not want nature to be entirely without them even if they provided him no prospect of benefit but instead perhaps even some harm. Such a person is taking a direct interest in the beauty of nature. (*CJ, KdU,* §42, 299)

In order further to clarify the difference between our interest in natural beauty and our interest in fine art, Kant produces yet another example. Let us imagine, he suggests, that upon aesthetically enjoying the beautiful forms of nature, the lover of natural beauty suddenly realizes that he is deceived by someone "sticking in the ground artificial flowers . . . or perching artfully carved birds on the branches of trees" (ibid.). Upon discovering the hoax, the lover of natural beauty would find that the "direct interest he previously took in these things *would promptly vanish*" and be replaced by "an interest of vanity, to use these things to decorate his room for the eyes of others" (ibid., emphasis added). Even if the formal qualities of the beautiful object were the same, nothing would remain of the direct interest that he previously took in the object. This is the case because the a priori interest we take in natural beauty necessarily presupposes that this beauty is void of human intentionality and meaning.

On contemplating the beauty of nature, we see no trace of human intentionality. Instead, we face the other of humanity. Yet this other addresses us in a pleasing, almost meaningful way. Nature seems to have overcome its muteness. However, in order to contemplate "that cipher through which nature speaks to us figuratively in its beautiful forms" (*CJ, KdU,* §42, 301), one must possess specific sensibilities. These sensibilities, Kant continues, are morally attuned. Only thus may the interest in the beauty of nature be the mark of a good soul; only thus may the interest in natural beauty be "peculiar to those whose way of thinking is either already trained to the good or exceptionally receptive to this training" (ibid.).

The direct interest in natural beauty is, in other words, generated by the fact that forms, which, as such, hold no human intention, nonetheless appear as if they were meaningful – that they appear as if they were signs of a higher purpose (or freedom) behind the very same nature that, when regarded from the perspective of physical science, is governed by blind causality. The possibility of such an "as if" is the reason why Kant, after the deduction of the pure judgment of taste, places natural beauty over the artistically beautiful. The priority of natural beauty rests with the possibility that nature, even as the other of human subjectivity, may appear as if exhibiting a purpose, which we, elsewhere, "do not find . . . anywhere outside us" (ibid.). As Gadamer summarizes, Kant's preference for natural beauty hinges on the idea that "'nature,' whose innocence consists in the fact that it knows nothing of man or his social vices . . . has something to say to us. As beautiful, nature finds a *language* that brings to *us* an intelligible idea of what mankind is to be" (*TM*, 51; *WM*, 57).

Returning to Hegel

In considering the notion of natural beauty, Gadamer next reviews the validity and relevance of Kant's argument. In his view, the fascination with pure nature carries Kant several steps too far. Ultimately, the preference for natural beauty is based on a faulty premise, namely that it takes a non-human medium, a medium that is devoid of human intentionality, to confirm and acknowledge humanity as such. Although Kant is, admittedly, right in claiming that "When man encounters himself in art, this is not the confirmation of himself by another" (ibid.), one cannot deem this, as Kant does, a deficiency or weakness. At this point, Gadamer claims, Kant no longer "employs the appropriate criteria [*Maßstab*] for the phenomenon of art" (ibid.). The work of art is assessed from the standpoint of natural beauty, and not, as in §17, on the basis of its intrinsically hermeneutic character. If, however, we turn this evaluative hierarchy around, judging natural beauty in terms of the idea of a human self-encounter, then, Gadamer reasons, the indeterminacy of natural beauty no longer appears as a strength, but presents us with a major aesthetic weakness.

Since the beautiful forms of nature do not "say anything," they offer themselves "freely and indeterminately for [any] interpretation according to one's mood" (ibid.). Thus the reflective or dialogical potential of natural beauty turns out to be an illusion. Its meaning, marked by an inescapable "as if," may be interpreted in accordance with the changing modes and feelings of the individual spectator. If natural beauty offers to humanity a confirmation of itself through its other, then this other, in its lack of intellectual constraints, may easily turn out to be a screen that is open to each and every projection. Allegedly presenting us with a most tangible sign of our moral determination, natural beauty may prove but an empty reflection of our own ideas and desires. What Kant takes to be the advantage of natural beauty – namely that nature, because it does not say anything specific, should, so to speak, be able to say everything – is nothing but "the other side of natural beauty's inability to express something specific" (ibid.). For the experience of beauty to offer some kind of recognition, it needs a dimension of meaning (even if this intention or meaning cannot be the content of a propositional judgment); there must be some kind of expression which, although it cannot be conceptually exhausted, still "speaks to us in a significant and definite way" (ibid.).

According to Gadamer, the experience of the beautiful is, as we have seen, a dialogical experience. It is the experience of being addressed in a definitive, yet not conceptually determinate, way. However, in encountering the beauty of nature, at least as expounded by (Gadamer's) Kant, the dialogical aspect of beauty gives way to a monological encounter. What we get back from this encounter might prove to be no more than we invest in it. Our interest in natural beauty therefore cannot be on a par with our interest in art. Only in the work of art does spirit encounter spirit; only here can spirit participate in the kind of truth that is intrinsic to the ongoing process of dialogical self-reflection and understanding. And only by pondering the experience of art as dialogical can we steer clear of the subjectivization of aesthetics, which, according to Gadamer, is inherent to Kant's doctrine of the pure judgment of taste (but not to his idea of the impure judgment that is passed on the basis of a moral reference).

Earlier in this chapter, we saw how Gadamer's interpretation of the moral relevance of the beautiful – the point at which Kant so to speak ceases to be an orthodox Kantian – draws heavily on Hegel. How, then, about Gadamer's critique of Kant's notion of natural beauty? Like his reading of Kant's discussion of the moral relevance of art,

Gadamer's critique of Kant's concept of natural beauty is Hegelian in spirit. Hegel's skepticism towards natural beauty is palpable right from the beginning of his lectures on aesthetics. In the very first paragraphs, Hegel makes it clear that he will exclude the beauty of nature from his investigation and consider only the artistically beautiful (i.e., the area Kant discusses in the parts of the Critique that Gadamer seeks hermeneutically to appropriate) (*LFA*, vol. I, 1; *VsK*, vol. I, 13). The beauty of art, Hegel continues, is the beauty of spirit's own radiation – the sensuous appearance of the idea. This is a beauty that ranks higher than the beauty of nature. Indeed, in Hegel's view, the superiority of such a beauty is so overwhelming that when "considered *formally* [i.e., no matter what it says], even a useless notion ['schlechter Einfall'] that enters a man's head is higher than any product of nature, because in such a notion spirituality and freedom are always present" (*LFA*, vol. I, 2; *VsK*, vol. I, 14). As a product of spirituality and freedom, the work of art carries an intrinsic potential for knowledge and cognition: spirit encounters spirit. In this sense, the meaning of the work is binding. This is not, however, the case with natural beauty. Here, Hegel claims, spirit does not encounter spirit, but that which is, potentially, spirit-less. Consequently, when we experience natural beauty "we feel ourselves too much in a vague sphere, without a *criterion* ['ohne *Kriterium*']" (*LFA*, vol. I, 3; *VsK*, vol. I, 15).

Nature and knowledge in the third Critique

Gadamer's critique of the Kantian understanding of natural beauty must be related to the way in which he traces Kant's "subjectivization of taste" back to his understanding of knowledge in the first Critique. In Gadamer's account, Kant discredited "any kind of theoretical knowledge except that of natural science" (*TM*, 41; *WM*, 47). In Kant's critical philosophy, the concept of knowledge is reserved for the activity of the natural sciences whose conditions of objective validity are grounded in the deduction of the transcendental categories. The realm of concrete historical intersubjectivity – of human practice and interaction, of tradition, religion, and ethical life – is deprived of any straightforward cognitive claim. Gadamer believes that this concept of knowledge must necessarily put constraints on Kant's approach to art and beauty. With the exception of the brief but important discussion of the ideal of beauty, there is, Gadamer argues, no room within Kant's model to ponder the thought, later to be associated with Hegel, of the dialogical truth of art, i.e., the way in which it yields knowledge and self-understanding. Now, it can hardly be denied that, according to Kant, our relation to beauty is not of a direct cognitive nature. Yet it is an open question as to what extent Gadamer, given his focus on the hermeneutic nature of art, really is able to offer an adequate interpretation of Kant's approach to beauty. For Gadamer's critique rests on the assumption – and this, again, is something he inherits from Hegel – that in order for our experience of beauty to be of importance for our self-understanding, it must be granted a direct cognitive claim. If not, Gadamer reasons, our encounter with the beautiful and the sublime is bound to undergo a qualitative devaluation.

In the *Critique of Pure Reason*, Kant accounts for the a priori possibility of cognition in general. As he puts it, the *Critique of Pure Reason* is "a treatise on the method, not a system of the science itself" (*CPR*; *KdrV*, B xxii). Although the deduction of the pure concepts of understanding demonstrates the conditions of possibility for natural science, it cannot prevent the possibility of a certain openness in our empirical study of nature. With regard to the concept of causality, for example, the transcendental deduction has shown a priori that every effect must have a cause. It has not, however, provided any claims regarding the uniformity of natural events and hence the possibility of inductive rationality. There is, in other words, a possible gap, a "looseness of fit,"[43] between the minimal account offered by the *Critique of Pure Reason* and the demand of normal science for a foundation of scientific induction and hypothesis-formation.

Kant wrote two different versions of the introduction to the *Critique of Judgment*. The first version was rejected because it proved too long. Kant therefore went on to produce a shorter, more poignant introduction about half a year later.[44] The first introduction to the *Critique of Judgment*, which was not originally published with the book, is valuable because it shows more clearly how Kant conceives of the possibility that the third Critique, in its focus on our experience of the beauty (purposiveness) of natural forms, responds to the problem of diversity at the level of empirical science, and thus also to the question of knowledge which, in Gadamer's reading, appears to be completely absent from Kant's account.

---

43 The expression is borrowed from Gerd Buchdahl, *Metaphysics and the Philosophy of Science* (Oxford: Basil Blackwell, 1969), 651f.
44 See "Kant's Explanation of Aesthetic Judgment," in Henrich, *Aesthetic Judgment*, 46.

According to Kant, the problem of empirical diversity is that "there are such diverse forms of nature, so many modifications as it were of the universal transcendental concepts of nature, which are left undetermined by these laws, that surely there must be laws for these forms too" (*CJ*; *KdU*, Introduction, IV, 179f.). Determinative judgment proceeds by subsuming the particular under a universal law. Reflective judgment, by contrast, issues from the particular and moves towards the universal. On encountering the diversity of natural forms, only reflective judgment indicates the possibility of a higher unity or purpose. This purpose cannot be of an objective nature. It can only be proved to be subjective, a purposiveness related to our endeavor to grasp empirical nature as an intelligible order – the idea of nature as a well-organized unity rather than a "crude chaotic aggregate without the slightest trace of a system" (*CJ*; *KdU*, First Introduction, IV, 209). Furthermore, Kant argues that the idea (or maxim) that nature, in its diversity, is organized as a coherent whole is equivalent to the idea that it is organized in a system of genera and species. The subjective purposiveness of nature is identified with the idea of an order by means of which our (empirical) concepts or laws can be organized in terms of their increasing extension. If nature were organized in order to ease the work of our cognitive powers, it would make up an inductively predictable structure, a well-ordered hierarchy that points the way towards an increasing generality and scope of applicability for our (empirical) laws and concepts.

It is already in the *Critique of Pure Reason* that Kant discusses the idea of such a structure. Here he assigns to reason (in its regulative use) the task of anticipating an order in our empirical cognition. It is, as Kant puts it, "the business of reason to render the unity of all possible empirical acts of the understanding systematic; just as it is of the understanding to connect the manifold of the appearances by means of concepts, and to bring it under empirical laws" (*CPR*; *KdrV*, A 664/ B 692). In the *Critique of Judgment*, however, the idea of such a unity is no longer limited to the regulative use of reason. It is seen as a transcendental principle, the (subjective) principle of judgment power. The idea of an order of nature is not exhausted by the appeal to reason's idea of a maximum, but is traced back to a particular relation between the cognitive powers: the free play between the imagination, in its schematizing capacity, and the understanding – a play that is only elicited by our disinterested and non-instrumental contemplation of nature.

The free play of the cognitive faculties is, as we have seen, induced by the experience of nature appearing as if it were organized so as to facilitate their work. It is an experience in which the forms of nature, in spite of representing the other of human reason and rationality, appear not as if they were the products of blind contingency, but rather as the result of an intentional and purposive activity. As such, the experience of natural beauty is that of nature appearing as art. Hence Kant speaks of a *technique* of nature, where technique is distinguished from a mechanical application of rules.[45] In Kant's own words, we may speak of a technique of nature in the cases where "we merely *judge* (certain) objects of nature *as if* they were made possible through art" (*CJ; KdU*, First Introduction, I, 200). In the *Critique of Judgment*, the concept of nature as the realm of blind law-likeness is supplemented by the idea of nature appearing as though it were the realm of intentionality and meaning. This, in turn, incites the hope that morality may be realized in the realm of nature – the hope of a reconciliation of the laws of nature and the law of freedom.

By ascribing aesthetic judgment a transcendental principle of its own, Kant concomitantly explores the possibility of a non-instrumental relation to nature. As Gadamer correctly points out, this relation to nature is not cognitively constituted. Yet, even if it escapes the formal demands of cognition, Kant does not take natural beauty to be devoid of cognitive relevance. Gadamer is therefore not right in claiming that the doctrine of Kant's aesthetics presupposes a rigid understanding of truth and rationality in terms of natural science. Nor is he right in regarding the encounter with natural beauty as an immediate experience, at least not with the meaning that Gadamer ascribes to this term. The *Critique of Judgment* is the work in which Kant, within the framework of transcendental idealism, explores the possibility of an irreducibly non-instrumental, non-subsumptive relation to nature. Although our aesthetic relation to nature cannot be granted a direct and explicit cognitive validity, it serves as a guiding premise, even a rational guiding premise, for our cognitive orientations. What Kant is driving at in the

45 According to Kant, the technique of nature "contrasts with the mechanisms of nature, which consists in the causality nature has insofar as it connects the diverse without [there being] a concept underlying the manner of this unification, roughly as when we call certain lifting devices – e.g., a lever or an inclined plane – machines but not works of art, since they can produce their purpose-directed effect even without [there being] an underlying idea; for while these devices can be used for purposes, their [own] possibility does not require a reference to purposes" (*CJ; KdU*, First Introduction, VII, 219).

Critique of Judgment is the idea of a pre-predicative synthesis that transcends the grasp of determinative judgment but that nonetheless is relevant to it. Even if this cannot be called a hermeneutics in any ontological meaning of the term, it still anticipates Gadamer's own effort to rekindle a kind of experience that "methodological dispute serves only to conceal and neglect, something that does not so much confine or limit modern science as precede it and make it possible" (*TM*, xxix; *WM*, vol. II, 439).

The problem with Gadamer's reading of Kant is therefore not, as Bürger suggests, that he categorically disapproves of the hermeneutic potential of the third Critique. Rather, the problem is that he, like Hegel, hypostatizes a contrast between Kant's account of art, on the one hand, and his understanding of natural beauty, on the other. Thus he prevents himself from acknowledging how the experience of natural beauty, for Kant, is an experience of nature as art (or, as Kant also puts it, as technique – that is, an experience of nature as if it were endowed with an intrinsic meaning and intentional organization that enables inductive research, as well as providing a bridge between freedom and nature as subjected to causal laws). If Gadamer argues that Kant, in §§41 and 42 of the *Critique of Judgment*, illegitimately judges art from the perspective of natural beauty, then the opposite seems to apply to Gadamer himself. Like Hegel, he ends up evaluating Kant's concept of natural beauty from the standpoint of fine art. In his eagerness to rehabilitate the hermeneutic aspect of Kant's discussion of art and morality (the ideal of beauty), he overlooks the hermeneutic potential of Kant's discussion of natural beauty. In the chapters to come, we will see how this misreading hampers Gadamer's engagement with post-Kantian philosophy.

BEYOND THE THIRD CRITIQUE: EPISTEMOLOGICAL SKEPTICISM AND AESTHETIC CONSCIOUSNESS

In Chapter 1 we saw that Gadamer distinguishes too sharply between Kant's account of art and his account of natural beauty, and that, as a consequence of this, he wrongly ascribes to Kant a radically non-hermeneutic conception of natural beauty. However, the fact that Gadamer misreads Kant's notion of natural beauty does not mean that the basic orientation of his critique – the more general philosophical point that he is after – is illegitimate as such. In this second chapter, I argue that Gadamer's misreading of Kant's approach to natural beauty paves the way for a more promising critique of aesthetic subjectivism and immediacy, notions that Gadamer traces back to the paradigm of aesthetic consciousness.

As opposed to the discussion of the *Critique of Judgment*, Gadamer's critique of aesthetic consciousness does not deal in detail with selected sections of a particular philosophical work. It does not address a specific thinker or a specific historical epoch. At stake is an attempt to clarify and make explicit the comprehensive intellectual framework by which post-Kantian aesthetics has had a tendency to be delimited.

Emerging within the romantic period, aesthetic consciousness questions the rigid scientific understanding of human life and its place in nature, and emphasizes instead our capacity for spontaneity, freedom, and creativity. In drawing attention to the role of art in human life, aesthetic consciousness stresses the immediacy of aesthetic creation and experience, claiming that the work of art is presented to consciousness in terms of pure aesthetic qualities. Yet in focusing on the idea of pure aesthetic qualities, aesthetic consciousness fails to account for the linguistic mediation of experience. It ends up defending an aesthetic immediacy akin to the one that Hegel criticizes in his discussion of romanticism and the beautiful soul.[1] Like Hegel, Gadamer wants to overcome this way of thinking and defend, against aesthetic subjectivism and the turn to aesthetic immediacy, the cognitive relevance of art. For even if aesthetic consciousness initially aimed at developing an alternative to the scientific view of the world, it fails to consider the possibility, suggested by Kant's account of the ideal of beauty, that the experience of art might give rise to a particular kind of knowledge and self-understanding.

Although Gadamer's discussion of aesthetic consciousness offers a promising critique of the turn towards aesthetic subjectivity and immediacy, it is not without problems. This becomes clear upon comparing Gadamer's position to that of Hegel. For if Hegel persistently criticizes the romantic withdrawal to the sphere of subjectivity and immediacy, he never loses sight of how post-Kantian aesthetics responds to the situation of art in modernity. Gadamer does not address this aspect of romantic philosophy. As a result, he entertains a far too narrow understanding of modern aesthetics. Nowhere is this more evident than in his critique of the museum – the expression, par excellence, of the predicament of art in the modern era. While he disapproves of the way in which the museum leaves us with the illusion of a work without a world, Gadamer never asks what the alternatives are, in modernity, to the idea of the museum as a place for art and aesthetic appreciation.

This chapter opens with an account of Gadamer's use of the term "aesthetic consciousness" and proceeds to discuss the historical-systematic roots of this paradigm in the romantic (mis)reading of Kant and Fichte. Gadamer's reconstruction of the historical development of aesthetic consciousness is then reviewed. While Gadamer's critique of aesthetic consciousness is impeded by a number of historical shortcomings, this should not keep us from acknowledging the systematic relevance of his argument. Gadamer convincingly critiques aesthetic subjectivism and the notion of aesthetic autonomy. Moreover, he aptly criticizes the notion of pure, aesthetic givenness or immediacy. According to Gadamer, the problems of aesthetic consciousness can be overcome only by conducting a shift from aesthetics, in the narrow meaning of the term,

---

1 For a discussion that traces the beautiful soul back to its roots in the English–Scottish idea of the beautiful moral sciences, see Robert E. Norton, *The Beautiful Soul: Aesthetic Morality in the Eighteenth Century* (Ithaca: Cornell University Press, 1995).

to hermeneutics – that is, to a broader theory of the linguistic mediatedness of experience. Yet, in spite of these valuable points, Gadamer's critique of aesthetic consciousness remains hampered by a fundamental flaw: even though he is indebted to Hegel's objections to romantic aesthetics, Gadamer ultimately fails to live up to Hegel's awareness of the particular challenges of art in modernity.

Aesthetic consciousness and the romantic misunderstanding of Kant's Critique

We have seen that Gadamer begins his philosophical training as a student of ancient Greek philosophy and a great admirer of Platonic dialogue. As it is, the term "aesthetic consciousness" is initially introduced in order to characterize the subjectivist turn among the poets in Plato's Athens: that is, the position against which Plato's critique of poetry was initially directed.[2] However, in turning to aesthetic consciousness, Gadamer's aim is not to address a bygone intellectual era. Rather, aesthetic consciousness, in his work, refers to a set of fundamental premises – prejudices, one might even say – that have misled our understanding of art and beauty throughout the entire tradition of Western philosophy, and never more so than in the period of post-Kantian thought.

Hegel, we saw in Chapter 1, plays an important role in Gadamer's reading of Kant's *Critique of Judgment*. Gadamer's wish to address the premises of our own philosophical horizon in terms of their historical presuppositions is also influenced by Hegel, this time by Hegel's reconstruction of spirit's organic unfolding in history. In the *Phenomenology of Spirit*, Hegel traces the development of spirit through a set of concrete forms of reflection – intellectual figures or *Gestalten*, as he puts it. Each of these figures is approached in terms of its inherent philosophical *Maßstab*, its implicit notion of what counts as a valid argument, belief, or ground for action. Hegel's strategy is that of an immanent critique: he wishes to show how each figure, while failing to redeem its own inherent criteria, points the way towards the sublation of spirit into new and more adequate forms of reflection. According

---

2 See "Plato and the Poets" (1934), trans. P. Christopher Smith, *DD*, 65; "Plato und die Dichter," *GW*, vol. V, 206. Although Gadamer uses the concept of aesthetic consciousness as early as 1934, it is not given a systematic exposition until the end of the 1950s.

to Hegel, this is the method of dialectics in the most comprehensive sense of the term.[3]

Hegel's philosophy was deliberately designed not only as an alternative to transcendental idealism, but also to the intellectual strategies of the Jena romantics. Although he himself had started out as a young, romantic scholar in Tübingen, Hegel soon became more skeptical in his attitude towards what he perceived as lighthearted romantic aestheticism. His rampant critique of romantic philosophy in the *History of Philosophy* gives a clear expression of this, but so does his discussion of the beautiful soul in the *Phenomenology of Spirit*. For Hegel, the beautiful soul represents a subjectivist understanding of ethical life and morality. The beautiful soul is driven by contempt for a society that can no longer be perceived as an organic, harmonious totality and turns its back on the ethical-political realm of intersubjectivity. What matters to the beautiful soul is the pristine domain of the inner. But the retreat to the inner offers no long-term solutions to the ills of modernity. The beautiful soul is unable to achieve any mediation of its moral consciousness and, as a consequence, ends up living "in dread of besmirching the splendour of its inner being by action and an existence; and, in order to preserve the purity of its heart, it flees from contact with the actual world" (*PS*, 400; *PhG*, 483).

By and large, Gadamer follows Hegel's critique of the beautiful soul. In *Truth and Method*, the concept of aesthetic consciousness designates a tendency to consider our relation to art and beauty in terms of subjective feeling. Nonetheless, aesthetic consciousness is not a position that, as Alan How suggests, reduces our judgments of taste to "matters of personal opinion."[4] Gadamer's critique of aesthetic consciousness is not limited to an empiricist position of this sort. If it

---

3 As Terry Pinkard expounds, dialectics is based on the idea that "A reflective form of life takes such and such to be authoritative reasons for belief and action; those types of reasoning then generate within their own terms skeptical objections against themselves (as Hegel puts it, they generate their own 'negation'); that form of reflective life, however, turns out to be unable to reassure itself about what it had taken as authoritative for itself; the new form of reflective life that replaces it and claims to complete it, however, takes *its* account of what *for it* have come to be authoritative reasons to be that which was necessary to successfully resolve the issues that were self-undermining for the older form of life; but this new reflective form of life in turn generates self-undermining skepticism about its own accounts, and the progression continues." Terry Pinkard, *Hegel's Phenomenology: The Sociality of Reason* (Cambridge: Cambridge University Press, 1996), 12.

4 Alan How, *The Habermas–Gadamer Debate and the Nature of the Social* (Aldershot: Ashgate Publishing Company, 1995), 25.

were directed against Hume and the empiricists, then the standpoint of the third Critique, where Kant ascribes to taste an a priori dimension of validity, would itself represent an overcoming of aesthetic consciousness. However, in Gadamer's view, Kant's third Critique represents no such overcoming. Rather, by grounding the pure judgment of taste in a universal, subjective principle and by gearing aesthetics towards the alleged immediacy of natural beauty, Kant furnishes aesthetic consciousness with its ultimate philosophical foundation.

Can we, then, assume that aesthetic consciousness can be traced back to the interest in natural beauty and the concept of pure aesthetic judgment that is developed in the *Critique of Judgment*, i.e., to the dimension of this work that makes Kant abstain from further elaborating the hermeneutic nature of art and beauty that he discloses in the discussion of the ideal of beauty? Richard Bernstein, for one, suggests a close connection between Kant and aesthetic consciousness. "It is," he claims, Kant's "'radical subjectivization' of aesthetic judgment that Gadamer calls 'aesthetic consciousness.'"[5] In light of Gadamer's early discussion of aesthetic consciousness, such a claim may prove sustainable. In an essay from 1958, "Zur Fragwürdigkeit des ästhetischen Bewußtseins," aesthetic consciousness is identified with aesthetic judging, and, as autonomous, this capacity is given its first systematic justification in Kant's third Critique.[6] However, this understanding of aesthetic consciousness cannot be extended to Gadamer's later work. Only a few years later, in *Truth and Method*, Gadamer leaves us in no doubt that aesthetic consciousness belongs to the standpoint of art, which, in turn, is not the same as the standpoint of taste (*TM*, 81; *WM*, 86f.). Even though Gadamer, a few lines later, admits that the concept of art is itself "a product of aesthetic consciousness" (*TM*, 81; *WM*, 87), this claim also underlines the close relation between aesthetic consciousness and the standpoint of art.

The standpoint of art, Gadamer argues, is developed in the wake of (and not with) the third Critique. Kant, as we have seen, was primarily interested in the normativity-claim that inheres in our disinterested judging of natural beauty. In spite of his promising remarks about taste's relation to morality, Kant did not enter into a fully-fledged

---

5 Richard Bernstein, *Beyond Objectivism and Relativism: Science, Hermeneutics and Praxis* (Philadelphia: University of Pennsylvania Press, 1983), 119.

6 As Gadamer here puts it, "Das ästhetische Urteil ist eine Funktion des ästhetischen Bewußtseins." "Zur Fragwürdigkeit des ästhetischen Bewußtseins," *GW*, vol. VIII, 9.

discussion of art. It is, Gadamer maintains, first with Friedrich Schiller that we witness a shift from an interest in taste and judgment to an interest in artistic beauty (*TM*, 84; *WM*, 90). From now on "[a]esthetics is ultimately possible *only as the philosophy of art*" (*TM*, 58; *WM*, 64, emphasis added). Aesthetics is no longer concerned with such questions as "Can a dimension of validity be ascribed to taste and reflective judgment?" but, rather, asks "What is a work of art?" and "Why do works of art matter to us at all?" Gadamer finds this transition to be most decisive. As it is, Gadamer's own hermeneutics deals with the question of art, and so do Hegel's lectures on aesthetics (*TM*, 98; *WM*, 103). Indeed, one could even argue that Gadamer's own appropriation of the third Critique – focusing, as it does, on the relation between art and morality in §§16 and 17 – presupposes the standpoint of art. Only against this background does Gadamer's reading of Kant emerge as an attempt to trace a hermeneutic philosophy of art in the third Critique, even though the overall perspective of the Critique is that of reflective judgment and the teleology of nature.

The romantic philosophers left behind the interest in natural beauty and turned instead to art and artistic beauty. Yet, in doing so, they failed to acknowledge the full philosophical potential inherent in this shift. While moving from an investigation into the normativity of taste to an interest in art, they remained faithful to the framework staked out by Kant's doctrine of pure aesthetic judgment (rather than his hermeneutic account of the impure, morally related interest in art). Aesthetic consciousness ignores Kant's own demand for a relation between art and reason; it ignores what Gadamer takes to be Kant's own suggestion that "In order to do justice to *art*, aesthetics must go *beyond* itself and surrender the 'purity' of the aesthetic" (*TM*, 92; *WM*, 98, emphasis added). Because it turns its back on the hermeneutic impulse of the third Critique and focuses, rather, on Kant's notion of pure aesthetic judging, aesthetic consciousness is, in Gadamer's view, left with the idea that beautiful art must be considered from the perspective of natural beauty. According to Gadamer, this implies that it must be viewed as the art of genius. With romantic aesthetics, genius is turned into the criterion of artistic production, that by which a work of art is distinguished from other kinds of objects and representations. As such, the notion of genius provides post-Kantian philosophy with a "transcendental principle for aesthetics in general" (*TM*, 58; *WM*, 64).

The first step in Gadamer's critique of post-Kantian aesthetics is, in other words, to pin down aesthetic consciousness as a model that leaves behind Kant's interest in taste and judgment power but none-theless remains influenced by his reflections on natural beauty and aesthetic genius. But, he continues, not until it is detached from its Kantian framework and perceived through the lens of post-Kantian philosophy does the notion of aesthetic genius reach its full impact. How, then, does Gadamer account for this development?

Misreading Kant and Fichte: subjectivity and aesthetic genius

To see why Gadamer takes the concept of genius to be of crucial importance for aesthetic consciousness, one must bear in mind that the notion of aesthetic genius is a relatively recent addition to the philosophical vocabulary. Admittedly, earlier philosophy entertained a general notion of genius, but only in post-Kantian aesthetics is cre-ative production, hence also the notion of genius itself, restricted to the realm of art.[7] In the *Critique of Judgment*, Kant famously claims that fine art is the art of genius (*CJ, KdU*, §46, 307). This claim proves more important than Kant would ever have been able to foresee. With the romantic adaptation of the third Critique, the notion of creative genius soon shapes and lends voice to a whole new *Zeitgeist* in aesthetics.

In the course of the previous chapter, little attention was paid to Kant's account of genius. However, in order to come fully to terms with Gadamer's critique of aesthetic consciousness, the contours of this account must be retrieved. Kant deals with aesthetic genius in the "Deduction of Pure Aesthetic Judgments," that is, §§46–51 of the *Critique of Judgment*. In the section immediately prior to this discussion, Kant repeats his claim, first put forth in §16, that only free beauty, i.e., beauty that is contemplated without regard to a concept, can be an object of pure aesthetic judging. Nature provides the privileged examples of free beauty: the harmonious shapes of a petal or the tortuous forms of a conch – that is, beautiful forms that have not been intentionally brought forth and are not designed in order to fulfill a particular purpose. If a work of art, i.e., a product of human intention,

---

7 As Wladyslaw Tatarkiewicz sums up this point: "Only in the nineteenth century did the term 'creator' enter the language of *art*. But it then became the *exclusive* property (in the human world) of art: creator became a synonym for artist. New expressions, for-merly superfluous, were formed, such as the adjective 'creative' and the noun 'creativity'; these were used exclusively in reference to artists and their labor." Wla-dyslaw Tatarkiewicz, *A History of Six Ideas: An Essay in Aesthetics*, trans. Christopher Kasparek (The Hague: Martinus Nijhoff, 1980), 251.

is to appear beautiful, then it needs to display a similar freedom. The work of art cannot appear to be produced so as to satisfy some pre-existing concept, law, or notion. Can, then, the work of art be an object of pure aesthetic judgment? In Kant's view it can, but only to the extent that it looks to us like nature (*CJ; KdU*, §45, 306). The work of art must display a spontaneity, a lack of (conceptual) constraints, that makes us see in it a freedom akin to the freedom we perceive in natural beauty.[8] This is an aspect of Kant's aesthetics that Gadamer adopts. He claims that:

> Kant is right when he says that art must be capable of "being regarded as nature" – i.e., please without betraying the constraints of rules. We do not consider the intentional agreement between what is represented and the reality we know, we do not look to see what it resembles, we do not measure its claim to significance by a criterion that we already know well. (*TM*, 52; *WM*, 57)

According to Gadamer, however, the next step in Kant's analysis is more problematic. Being a product of human intentionality, art must somehow be thought through and organized. It must, as Kant puts it, display a rule (*Regel*). Yet, if it is not to hinder the nature-like appearance of the work, the rule must show "no hint that [it] was hovering before the artist's eyes and putting fetters on his mental powers" (*CJ; KdU*, §45, 307). This is where aesthetic genius enters the picture. Aesthetic genius provides a rule that shows no sign of having been consciously conceived by the artist. Thus nature is introduced within the realm of culture. According to Kant, genius is the talent "through which nature gives the rule to art" (*CJ; KdU*, §46, 307). In the work of genius, the rule of art is intrinsically related to the immediacy of aesthetic creation.

Among the romantic philosophers, Kant's idea of creative genius quickly gained currency – it reached "a true apotheosis," as Gadamer at one point puts it (*TM*, 59; *WM*, 65). In Gadamer's view, the growing interest in creative genius must be explained in light of Fichte's theory of subjectivity. Again Gadamer pursues a Hegelian line of reasoning.

---

8 Allison helpfully discusses the point that fine art must seem like nature, yet we must be conscious of it as art: this statement does not simply entail "the trivial point that it must *be art*, but rather the substantive claim that we must be *conscious* of it as such. As Kant makes clear, this is because such a consciousness is a precondition of its evaluation as beautiful, or, equivalently, as fine art. For unless we were aware of it as the product of a conscious intent, we could not begin to appreciate it as art." *Kant's Theory of Taste*, 274f.

According to Hegel, Fichte is the true successor of the Kantian project. "The shortcoming in the Kantian philosophy," Hegel claims, "was its unthinking inconsistency ['gedankenlose Inkonsequenz'], through which speculative unity was lacking to the whole system; and this short-coming was removed by Fichte."[9] Gadamer, however, is more interested in another aspect of the Kant–Fichte connection. In Gadamer's reading, Fichte's emphasizing of spontaneous subjectivity is but a universalization of the Kantian theory of genius. Fichte, Gadamer claims, elevates "genius and what genius created to a universal transcendental position" (*TM*, 60; *WM*, 65). The idea of an unlimited, immediate spontaneity is turned into "a universal concept of value" (*TM*, 59; *WM*, 65).

The romantics worried about the way in which scientific reason monopolizes our understanding of ourselves and the world. Even though scientific rationality may well increase our understanding of physical nature (as perceived under causal laws), it fails to account for the full scope of human nature and in particular for the dimensions of freedom and spontaneity.[10] Classicist aesthetics, with its search for a "Newton of art,"[11] emerges as inadequate. The concept of genius, by contrast, fits in nicely with these novel aesthetic sensitivities. Art no longer emerges as a further manifestation of scientific rationality, but appears as something that exceeds the logic of such a rationality altogether. Against the conception of nature and human being in terms of causality and natural laws, aesthetic genius represents a spirit of freedom and transgression. If, as Lessing suggests, the educated, enlightened society has made "machines out of men," then the aes-thetics of genius penetrates this lifeless existence in order to "make men again out of these machines."[12] The creativity of genius attests to

9 G. W. F. Hegel, *Lectures on the History of Philosophy*, trans. E. S. Haldane and Frances H. Simson (Lincoln: University of Nebraska Press, 1995), vol. III, 481; *Vorlesungen über die Geschichte der Philosophie*, vol. III, *Werke* [vol. XX], 388. Friedrich Schlegel expounds the same problem in Athenaeum Fragment no. 281, *Lucinde and the Fragments*, trans. Peter Firchow (Minneapolis: University of Minnesota Press, 1971), 202; *Kritische und theo-retische Schriften* (Stuttgart: Reclam, 1978), 111.

10 Charles Taylor, whose analysis of romanticism holds much in common with Gadamer's critique of aesthetic consciousness, expounds this aspect of romantic philosophy in *Sources of the Self: The Making of the Modern Identity* (Cambridge: Cam-bridge University Press, 1989), chapter 21.

11 This expression is borrowed from Ernst Cassirer, *The Philosophy of the Enlightenment*, trans. Fritz C. A. Koelln and James Pettegrove (Princeton: Princeton University Press, 1979), 280; *Die Philosophie der Aufklärung* (Tübingen: J. C. B. Mohr, 1932), 375.

12 Gottfried Lessing's *Hamburg Dramaturgy*, quoted in *The Philosophy of the Enlightenment*, 296; *Die Philosophie der Aufklärung*, 395.

a dimension of human being that is repressed or even destroyed by scientific reason; it reflects a dimension of nature that has largely been left unaccounted for by the ascendant natural sciences.[13] Attuned to the idea of the immediacy of nature, the romantic aesthetics of genius continues and further develops the Rousseauian spirit, which, as we have seen, Gadamer, rightly or not, takes to be at the core of Kant's interest in natural beauty.

However, in his critique of aesthetic consciousness, Gadamer, in line with his previous strategy of reading, turns precisely to Kant's *Critique of Judgment.* He wants to show that even though creative genius plays an important role within the first part of the *Critique of Judgment,* Kant himself would never go so far as to ascribe to genius a sovereign position vis-à-vis taste and critical judgment. Kant, Gadamer insists, had "steadfastly maintained the concept of taste which the Sturm und Drang not only violently dismissed but also violently demolished" (*TM,* 57; *WM,* 62). For Kant, genius is a necessary condition for something to count as art, yet by no means a sufficient one. Only "shallow minds ['seichte Köpfe']," Kant claims (referring, apparently, to some prominent representatives of the *Sturm und Drang*),[14] would understand art only in terms of originality and immediacy (*CJ; KdU,* §47, 310). Genius furnishes the material for products of art but can hardly vouch for aesthetic form (ibid.). Aesthetic form requires discipline and a talent that is academically trained (ibid.), i.e., a capacity for judgment. In spite of his Rousseauian avoidance of everything polished and cultured, when it comes to art Kant unwaveringly emphasizes the role of critical judgment. Hence, the dream of an immediate and entirely

---

13 This was the heart of the debate about the genius of Pope versus the genius of Shakespeare, the former being a schooled genius, the latter an unschooled one. Zammito briefly discusses this debate (and its possible influence on Kant) in *The Genesis of Kant's "Critique of Judgment,"* 28ff. Gadamer acknowledges the importance of Shakespeare for the German romantic movement in *TM,* 56f.; *WM,* 62. For a more detailed account of Shakespeare's importance for eighteenth-century German aesthetics, see my "Reading Shakespeare; Reading Modernity," *Angelaki: Journal of the Theoretical Humanities,* vol. 9, no. 3, 2004, 17–31.

14 As Zammito puts it, "Kant's hostility to the *Sturm und Drang* is the decisive context in which one must read not only his distinction of art from science in §43, but also his whole treatment of genius in §§46–47. Kant has a very definite target in mind, even within the *Sturm und Drang*: Johann Herder. His juxtaposition of science and art can be read – should be read – as a juxtaposition, as well, of his own *method* with Herder's *manner.*" *The Genesis of Kant's "Critique of Judgment,"* 137. For a fuller account of Herder's aesthetics, see Robert E. Norton, *Herder's Aesthetics and the European Enlightenment* (Ithaca: Cornell University Press, 1991), chapters 1 and 4 in particular.

unconstrained aesthetic creation is incompatible with the spirit of the
Critique of Judgment. As Gadamer puts it, the "systematic predominance
of genius over the concept of taste" is "not Kantian" (*TM*, 59; *WM*, 65),
and, as a consequence, aesthetic consciousness turns out to be predicated on a misunderstanding of Kant's *Critique of Judgment.*

Romanticism regained

I have already mentioned that the first part of *Truth and Method,* in
which Gadamer works out his critique of aesthetic consciousness, was
conceived as early as the 1930s.[15] This is not only the decade in which
Heidegger developed his criticism of the aesthetic tradition from
Plato to Schopenhauer, but also a period when the romantic *Zeitgeist*
was subjected to systematic criticism.[16] During the past twenty years,
however, there has been a new interest in romantic philosophy.
Manfred Frank's study of the romantic continuations of Kant's third
Critique offers just one example.[17] Other examples would include
works by Stanley Cavell, Charles Larmore, and Frederick Beiser.[18] In
light of these studies, Gadamer's criticism may appear both biased and
exaggerated in its Hegelian gist.

Consider, to start with, Gadamer's claim that the romantics
approached Kant's notion of genius through the lens of Fichte's
theory of subjectivity. Fichte's theory of subjectivity changes
throughout his career and cannot be reduced to a single position.[19]

---

15 Gadamer, "Writing and the Living Voice," in Gadamer, *Hans-Georg Gadamer on Education, Poetry and History,* 64.
16 For an account of nineteenth- and twentieth-century criticism of romanticism in
German philosophy, see Karl Heinz Bohrer, *Die Kritik der Romantik* (Frankfurt am
Main: Suhrkamp Verlag, 1989).
17 See Frank, *Einführung in die frühromantische Ästhetik* and his interpretation of
Schleiermacher's hermeneutics in *Das individuelle Allgemeine* (Frankfurt am Main:
Suhrkamp Verlag, 1977).
18 Stanley Cavell, *In Quest of the Ordinary: Lines of Skepticism and Romanticism* (Chicago:
University of Chicago Press, 1988); Charles Larmore, *The Romantic Legacy* (New York:
Columbia University Press, 1996); Frederick Beiser, *The Romantic Imperative* (Cam-
bridge, Mass.: Harvard University Press, 2003). See also the essays collected in Nikolas
Kompridis (ed.), *Philosophical Romanticisms* (London: Routledge, 2006).
19 Dieter Henrich discusses the development of Fichte's concept of self-consciousness in
"Fichte's Original Insight," trans. David R. Lacherman, in Darrel E. Christensen (ed.),
Contemporary German Philosophy, vol. I (University Park, Pa.: Pennsylvania State Uni-
versity Press, 1982), 15–53; *Fichtes ursprüngliche Einsicht* (Frankfurt am Main: Vittorio
Klostermann, 1967).

However, Gadamer does little to accommodate this. Furthermore, he fails to mention that even though the *Wissenschaftslehre* explores the I's capacity for absolute self-positing,[20] Fichte also anticipates Hegel's understanding of intersubjectivity as being based upon mutual recognition.[21] In Gadamer's account, Fichte's thinking represents little else than a problematic subjective idealism.[22] But what if the romantics, in their approach to Fichte, were more subtle than Gadamer is willing to consider? What if they were influenced not only by Fichte's notion of transcendental subjectivity, but also by his turn towards intersubjective recognition? Could, then, philosophical romanticism still be characterized as aesthetic consciousness? These are issues that Gadamer fails to address. Another question that Gadamer systematically evades is whether the romantic philosophers, in their reading of the *Critique of Judgment*, really did focus that one-sidedly on the spontaneity of creative genius. What about Kant's notion of aesthetic ideas? To the extent that the romantics were interested in such a concept (the notion of an intuition for which an adequate concept can never be found), the recourse to aesthetic genius would not be the only way to distinguish a work of art from non-aesthetic objects and representations.

Even though these objections are valid and important, they fail to do full justice to Gadamer's critique of aesthetic consciousness. For what Gadamer is after is not really to offer a historical portrait of the romantic reception of Kant's *Critique of Judgment*. Rather, his point is of a more general nature, namely that modern aesthetics, as it develops in the wake of Kant's critique of aesthetic judgment, remains inclined to see the experience of art as something subjective, something that may well have to do with immediacy, inwardness, and feeling but that is of no relevance for our cognitive, ethical, or political orientations. This way of thinking cannot be reduced to one particular philosophical

20 See for instance Johann G. Fichte, "Zweite Einleitung in die Wissenschaftslehre," in *Sämtliche Werke*, ed. Immanuel Hermann Fichte (Berlin: Walter de Gruyter, 1971), vol. I, 463.

21 Allen Wood emphasizes the influence of Fichte's work on Hegel and suggests that although "much in Hegel's discussion of recognition is novel and provocative . . . both the concept of recognition and its use as the basis of a theory of natural right are derived from Fichte's *Foundations of Natural Right*." Allen Wood, *Hegel's Ethical Thought* (Cambridge: Cambridge University Press, 1991), 78.

22 Gadamer also plays on the idea of a fundamental opposition between Fichte and Hegel in a later work. See Gadamer, "Hegel's Dialectic of Self-Consciousness" (1973), *HDi*, 54; "Die Dialektik des Selbstbewußtseins," *GW*, vol. III, 47.

position, e.g., a romantic aesthetics of genius. Rather, the romantic aesthetics of genius offers an example that is meant to direct our attention towards a wider philosophical mindset that Gadamer finds characteristic of modernity as such: its understanding of truth in terms of the ideals of natural science only and its claim that art, being incapable of providing scientific truth, is void of cognitive content.

Subjectivism and the problem of aesthetic autonomy

In Gadamer's view, romanticism is motivated by a deep-seated dissatisfaction with the way scientific reason monopolizes our understanding of human existence and the world – art and aesthetic experience included. However, if romanticism, in its alleged turn to the spontaneous creation of genius, seeks to counter the monopoly of scientific reason, then a question arises. Is it really right to view, as Gadamer does, aesthetic consciousness and philosophical hermeneutics as radically opposed to one another?

According to Gadamer, the aim of philosophical hermeneutics is to defend, against the predominant notion of "reason in the age of science,"[23] all "modes of experience in which a truth is communicated that cannot be verified by the methodological means proper to science" (*TM*, xxii; *WM*, 2). This task is itself indebted to the romantic critique of the Enlightenment. Moreover, one could plausibly argue that had it not been for the affinities between romanticism and hermeneutics, it would not have been so important for Gadamer to criticize the mistakes of aesthetic consciousness in the first place – not only with regard to its alleged misreading of Kant's *Critique of Judgment*, but also with regard to the ambition that, in Gadamer's reading, initially triggered the turn to Kant's aesthetics: the desire to curb the rapidly expanding influence of the scientific understanding of the world. How, then, does Gadamer understand the modern notion of scientific reason? And, why, in his view, does aesthetic consciousness fail in its attempt to overcome the limitations of the scientific world-view?

I have already mentioned that Gadamer, in spite of his call for a move beyond Heidegger's philosophical style, remains influenced by

---

23 "Reason in the Age of Science" is the title of a collection of essays published in 1976. Hans-Georg Gadamer, *Reason in the Age of Science*, trans. Frederick G. Lawrence (Cambridge, Mass.: MIT Press, 1981); *Vernunft im Zeitalter der Wissenschaft* (Frankfurt am Main: Suhrkamp Verlag, 1976).

his critique of the aesthetic tradition. Gadamer also draws on Heidegger in his treatment of modern epistemology. In *Being and Time*, Heidegger claims that Cartesian ontology "in principle, is still the usual one today" (*BT*; *SZ*, §21, 100). Like Heidegger, Gadamer takes modern scientific reason to rest on a "Cartesian basis" (*TM*, 461; *WM*, 465). The idea of such an intellectual basis should not, however, be interpreted too literally. In alignment with his reference to aesthetic consciousness, Gadamer's notion of the Cartesian basis of modern science designates a general mindset or framework on which our reflection on such issues as truth, rationality, and knowledge has a tendency to draw. For, as Richard Bernstein points out, even though "[f]ew philosophers since Descartes have accepted his [Descartes'] substantive claims ... there can be little doubt that the problems, metaphors, and questions that he bequeathed to us have been at the very center of philosophy since Descartes."[24]

Within the larger phenomenological movement, Descartes appears, from the very beginning, as an ambiguous figure. Although critical of Descartes' turn to the epistemic cogito, Husserl had famously described his phenomenology as neo-Cartesian in spirit.[25] And while he was still working closely with Husserl, Heidegger had been rather positive about Descartes and what he took to be an almost existentialist retrieval of the meaning of the being of the 'I am'.[26] As

---

24 Bernstein, *Beyond Objectivism and Relativism*, 17.

25 Husserl discusses Descartes in *Ideas* and in *Erste Philosophie* (1923–24), turns him into a major ally in *Cartesian Meditations* (1929, published in French in 1931), and, finally, concludes his reading of Descartes in the posthumously published *Crisis* (1934–37). As Husserl puts it in *Cartesian Meditations*: "one might almost call transcendental phenomenology a neo-Cartesianism." See Edmund Husserl, *Cartesian Meditations: An Introduction to Phenomenology*, trans. Dorion Cairns (Dordrecht: Martinus Nijhoff, 1988), 43. See also *The Paris Lectures*, trans. Peter Koestenbaum (Dordrecht: Martinus Nijhoff, 1964). The German texts are published as *Cartesianische Meditationen und Pariser Vorträge, Husserliana I* (The Hague: Martinus Nijhoff, 1973). See also *Erste Philosophie. 1. Teil, Husserliana VII*, ed. Rudolf Boehm (The Hague: Martinus Nijhoff, 1956), 6–8 and *Erste Philosophie. 2. Teil, Husserliana VIII*, ed. Rudolf Boehm (The Hague: Martinus Nijhoff, 1959).

26 Heidegger claims that "The question of the ontological sense of factical life [i.e., the question of phenomenology] can be grasped, by way of a formal indication, as the question of the sense of the 'I am! ["die Frage nach dem Sinn des 'ich bin'"]'." The task of phenomenology is nothing but "that of pursuing the sense of the sum of the *cogito-sum* ['dem Sinn des "sum" im "cogito sum"']." In doing so, phenomenology ought to return to Descartes. For, Heidegger explains, "The sum is indeed the first, even for Descartes ['Das "sum" is das erste zwar auch für Descartes']." Heidegger, *Phenomenological Interpretations of Aristotle*, 130; *Phänomenologische Interpretationen zu Aristoteles, GA*, vol. LXI, 172f.

far as Cartesian epistemology goes, however, Heidegger is critical. This is clear in *Being and Time* (*BT*; *SZ*, §§ 19–21) but even more so in the later works. Gadamer follows the line staked out by the later Heidegger.

In his 1938 essay "The Age of the World View," Heidegger argues that the Cartesian basis of modern thinking is characterized by two closely related assertions. First, objectivity is established with reference to subjectivity itself. Second, it is understood in terms of a given set of rules or methodological guidelines. In Heidegger's reading, the Cartesian basis of modern science is related to a conception of truth, rationality, and knowledge that is grounded in the mutual depend-ence of a certain kind of subjectivism, on the one hand, and a certain kind of positivism, on the other. Its subjectivism is traced back to the way in which "[m]an becomes the representative of the existent in the sense of the objective."[27] Its positivism rests with its identification of reason with the adoption of a rational method, and the related assertion that whatever transcends the bounds of methodological behavior is beyond the pale of truth and knowledge.[28] Although it would be incorrect to suggest that Cartesian philosophy, as such, can be reduced to the consideration of a rational method for the natural sciences – thereby overlooking how the *Meditations* develops several motives from a philosopher such as Augustine,[29] and how Descartes

---

27 Martin Heidegger, "The Age of the World View," trans. Marjorie Grene, *Boundary 2*, vol. 4, no. 2, winter 1976, 352; "Die Zeit des Weltbildes," *Holzwege, GA*, vol. V, 88.

28 As Heidegger puts it in a quotation that may also shed light on the title of Gadamer's opus magnum, "theoretical behavior is just looking, without circumspection ['umsichtiges Nur-hinsehen']. But the fact that this looking is non-circumspective does not mean that it follows no rules: it constructs a canon for itself in the form of *method*" (*BT*; *SZ*, §15, 69).

29 According to a study by Stephen Menn, the step from *Rules* to *The Meditations* is Descartes' step towards a retrieval of Augustinian and Plotinian neo-Platonism (against the Aristo-telian physics of matter and forms). As he puts it, "Augustine's metaphysics of God and the soul is a possible candidate to be Descartes' foundational discipline, because it does not depend on any doctrine of the physical world, and indeed results from a discipline of *aversio* from the senses. So Descartes can base his physics on this metaphysics without danger of circularity; this is important, not just because circles are bad in principle, but because Descartes cannot effectively challenge 'our appetites and our teachers,' the Aristotelian physics and the prejudices of the senses, if this starting-point is itself con-taminated by Aristotle and the senses. Philosophically and sociologically, Augustine's metaphysics gives Descartes an Archimedean point: both its intellectual justifications and its prestige within society are independent of Aristotelianism, and can be used to subvert it." Stephen Menn, *Descartes and Augustine* (Cambridge: Cambridge University Press, 1998), 209f. See also Gareth B. Matthews, *Thought's Ego in Augustine and Descartes* (Ithaca:

situates his work within the ancient genre of meditative literature[30] – Gadamer assumes that the enlightenment concept of reason, being based on the idea that reason authorizes its own activity in an act of "absolute self-construction" (*TM*, 277; *WM*, 281), may be illuminated by a recounting of its Cartesian origins.

In considering Gadamer's critique of the Cartesian basis of scientific thinking, it is helpful to keep in mind how Descartes, looking back on his philosophical education, stages his battle with philosophical skepticism. The skeptic, in his view, is a person who doubts only for the sake of doubting.[31] This, Descartes argues, must be distinguished from his own efforts to "reach certainty – to cast aside the loose earth and sand so as to come upon rock or clay."[32] Keen to uncover a stable intellectual foothold, Descartes remains unimpressed by the resources offered by the tradition-based consensus of his intellectual community. Neither the kind of normativity that pertains to a given tradition nor the authority of his teachers can curb the doubt that plagues him. Only upon arriving at the ego's reflective turn towards its own thinking does Descartes uncover a kind of certainty that withstands all skeptical doubt.[33] In Gadamer's view – and at this point we see how his critique of Descartes is related to his critique of

Cornell University Press, 1992). Augustine also exercised a vast influence on Heidegger and Gadamer. For an overview of Heidegger's understanding of Augustine in the period leading up to *Being and Time*, see Theodore Kisiel, *The Genesis of Heidegger's "Being and Time"* (Berkeley: University of California Press, 1993), 192ff. Gadamer draws on Augustine both in *Truth and Method* and in a number of subsequent essays. Jean Grondin discourses on the general importance of Augustine for Gadamer's hermeneutics in *Sources of Hermeneutics* (Albany, N.Y.: SUNY Press, 1995), chapter 7.

30 For a discussion of this point, see Amélie Oksenberg Rorty, "The Structure of Descartes' *Meditations*," in Oksenberg Rorty (ed.), *Essays on Descartes' "Meditations"* (Berkeley: University of California Press, 1986), 1–20.

31 René Descartes, *Discourse on the Method*, trans. John Cottingham, Robert Stoothoff, and Dugald Murdoch, in *The Philosophical Writings* (Cambridge: Cambridge University Press, 1985), vol. I, 125; *Discours de la méthode, Œuvres*, ed. Charles Adam and Paul Tannery (Paris: J. Vrin, 1973), vol. VI, 29.

32 Ibid.

33 *Discourse on the Method*, 127; *Discours de la méthode*, 33. While approaching this part of Descartes' philosophy, it is, as Bernard Williams points out, important to keep in mind that the Latin term "cogitatio" (as in "cogito ergo sum") has "a wider significance than the English *think* or *thought*. In English, such terms are specially connected with ratiocinative or cognitive processes. For Descartes, however, a *cogitatio* or *pensée* is any sort of conscious state or activity whatsoever; it can as well be a sensation (at least, in its purely psychological aspect) or an act or will, as judgment or belief or intellectual questioning." Bernard Williams, *Descartes: The Project of Pure Enquiry* (London: Penguin, 1978), 78.

Kant – what matters here is the idea of normativity by which Descartes' thinking is driven. Descartes, Gadamer claims, understands normativity in terms of a categorical *either–or*. *Either* we uncover an absolute ahistorical Archimedean point of thinking, an apodictic truth upon which all other propositions may be grounded, *or* we face an epistemic uncertainty so overwhelming that it resembles the feeling of having, in Descartes' own words, "fallen unexpectedly into a deep whirlpool which tumbles [one] around so that [one] can neither stand on the bottom nor swim up to the top."[34] Hence, as Gadamer reads him, Descartes bases the distinction between a skeptical and a non-skeptical position on the ability to uncover a set of absolute criteria. Gadamer, however, is not convinced by this move. On his interpretation, it is the very quest for absolute criteria, regardless of whether such criteria may be uncovered, that characterizes philosophical skepticism. And, furthermore, as Gadamer develops his argument it turns out that it is precisely this – the idea that knowledge necessarily involves criteria of this kind – that aesthetic consciousness takes over from the "Cartesian basis" of modern science, thereby embracing the deepest-held convictions of the position it initially wanted to defeat.

Gadamer's understanding of Descartes is one-sided. I return to this problem in Chapter 4. Of importance at this point is only the way in which Gadamer links up his critique of aesthetic consciousness with his objections to post-Cartesian epistemology. The rationale behind this alignment is the following: aesthetic consciousness reckons that the experience of art does not involve indubitable criteria of the kind endorsed by the Cartesian philosopher. Indeed, the very effort to uncover such criteria within the sphere of art would amount to a misunderstanding. On this basis, aesthetic consciousness draws the conclusion that the experience of art occasions subjective feeling rather than cognitive commitment. It is here, aesthetic consciousness assumes, that we find the real relevance of art for our understanding of human being. Given its non-cognitive nature, the work of art conveys an aspect of subjectivity that transcends the realm of law-oriented, scientific reasoning.

However, upon affirming (rather than rejecting) the idea of the non-cognitive status of art, aesthetic consciousness fails to challenge the concepts of truth, rationality, and knowledge that dominate

---

34 Descartes, *Meditations on First Philosophy*, trans. John Cottingham, Robert Stoothoff, and Dugald Murdoch, in *The Philosophical Writings*, vol. II, 16.

post-Cartesian epistemology. Against its own intentions, laudable as they may be, aesthetic consciousness proves to have "its theoretical basis in the fact that the domination of the scientific model of epistemology leads to discrediting all the possibilities of knowing that lie outside this new methodology" (*TM*, 84; *WM*, 89f.). It naïvely accepts the idea that modern scientific rationality gives us privileged access to rationality. Hence aesthetic consciousness remains caught up with the most fundamental presuppositions of the scientistic paradigm that it initially set out to overcome. For there is simply no room within this model to raise the question – which Kant, in Gadamer's reading, alludes to in his discussion of the ideal of beauty – of whether it would be possible to conceive of truth, knowledge, and rationality in a way that would not a priori exclude the experience of art and beauty, and that would therefore challenge the understanding of normativity in terms of absolute criteria. As Gadamer distills this point, "[u]nder the domination of nominalist prejudices, aesthetic being ['das ästhetische Sein'] can be only inadequately and imperfectly understood" (*TM*, 83; *WM*, 89). To overcome the subjectivization of art what is needed is not only an effort to get beyond a problematic conception of art, but also a questioning of the limitations pertaining to the post-Cartesian understanding of truth, knowledge, and rationality.

Immediacy and the myth of the aesthetically given

Aesthetic consciousness fails to realize that the Cartesian picture of reason cannot be defeated as long as it excludes from its understanding of truth, knowledge, and rationality all aspects of the life-world that cannot be explained in light of the natural sciences. By emphasizing this aspect of aesthetic consciousness, Gadamer, by the same token, highlights a fundamental difference between hermeneutics and aesthetic consciousness. It is not aesthetic consciousness but philosophical hermeneutics that takes on the task of developing a notion of truth and rationality that is comprehensive enough to encompass our experience of art and beauty, hence also challenging a narrow scientific understanding of rationality. (I return to this point in Chapters 3 and 4.) However, to fulfill the requirements of an immanent critique, Gadamer cannot stop at this point. Having moved from a historical to a systematic level of criticism, he cannot only argue, as he has done so far, that aesthetic consciousness presupposes too narrow a notion of rationality, thus excluding art from the area of

cognition. In addition to this, he must show that aesthetic consciousness, even on an internal level (that is, with regard to the
inherent premises of its understanding of art and aesthetic experience), is hampered by the very position it is determined to
trump. Gadamer does this by returning, once again, to the contrast
between a humanist conception of taste and a Kantian understanding
of beauty.

In its seventeenth-century humanist garb, taste, in Gadamer's
interpretation, appears as "a testimony to the mutability of all human
things and the relativity of all human values" (*TM*, 58; *WM*, 63). There
are no final rules, no ahistorical principles within the realm of taste.
Yet there exists a deeper agreement, a common horizon, that lends
normativity to our judgments within this area. This is a kind of normativity that is grounded in a concrete, historically developed life-
world. Rather than being based on an abstract law or principle –
ultimately the kind of either–or thinking that Gadamer ascribes to
Descartes – this type of normativity refers to the historical *sensus
communis*, the "we" that understands itself in light of the values
expressed by this particular judgment. Kant and aesthetic consciousness let go of this kind of normativity, and in doing so, concomitantly
give in to a problematic "aesthetic skepticism" (*TM*, 57; *WM*, 63).

In Gadamer's view, Kant is the first to reject the normativity
inherent in taste's relation to a concrete, socially embodied *sensus
communis*. Even if it would be wrong to claim that Kant renounces the
idea of a relation between taste and *sensus communis* altogether, he
does trace *sensus communis* back to the free play of the cognitive faculties.[35] When aesthetic consciousness appeals to Kant's *Critique of
Judgment*, it finds a notion of *sensus communis* that is so formal that it
can hardly provide a basis for reflection on the nature of art. As a
consequence, art is torn loose from its relation to a concrete life-
world. The work is not considered in terms of a larger context of
meaning that is relevant to our understanding of ourselves as finite,
historical beings, but is thought to present itself to us (as aesthetic)

---

35 The attuning of the cognitive faculties (inducing the aesthetic feeling) must, for Kant,
"be universally communicable." The communicability of a feeling, Kant continues,
presupposes a common sense. Hence, he argues, "we do have a basis for assuming
such a sense, and for assuming it without relying on psychological observations, but as
the necessary condition of the universal communicability of our cognition, which
must be presupposed in any logic and any principle of cognition that is not skeptical"
(*CJ*; *KdU*, §21, 239).

only to the extent that we abstract from our own situatedness within a historical culture, i.e., to the extent that we contemplate it in terms of pure aesthetic qualities. In abstraction from its historical context and the tradition through which it is handed down, the work is conceived as a mere aesthetically given.[36]

It is only when keeping in mind this analysis of aesthetic consciousness that it is possible fully to grasp the meaning of Gadamer's claim that "aesthetic being" is inadequately understood as long as we subscribe to the paradigm of a (quasi-)Cartesian, scientific reason. By detaching art from every concrete historical context, aesthetic consciousness falls prey to the skepticism that, in Gadamer's account, has beleaguered modern epistemology.[37] When judged in terms of its own intrinsic *Maßstab*, the problem with aesthetic consciousness is therefore that it imports the premises of scientific rationality into an area where such premises do not belong. In the name of aesthetic subjectivity, it adopts the kind of attitude that Gadamer understands as a prejudice against prejudice. In Chapter 4, I return to Gadamer's critique of the prejudice against prejudice. In this context, however, I wish to focus on another aspect of Gadamer's discussion of aesthetic consciousness, namely, his critique of the desire for a pure, aesthetic givenness and an aesthetics of immediacy and subjective feelings.

According to aesthetic consciousness, this is what characterizes a work of art: "that its meaning [*Bedeutung*] lies in the phenomenon itself and is not arbitrarily read into it" (*TM*, 77; *WM*, 83). As the expression of creative genius, a work of art is self-contained. To appreciate its aesthetic qualities, one does not have to take into

---

36 This approach to aesthetic consciousness is further supported by Gadamer's reading of Wilhelm Dilthey. In Gadamer's interpretation, Dilthey's attempt to grant to the human sciences a validity dimension of their own is based on the idea that even within the historical sciences we may operate with an immediately "given." See "Wilhelm Dilthey nach 150 Jahren (Zwischen Romantik und Positivismus. Ein Diskussionsbeitrag)," in Ernst Wolfgang Orth (ed.), *Dilthey und die Philosophie der Gegenwart* (Freiburg: Karl Alber, 1985), 164. For an alternative view of Dilthey's understanding of the human sciences, see Rudolf A. Makkreel, *Dilthey: Philosopher of the Human Studies* (Princeton: Princeton University Press, 1975), 418ff.

37 I return to the problem of skepticism in Chapter 6. The problem of skepticism is one of the areas where the difference between Gadamer's hermeneutics and the legacy of German Idealism becomes evident. Gadamer wishes to dissolve skepticism by pointing out how it overlooks the situatedness of reason within a concrete, historical life-world. Hegel and Schleiermacher, by contrast, view philosophy as the completion of skepticism (albeit an ancient, rather than a modern, Cartesian, skepticism).

account the relations in which the artwork stands. Upon encountering the product of aesthetic genius, what matters is the disinterested appreciation of its formal qualities. Aesthetic expression and experience are distinguished "from the non-aesthetic relationship" in which they stand (*TM*, 89; *WM*, 95). As such, aesthetic consciousness undertakes an aesthetic differentiation ("ästhetische Unterscheidung," *TM*, 85; *WM*, 91). Gadamer elucidates this concept by offering two concrete examples: Richard Hamann's understanding of the *Eigenbedeutsamkeit* of the aesthetic and the romantic interest in the symbol as a paradigm case of the aesthetic as such.

Richard Hamann, one of Gadamer's teachers in Marburg, is now a largely forgotten figure within the world of Anglophone philosophy. In the context of Gadamer's hermeneutics, however, Hamann plays an important role – not least because of the way in which he appropriates the ideas of his teacher, Wilhelm Dilthey.[38] When turning to Hamann's work, Gadamer highlights his understanding of aesthetic experience as *eigenbedeutsam* or significant in itself (*TM*, 89; *WM*, 95). According to Hamann, the aesthetic object is not *fremdbedeutsam*: it is not significant in relation to something else (*TM*, 90; *WM*, 95). No hermeneutic activity or synthesis is involved in distinguishing a given object as a work of art. Aesthetic experience is thought to be independent of intellectual or linguistic mediation. It "has a definitive immediacy which eludes every opinion about its meaning ['hat eine betonte Unmittelbarkeit, die sich allem Meinen seiner Bedeutung entzieht']" (*TM*, 67; *WM*, 72). Any reference to the meaning of this experience would threaten the particular kind of presence with which beauty is given to consciousness.

In Gadamer's view, a different, but nonetheless related, idea of pure aesthetic presence is found in the romantic celebration of the symbol. As he argues, the romantic understanding of the symbol presupposes the idea of a "coincidence of the sensible and the non-sensible" (*TM*, 74; *WM*, 80). Given this coincidence, there is a close relation between the aesthetics of the symbol, on the one hand, and the idea of an "aesthetic autonomy against the claims of the concept," on the other (*TM*, 79; *WM*, 84). The symbol testifies to a "relation of the ineffable to language" (ibid.). The notion of a symbolic "relation

---

38 For an account of Gadamer's relation to Hamann, see Jean Grondin, *Hans-Georg Gadamer: A Biography*, trans. Joel Weinsheimer (New Haven: Yale University Press, 2003), 88ff.

of the ineffable to language" effects a correspondingly negative evaluation of allegory. The allegorical expression rests upon the possibility of replacing one order of signs with another, and the interpretation of allegory is a matter of convention. Unraveling allegorical meaning requires no pure aesthetic feeling. Allegorical meaning is only accessible to those who already belong to a community of interpretation; it has "a dogmatic aspect" (*TM*, 79; *WM*, 85) that makes the romantics attribute to it an "external and artificial significance" (*TM*, 74; *WM*, 80). The very distinction between art and non-art is conceived along the lines of the symbolic/allegorical distinction. As the romantics would argue, what is allegorical cannot be art. This, in short, is Gadamer's reading of the romantic aesthetics of symbol.

Gadamer's understanding of the romantic conception of symbol and allegory is not without problems. (I discuss some of them in Chapter 3.) However, in this context what matters is simply how Gadamer uses a certain notion of *Eigenbedeutsamkeit* and symbolic meaning to illuminate a more comprehensive desire for pure aesthetic presence or givenness. This, he suggests, is what is ultimately at stake in the romantic misreading of Kant: the idea that either aesthetic qualities present themselves as free from conceptual and intellectual reference or else they are not aesthetic qualities proper. But according to Gadamer, Kant's point had not been to cut aesthetic experience off from intellectual reference and linguistic mediation, but to show that as an object of pure aesthetic judgment art cannot be perceived in terms of a specific objective concept or purpose. The argument could even be extended to the realm of natural beauty: in the *Critique of Judgment,* the aesthetic experience is not detached from our linguistic capacities, but is subtly related to the conditions of possibility for the application of empirical concepts.[39]

Aesthetic consciousness fails to see this. Misunderstanding Kant even more seriously than Gadamer initially indicates, it reckons that because a work of art cannot be approached in terms of specific (empirical) ends or concepts by which its meaning would once and for all be determined, it must be detached from linguistic mediation as such. Thus, aesthetic consciousness mirrors the skepticism of Cartesian epistemology in that it is based on the problematic assumption that either a work of art is conceptually determinable (which, as Kant

---

39 See Allison, *Kant's Theory of Taste,* 21–28.

has shown, it is not) or it has nothing to do with our linguistic capacities at all. It overlooks the third route that Kant, in Gadamer's reading, hints at in his discussion of the ideal of beauty. It is this *tertium non datur*, this aesthetic skepticism, rather than the particular problems of an aesthetics of genius, that Gadamer criticizes. Thus the attempt at overcoming aesthetic consciousness cannot culminate in the critique of a problematic notion of aesthetic genius, but must lead to a much wider account of experience – that is, it must occasion a turn from aesthetics to hermeneutics.

Overcoming the myth of the aesthetically given

According to Gadamer, the notion of pure aesthetic givenness is phenomenologically inadequate.[40] Recalling the insights of Aristotle's *De Anima*, a work that had been given a new phenomenological reading by Heidegger, Gadamer maintains that "all aisthesis tends toward a universal, even if every sense has its own specific field and thus what is immediately given in it is not universal" (*TM*, 90; *WM*, 95). The idea of an aisthesis that is present as merely given is an abstraction. No object of perception is present in this way. Rather, "we see sensory particulars in relation to something universal" (ibid.). A universal does not need to be a determinative law or concept (as aesthetic consciousness assumes). Admittedly, aesthetic consciousness is correct in pointing out that aesthetic experience is "characterized by not hurrying to relate what one sees to a universal, the known significance, the intended purpose, etc., but by dwelling on it as something aesthetic" (*TM*, 90; *WM*, 96). However, as Gadamer argues, this dwelling does "not stop us from seeing relationships" (ibid.). All perception involves contextual reference. Perception is "never a simple reflection of what is given to the senses" (ibid.), but requires a synthesis in which one "looks-away-from ['wegsieht von . . .'], looks-at ['hinsieht auf . . .'], sees-together-as ['zusammensieht als']" (*TM*, 91; *WM*, 96). This also applies to aesthetic experience. According to Gadamer, we do not, on the most fundamental phenomenological level, perceive a pure aesthetic form that induces in us an equally pure aesthetic feeling or liking. What we perceive is a beautiful flower, a beautiful poem, or a beautiful

---

40 See Françoise Dastur, "Esthétique et herméneutique. La critique de la conscience esthétique chez Gadamer," in Renaud Barbaras *et al.* (eds.), *Phénoménologie et esthétique* (Paris: Encre Marine, 1998), 41–60.

artistic presentation. The notion of a perception that involves no intellectual reference is, Gadamer argues, "an abstraction" (*TM*, 90; *WM*, 95).

Upon encountering, say, a piece of literature, we do not perceive it as a work of art because we have some sort of immediate access to its aesthetic qualities (designed so as to induce a feeling of presence or *Eigenbedeutsamkeit* in us). As Gadamer puts it, only when we "*understand* a text," only when we are "at least in command of its language," can it be a work of literary art for us (*TM*, 91; *WM*, 97, emphasis added). This is also the case upon proceeding to non-linguistic art. Turning to the visual arts, Gadamer continues, it applies that "Only if we '*recognize* [*erkennen*]' what is presented ['das Dargestellte'] are we able to 'read' a picture; in fact, that is what ultimately makes it a picture" (ibid., trans. modified). And as far as music is concerned, Gadamer suggests that even "in listening to absolute music we must 'understand' it. And only when we understand it, when it is 'clear' to us, does it exist as an artistic creation for us" (ibid.).

On the face of it, the emphasis on understanding might seem to create a tension in Gadamer's philosophy of art. For has not Gadamer, siding at this point with Kant and aesthetic consciousness (and going against Hegel), emphasized that the truth of art can never be fully exhausted by conceptual reason? Indeed, he has. And as famously articulated in Adorno's critique of hermeneutics, the orientation towards understanding seems contrary to the insistence on the non-conceptual nature of art. In Adorno's polemical exposition, the task of aesthetics "is not to comprehend [*begreifen*] artworks as hermeneutical objects."[41] Being distinguished by their constitutive *in*comprehensibility, advanced works of art are, as he puts it, "enigmas."[42] Hermeneutics does not realize this; it does not see that "understanding [*Verstehen*] is itself a problematic category in the face of art's enigmaticalness."[43] Rather than acknowledging the enigma of art, hermeneutics rejects it, thus potentially undermining the very phenomenon that it set out to recover, i.e., the phenomenon of art. Those who "peruse art solely with comprehension," Adorno claims, are forced to see it "disappear."[44] They make art "into something

---

41 Theodor W. Adorno, *Aesthetic Theory*, trans. Robert Hullot-Kentor (Minneapolis: University of Minnesota Press, 1997), 118; *Ästhetische Theorie* (Frankfurt am Main: Suhrkamp Verlag, 1970), 179.
42 Ibid., 120; ibid., 182.   43 Ibid., 121; ibid., 184.   44 Ibid., 122; ibid., 185.

straightforward ['zu einem Selbstverständlichen'], which is furthest from what it is."[45]

Exaggerated as it is, Adorno's criticism presupposes that the aim of hermeneutics is to grasp conceptually the meaning of the work as such. But is this really what is implied by the concept of under-standing? Gadamer's point – and this is where he, along the lines staked out by the ideal of beauty sections of the third Critique, tran-scends the kind of either–or thinking that characterizes aesthetic consciousness – is not that we, on the fundamental level of under-standing, have to (or are able to) grasp the full meaning of the work, i.e., that we have to (or are able to) see the work in terms of concepts. As it is, concepts do not belong to the realm of art, nor, for that sake, to the larger realm of symbolic expression. This is the very point of Gadamer's attempt, in *Truth and Method* and other places, to rethink the circle of understanding.[46] He calls for a redefinition of herme-neutics, a shift from a didactic-methodological exposition of the way in which the interpreter moves back and forth between the parts of a text and its meaning as a larger unity (until he or she has grasped its meaning),[47] to an awareness of the intrinsically temporal aspect of understanding.

The meaning of a text is never fixed, Gadamer claims. It is not something that lurks behind the work, only to be teased out by the clever interpreter. In the realm of art, meaning is made possible by a fusion between the horizon of the interpreter, his or her larger system of beliefs and practices,[48] and the horizon of the text, as it is mediated by tradition.[49] The meaning of a text or a work of art is, in other

---

45 Ibid.

46 Gadamer discusses the hermeneutic circle in *Truth and Method* (*TM*, 190ff., 265f., 291f.; *WM*, 194ff., 270f., 296f.) but also in the essay "On the Circle of Understanding," trans. J. M. Connolly and T. Keutner, in Connolly and Keutner (eds.), *Hermeneutics versus Science?* (Indiana: University of Notre Dame Press, 1988), 68–78; "Vom Zirkel des Verstehens" (1959), *GW*, vol. II, 57–65.

47 Such an understanding of the hermeneutic circle is found in Friedrich Ast's work. See Joachim Wach, *Das Verstehen. Grundzüge einer Geschichte der hermeneutischen Theorie im 19. Jahrhundert* (Tübingen: J. C. B. Mohr, 1926), vol. I, 41ff.

48 A horizon, Gadamer explains, "is determined by the prejudices we bring with us . . . they represent that beyond which it is impossible to see" (*TM*, 306; *WM*, 311). Yet a horizon is no fixed border of comprehension. Rather, it is "continually in the process of being formed because we are continually having to test all our prejudices" (ibid.).

49 "Understanding is always the fusion of . . . horizons supposedly existing by themselves," Gadamer argues (ibid.). Such a fusion of horizons, such a transposing ourselves into the historical situation of the text ("solches sichversetzen," as Gadamer

words, not one over against which the interpreter relates as a neutrally investigating subject. Such a view, Gadamer reasons, only testifies to the "aesthetic-historical positivism" of aesthetic consciousness (*TM*, 307; *WM*, 312). At stake, rather, is a kind of signification that reflects back on the self-understanding of the interpreter him- or herself, altering the standpoint from which he or she, on another occasion, may return to the work. Hence there is a constitutive temporal displacement woven into the structure of hermeneutic labor. In understanding we never understand the same. What we understand, upon returning to the work, is always something different. Or, as Gadamer puts it, "understanding, as it occurs in the human sciences, is essentially historical . . . in them a text is understood only if it is understood in a different way" (*TM*, 309; *WM*, 314). This displacement in understanding, Gadamer argues, is not a weakness, i.e., something that hermeneutics ought to overcome. It is, rather, what keeps us returning to the work, what makes understanding a genuinely historical phenomenon. It is this focus on the historicity of understanding that Gadamer has in mind when he admits that even though his hermeneutics is thoroughly inspired by Hegel,[50] it also, drawing on the idea of an ongoing dialogical process, ventures into vistas of our historicity that Hegel would have characterized as "bad infinity."[51]

I return to Gadamer's discussion of Hegel in Chapter 4 and to his claim about understanding as understanding differently in Chapter 6. So far, it suffices to say that Gadamer seeks to overcome the aesthetic consciousness of modern philosophy by emphasizing the historical-temporal aspect of hermeneutics. However, having argued that aesthetic consciousness is trapped in a false opposition between immediacy and conceptual determination, Gadamer needs to indicate how hermeneutics, in his version, points beyond these false alternatives. He does so by expounding the way in which understanding constitutes

puts it), consists "neither in the empathy of one individual for another nor in subordinating another person to our own standards; rather, it always involves rising to a higher universality that overcomes not only our own particularity but also that of the other" (*TM*, 305; *WM*, 311).

50 "This almost defines the aim of philosophical hermeneutics: its task is to retrace the path of Hegel's phenomenology of spirit ['Phänomenologie des Geistes'] until we discover in all that is subjective the substantiality that determines it" (*TM*, 302; *WM*, 307, trans. modified).

51 "Hermeneutics and Logocentrism," trans. Diane Michelfelder and Richard E. Palmer, in *Dialogue and Deconstruction*, ed. Diane Michelfelder and Richard E. Palmer (Albany, N.Y.: SUNY Press, 1989), 123ff.

the quasi-transcendental conditions of experience. This is what Gadamer has in mind when he claims that his "real concern" in *Truth and Method* "was and is philosophic: not what we do or what we ought to do, but what happens to us over and above our wanting and doing" (*TM*, xxviii; *WM*, vol. II, 438). In this connection, he explains:

> it seems . . . a mere misunderstanding to invoke the famous Kantian distinction between *quaestio juris* and *quaestio facti.* Kant certainly did not intend to prescribe what modern science must do in order to stand honorably before the judgment seat of reason. He asked a philosophical question: what are the conditions of our knowledge, by virtue of which modern science is possible, and how far does it extend? The following investigation also asks a philosophic question in the same sense . . . It asks (to put it in Kantian terms): how is understanding possible? (*TM*, xxixf.; *WM*, vol. II, 439)

Understanding, Gadamer argues, is neither a method nor the outcome of a willed procedure of reflection. It is in fact not something we consciously (methodologically) do or fail to do, but something we *are*. At this point, Gadamer follows Heidegger and claims that his "temporal analytics of Dasein has . . . shown convincingly that understanding is not just one of the various possible behaviors of the subject but the mode of being of Dasein itself" (*TM*, xxx; *WM*, vol. II, 440). The tacit and pre-reflective way in which we orient ourselves in the world is itself of a hermeneutic nature. Yet our understanding of the world implies no theoretical knowledge. It is a kind of know-how that is revealed through the way in which we, without the involvement of theoretical consideration, know our way around the world. As Gadamer puts it, it is "always a human . . . world that presents itself to us" (*TM*, 447; *WM*, 451). The world is familiar to us in a basic, intuitive way; it is saturated with meaning all the way through. According to Gadamer, this meaning is linguistically mediated. There is no gap between world and language. "Language," he argues, "is not just one of man's possessions in the world; rather, on it depends the fact that man has a *world* at all" (*TM*, 443; *WM*, 446). Language is not a set of signs or labels that we tag onto this or that particular object, be it a work of art or some other kind of thing (*TM*, 403; *WM*, 407), but a larger totality in which we live and through which we communicate (*TM*, 450; *WM*, 453f.).

Our basic familiarity with the world is brought to reflective consciousness in the work of interpretation (*Auslegung*). Interpretation, however, need not be of a propositional nature. At stake is the explicit experiential foregrounding of a given thing or object. The most famous discussion of this claim is not really in Gadamer's *Truth and Method*, but in the first division of Heidegger's *Being and Time*. Heidegger here discusses how the dysfunctional hammer forces us to stop hammering and reflect on the purpose of a hammer (*BT; SZ*, §§15–16). This sudden awareness, Heidegger claims, is not to be equated with interpretation. Yet it highlights a crucial dimension of interpretation, the way in which it makes things or objects appear *as* something (*BT; SZ*, §32, 149). Gadamer generally endorses this way of thinking. Drawing upon the conceptual resources of *Being and Time*, he argues that all perception is perception of something *as* something – "ein Auffassen *als* etwas" (*TM*, 90; *WM*, 96). Still this *as* is only possible against the background of the world as a totality of practices and intersubjective encounters, the world that is opened up by our being linguistically there.[52]

In the process of interpretation, understanding does not become something different. Gaining a new reflective level, it becomes, rather, itself. Against a hermeneutic model that keeps apart understanding and interpretation, Gadamer maintains that no absolute distinction can be drawn within this field. "*Understanding occurs in interpreting [Die Vollzugsweise des Verstehens ist die Auslegung]*," as he puts it (*TM*, 389; *WM*, 392).[53] Understanding and interpretation make up two different aspects of the pre-reflective synthesizing through which the world is disclosed as a totality of meaning, a space in which it is possible for us to recognize objects as hammers, tables, or works of art.

This is the conclusion of Gadamer's critique of aesthetic consciousness: only when there is some sort of synthesizing activity involved (that is, only when there is reference to some universal and not only an immediate "here and now") can something be an object of experience. Experience implies linguistic reference. Linguistic reference, however, is not the same as conceptual determination. The most fundamental meaning of a thing, its "as-structure," is not something we superimpose on a stratum of pure, immediate impressions. The

---

52 For a discussion of Heidegger's notion of the as-structure of experience, see Stephen Mulhall, *On Being in the World: Wittgenstein and Heidegger on Seeing Aspects* (London: Routledge, 1990).

53 A claim that echoes the Heideggerian idea that in interpretation "understanding appropriates understandingly that which is understood by it," so that interpretation means to make something "*explicitly* understood" (*BT; SZ*, §32, 148f.).

"as-structure" goes all the way down. This is also the case when we encounter aesthetic objects. Although, in aesthetic experience, one "does not simply 'look beyond' what one sees – e.g., to its general use for some end – but dwells within it," it is still the case that "Lingering vision and assimilation is not a simple perception of what is there, but is itself understanding-as" (*TM*, 91; *WM*, 96). Referring to Heidegger's distinction between an understanding of objects or things in the world as ready-to-hand (*zuhanden*) and an understanding of objects or things as present-to-hand (*vorhanden*) – in ordinary practice and circumspection we encounter things as ready-to-hand, in terms of their reference to a comprehensive context of use and meaning; the scientific gaze, by contrast, strips the world of this dimension, regarding it solely as present-to-hand (*BT*; *SZ*, §§21ff.) – Gadamer maintains that "The mode of being of what is observed 'aesthetically' is not presence-at-hand" (*TM*, 91; *WM*, 97). Thus by failing to take into account how the work of art presents itself through a more comprehensive, hermeneutic synthesis, aesthetic consciousness is bound, upon further philosophical analysis, to generate a feeling of ontological embarrassment ("ontologische Verlegenheit," *TM*, 83; *WM*, 89). As an attempt to reflect on the ontological embarrassment caused by the myth of the aesthetically given, Gadamer's critique of aesthetic consciousness is much more than a critique of the romantic aesthetics of genius. It is, in fact, a critique of any orientation towards pure, aesthetic immediacy. As such, its relevance exceeds the boundaries of eighteenth-century art and philosophy.

Romanticism and modernity

So far we have seen that Gadamer's misreading of Kant's concept of natural beauty paves the way for a more promising critique of the idea of a pure aesthetic givenness. I mentioned at the beginning of the chapter that Gadamer's discussion of aesthetic consciousness draws upon and further develops Hegel's critique of the beautiful soul. Nonetheless, it is precisely when comparing Gadamer's criticism to Hegel's reading of romanticism that we experience some of the most fundamental problems with the former. These problems, it ought to be said, do not, as such, affect Gadamer's systematic critique of aesthetic subjectivism and the idea of pure, aesthetic givenness, but relate to the extension of aesthetic consciousness (that is, the assumption that the entire post-Kantian field is dominated by a bad aesthetic consciousness).

In the *Phenomenology*, the *Lectures on the History of Philosophy*, and the *Lectures on Fine Art*, Hegel is critical of, and sometimes outright hostile to, romantic philosophy and aesthetics. Referring to the tragic fate of several romantic writers (as well as their indebtedness to Fichte's theory of the self-positing of the I), Hegel claims that romantic poetry and philosophy cultivate a subjectivity that "signifies the lack of a firm and steady basis ['einem Festen'], but likewise the desire for such."[54] As such, subjectivity is characterized by a yearning (*Sehnsucht*). This, Hegel continues, leads to a predicament in which "[t]he extravagances of subjectivity constantly pass into madness."[55] However, in spite of his critique of romanticism, Hegel never forgets that romantic aesthetics, in its turn to (immediate) subjectivity, is reflective of the condition of art in modernity. Indeed, in his view, modern art is, in a certain sense, romantic. Here Hegel is in line with philosophical and aesthetic romanticism. He develops an idea which was later to be reformulated in Charles Baudelaire's suggestion that romanticism, as "a mode of feeling," is "the most recent, the latest expression of the beautiful,"[56] and also in Walter Benjamin's claim that the romantic notion of art criticism mirrors the condition of modern art and aesthetic discourse per se.[57]

Like Gadamer, Hegel claims that romantic aesthetics, in its turn to subjectivity, responds to the most problematic aspects of the Enlightenment, i.e., to a situation in which reason is reduced to "dry understanding" and "cold utility."[58] It represents a reaction to a

---

54 Hegel, *Lectures on the History of Philosophy*, vol. III, 510; *Vorlesungen über die Geschichte der Philosophie*, vol. III, 418.

55 Ibid.

56 Charles Baudelaire, "The Salon of 1846," in *Art in Paris, 1845–1862* ed. and trans. Jonathan Mayne (Oxford: Phaidon, 1981), 46; "Salon de 1846," *Œuvres complètes* (Paris: Gallimard, 1976), vol. II, 420.

57 It is worth noting that although Benjamin traces the romantic concept of criticism back to Fichte's *Theory of Science*, it is, in his view, not a conception that culminates in the turn towards aesthetic immediacy that Gadamer criticizes. In Benjamin's understanding, the decisive aspect of the romantic appropriation of Fichte's theory is not the concept of an immediate spontaneity, but rather that of *reflection*. See Walter Benjamin, *The Concept of Criticism in German Romanticism*, trans. D. Lachterman, H. Eiland, and I. Balfour, in Marcus Bullock and Michael W. Jennings (eds.), *Selected Writings* (Cambridge, Mass.: Harvard University Press, 1996), vol. I; *Der Begriff der Kunstkritik in der deutschen Romantik*, in Walter Benjamin, *Gesammelte Schriften*, ed. Rolf Tiedemann and Hermann Schweppenhäuser (Frankfurt am Main: Suhrkamp Verlag, 1974), vol. I.1.

58 These expressions occur in Hegel's review of Hamann: "[In Deutschland wurde] das Geschäft der Aufklärung mit trockenem Verstande, mit Prinzipien kahler Nützlichkeit, mit Seichtigkeit des Geistes und Wissens, kleinlichen oder gemeinen

condition in which art no longer offers an adequate articulation of
the common horizon of a given historical community. But in Hegel's
view – and this is where he radically differs from Gadamer – a
moment of rationality must be ascribed to the romantic turn to
subjectivity. Because art in modernity can no longer serve as the most
advanced source of intersubjectively binding meaning Hegel, later
on, deems it a thing of the past. This does not imply that works of art
will no longer be produced. Nor does it imply that our fascination
with art has come to an end. What it means, rather, is that we have
reached a state in which the absolute has moved into the realm of
free subjectivity, hence also beyond the resources of sensuous presentation. It is reason that articulates the absolutes of late modernity.
Even though we, in this state, still understand ourselves through art
and culture, absolute spirit has at this point moved on to philosophical reason. Art is still produced and appreciated. Yet art no
longer presents us with the most advanced articulations of the
ethical and religious ideals of our society. Art, rather, has become
aesthetic. This is the aspect of romantic aesthetics left out of
Gadamer's critique of aesthetic consciousness.

Gadamer's failure to see romantic aesthetics in the context of
modernity (rather than simply rejecting it as an example of aesthetic
consciousness) is particularly problematic in his critique of the
modern museum. The institution of the museum is developed
approximately at the time when aesthetics gains status as an independent philosophical discipline. The Glyptothek in Munich was
constructed in the period from 1816 to 1830 and the British Museum
had already opened in 1759, that is, a few decades before Kant would
publish the *Critique of Judgment*.[59] In the museum, the work of art
traditionally appears as an aesthetic object. Although it may be situated within a historical or thematic context, it is no longer an integral

Leidenschaften, und wo es am respektabelsten war, mit einiger, doch nüchternen
Wärme des Gefühls betrieben, und trat gegen Alles, was sich von Genie, Talent,
Gediegenheit des Geistes und Gemütes auftat, in feindselige tracassierende, verhöh-
nende Opposition." Quoted from Otto Pöggeler, "Hegels Kritik der Romantik"
(Bonn: Friedrich Wilhelms-Universität, 1956 [Dissertation]), 35.

59 For an account of the development of the institution of the museum and its relation
to aesthetics in general, see Hans Sedlmayr, *Art in Crisis: The Lost Center*, trans. Brian
Battershaw (Chicago: Henry Regnery, 1958), 27ff.; *Verlust der Mitte. Die bildende Kunst
des 19. und 20. Jahrhunderts als Symptom und Symbol der Zeit* (Salzburg: Otto Müller
Verlag, 1951), 31ff. See also Tony Bennett, *The Birth of the Museum: History, Theory,
Politics* (London: Routledge, 1995).

part of a broader ethical-political horizon.[60] If the ego cogito of Cartesian philosophy is, as Heidegger once put it, a "worldless 'I'" (*BT; SZ,* §63, 316), and if the Kantian conception of the normativity of the pure judgment of taste appears to be a worldless normativity, then the institution of the museum thrives, as Gadamer sees it, on an analogous idea: that of the worldless work. Here, Gadamer claims, we no longer admit "that the work of art and its world belong to each other" (*TM,* 85; *WM,* 90). Aesthetic consciousness appears as "the experiencing ... center from which everything considered art is measured" (ibid.). It is perceived as sovereign and free to draw "aesthetic differentiation everywhere and to see everything 'aesthetically'" (*TM,* 86; *WM,* 91). The work is deprived of authority, and it is not considered in terms of what it says. Rather, the aesthetic qualities of the work are distinguished "from all the elements of content that induce us to take up a moral or religious stance towards it" (*TM,* 85; *WM,* 91). As such, the work is judged solely in terms of its "aesthetic being" (ibid.). Whereas the early humanists had approached the normativity of taste in terms of a criterion of content – presupposing "the unity of a style of life and an ideal of taste" (*TM,* 85; *WM,* 90) – aesthetic consciousness refuses to let its judgments be guided by anything but pure aesthetic qualities.

In focusing on pure aesthetic qualities, aesthetic consciousness creates for itself a sphere of simultaneity. However, by protecting this simultaneity through special spheres or institutions such as the museum, it underwrites its own powerlessness. The experience of art is valid only within the limits of an autonomous aesthetic sphere and finds no application within an extra-aesthetic reality. As in Schiller's letters *On the Aesthetic Education of Man,* any education *by* art ends up being an education *to* art (*TM,* 83; *WM,* 88).[61] Rather than being seen as expressive of the extra-aesthetic reality, art is contrasted to it. In Gadamer's words, "beneath the dualism of 'is' and 'ought' that Kant reconciles

---

60 As Gadamer puts it, "[i]t is obviously no coincidence that aesthetic consciousness, which develops the concept of art and the artistic as a way of understanding traditional structures and so performs aesthetic differentiation, is simultaneous with the creation of museum collections that gather together everything we look at in this way. Thus we make every work of art, as it were, into a picture. By detaching all art from its connections with life and the particular conditions of our approach to it, we frame it like a picture and hang it up" (*TM,* 135; *WM,* 140).

61 See also Friedrich Schiller, *On the Aesthetic Education of Man,* bilingual edition, trans. Elizabeth M. Wilkinson and L. A. Willoughby (Oxford: Clarendon Press, 1982), letter 27.

aesthetically, a more profound, unresolved dualism opens up. The poetry of aesthetic reconciliation must seek its own self-consciousness against the prose of alienated reality" (*TM*, 83; *WM*, 89).

Gadamer is right in pointing out the dangers of depriving the work of its world. He is right in pointing out the aporia that follows from the idea of a pure aesthetic givenness, and, furthermore, in pointing out how institutions such as the museum may be consonant with the limited perspective of aesthetic humanism.[62] Here, one can see how the development of philosophical hermeneutics is, at least in part, driven by the same kind of concerns that troubled Adorno throughout the 1950s and 1960s.[63] However, Gadamer is wrong to deny the relevance of the question of the possible alternatives to an autonomous aesthetic sphere in modernity. Instead, Gadamer's critique of the modern museum presupposes that it would be possible to retrieve a pre-modern celebration of art as the articulation of a unifying symbolic authority that would keep the members of a given society together. He presupposes that this aspect of the work is itself of an ahistorical nature, that it is the essence of art *as* art, regardless of the way in which we, in our aesthetic and hermeneutic practices, conceive of or relate to the work. And from this perspective, the nuances between the various versions of post-Kantian aesthetics – be they representative of a naïve aesthetic consciousness or a much more subtle notion of aesthetic autonomy – do not matter. Nor does it matter to ask, as I shall do later, whether romantic philosophy, such as that of Friedrich Schleiermacher, really fits the bill of aesthetic consciousness. The only thing that matters is to prepare the ground for a new ontological conception of the truth of art. This hampers Gadamer's critique of aesthetic consciousness – and, equally importantly, his own account of art and hermeneutic reason.

62 Gadamer employs the term "aesthetic humanism" in "Plato and the Poets," *DD*, 39; "Plato und die Dichter," *GW*, vol. V, 187. Given Gadamer's criticism of aesthetic humanism, one cannot agree with Grondin who claims, without further explanation, that "Gadamer is a humanist and Heidegger isn't." To the extent that Gadamer is a humanist, he is a humanist who wants to rescue this concept from its aesthetic, even aestheticist, connotations. Jean Grondin, "Gadamer on Humanism," *LLP*, 157. I return to the question of Gadamer's humanism in Chapter 5.

63 Although Adorno and the other representatives of the Frankfurt School were to provide an analysis of the modern world that radically differs from Gadamer's, they are concerned about the reduction of art to an object of amusement or subjective enjoyment. In a false world, Adorno claims in his *Aesthetic Theory*, all *hedone* is false. Since this is a condition in which art can never redeem its *promesse de bonheur*, it applies that "Whoever concretely enjoys artworks is a philistine." *Aesthetic Theory*, 13; *Ästhetische Theorie*, 26f.

3

OVERCOMING THE PROBLEMS OF MODERN PHILOSOPHY: ART, TRUTH, AND THE TURN TO ONTOLOGY

Gadamer's discussion of modern aesthetics is committed to a phenomenological notion of criticism. Criticism, in this interpretation, not only involves the negative task of demonstrating the internal tensions of a given position, but also comprises the mapping-out of a new and more adequate comprehension of the problem at stake.[1] Along similar lines, Gadamer's critique of aesthetic consciousness and the skepticism that, in his view, pervades modern philosophy leads to the articulation of an alternative account of truth, one that is comprehensive enough to take into consideration the hermeneutic happening in the encounter with the eminent works of the tradition. However, if his hermeneutic account of truth develops dialectically from his critique of Kant and aesthetic consciousness, then a number of questions emerge. First, to what extent do the problems with Gadamer's critique of aesthetic consciousness – his failure to take seriously the romantic response to art in modernity and his over-generalization of aesthetic consciousness – shape his attempt to carve out a notion of truth that comprises the experience of art? Second, to what extent does Gadamer, in working out a hermeneutically

---

1 According to Jean Hyppolite, the concept of a phenomenological criticism (from Lambert onwards) is based on the insight that "the presentation of an untruth as untruth is already a movement beyond the error, [so that] to be cognizant of one's error is to be cognizant of another truth." Jean Hyppolite, *Genesis and Structure of Hegel's "Phenomenology of Spirit,"* trans. Samuel Cherniak and John Heckman (Evanston: Northwestern University Press, 1974), 14; *Genèse et structure de la Phénoménologie de l'esprit de Hegel* (Paris: Aubier, 1946), 19. Gadamer makes a similar point when claiming that Hegel converts the negative "purpose of [ancient] dialectic into a positive one. For Hegel the point of dialectic is that precisely by pushing a position to the point of self-contradiction it makes possible the transition to a higher truth which unites the sides of that contradiction." "Hegel and Heidegger" (1971), *HD*, 105; "Hegel und Heidegger," *GW*, vol. III, 91f.

adequate conception of the relationship between art, truth, and reason, manage to overcome the problems of aesthetic consciousness – i.e., the problem of its subjectivism, and its turn towards immediacy and pure, aesthetic presence? And, finally, to what degree does his own hermeneutic idea of truth and rationality incorporate the dialogical structure that he endorses in his analysis of the *Critique of Judgment*?

I argue that Gadamer, in elaborating on how world-disclosive art puts forth an immediate source of authority, hypostatizes a notion of immediacy. This notion of immediacy closely resembles the one we find in aesthetic consciousness, only that in Gadamer's model, art is detached, as he puts it, from all subjective meaning and is seen instead as its own ontological origin. Art puts forth its claim to truth with a trans-subjective authority; it does not beg reflective criticism, but instead demands subjection, self-transformation, and authenticity. As such, the understanding of art in terms of a world-disclosive truth transcends the dialogical dialectics that Gadamer initially gleaned from Kant's *Critique of Judgment*, as well as from Plato's *Philebus*.

This chapter begins by retrieving Gadamer's effort to overcome the subjectivist model by appealing to the autotelic structure of the work of art. I then discuss the way in which he links the autoteleology of the work to its capacity for truth. Next, we see that Gadamer argues that truth, phenomenologically speaking, is bifurcated into a more traditional theory of adequation and a phenomenological understanding of truth as world-disclosure. According to Gadamer, art has a particular affinity with the latter. The remainder of the chapter discusses the problems inherent in Gadamer's conception of the truth of art. In developing the notion of the world-disclosive truth of art, Gadamer attempts to arrive at a definition that is comprehensive enough to cover pre-modern, modern, and modernist art. Yet his account betrays a problematic preference for pre-modern art – and, equally problematic, a too narrow understanding of what pre-modern art amounts to in the first place. But if Gadamer's model proves historically problematic, what, then, about its systematic relevance? Expounding the world-disclosive truth of art, Gadamer recasts the notions of play and playing that were crucial to the Kantian tradition in a non-subjectivist way. However, even though Gadamer, with this move, manages to overcome the subjectivization of art in post-Kantian aesthetics, he fails to overcome the immediacy problem that he also ascribes to aesthetic consciousness. As such, Gadamer's ontology of art brings out a deeper tension in his philosophy, between a commitment to dialogue and reflection, on the one hand, and a fascination with the idea of a sublime and non-dialogical world-disclosure, on the other.

Leaving behind aesthetic autonomy

In spite of his critical approach to aesthetic consciousness, Gadamer acknowledges that in turning the focus from taste and judgment to the work of art, romantic aesthetics conducts an important shift in the history of philosophy. After the era of romanticism, aesthetics is no longer concerned with the validity of the judgment of taste, but rather asks: "What is a work of art and how does it differ from the product of a craftsman or even from some 'potboiler' – i.e., something of inferior aesthetic value?" (*TM*, 94; *WM*, 99). Gadamer takes this problem seriously. We need, he acknowledges, with a nod to aesthetic consciousness, a way philosophically to distinguish art from non-art (things of "inferior aesthetic value") without appealing, as does aesthetic consciousness, to aesthetic subjectivity and genius. How can such a distinction be drawn? The answer must be sought within Gadamer's phenomenological turn in aesthetics, the fact that he takes as his starting-point the artwork's own mode of being, and not the subjectivity of the recipient, or aesthetic genius.[2]

According to Gadamer, aesthetic consciousness reduces the work to a mere thing, a being that is simply present-at-hand. Can we thus assume, in terms of a Heideggerian distinction between the present-at-hand and the ready-to-hand, between theoretical objectification and practical, pre-reflective concerns, that art should be understood along the lines of the latter? To a certain extent this is indeed the case, but only if one adds to this that even though the work of art is ready-to-hand, it is also more than simply a thing. According to Heidegger, "[a]ll works have this thingly character," yet the artwork is also "something else over and above the thingly element" (*OWA*, 19; *UdK*, 9f.). This "something else" distinguishes the work of art as art. Thus, in order to grasp the essence of the work, it is helpful to investigate the

2 In this context, where Gadamer so to speak calls for a return to the artwork itself, it is worth bearing in mind that the phenomenological motto "to the things themselves" should not be interpreted as a re-instantiation of a subject–object paradigm in philosophy; rather, it defines an "opposition to all theoretical constructions that serve a desire for philosophical explanation not satisfied by the phenomena." See "The Phenomenological Movement" (1963), *PH*, 145; "Die phänomenologische Bewegung," *GW*, vol. III, 118.

phenomenological-hermeneutic understanding of thinghood, so as to get a better grasp of the contrast between works of art and other things.

In *Being and Time*, Heidegger analyzes the way in which the world is disclosed to *Dasein* through its everyday practices and coping. *Dasein* surrounds itself with things of use: tools, implements, and equipment (*Zeug*).[3] The equipmentality of equipment "consists in its usefulness" (*OWA*, 33; *UdK*, 26). Now, the overall tendency of Gadamer's writing – from his 1930 work on Socratic dialogue to the essays of the late 1990s – is to resist the priority that the early Heidegger ascribes to *Dasein*'s practical comportment. Unlike the early Heidegger, Gadamer explicitly focuses on the importance of language for a proper understanding of our being-in-the-world.[4] Yet Heidegger's analysis of the *Zeugstruktur* forms the background of Gadamer's ontology of art.

In Heidegger's *Being and Time*, a thing of use (*Zeug*) is designed with an eye to the purpose it serves. The better a tool fulfills its purpose, the less we reflect on its presence. Only when a tool no longer works do we reflect on its being there and the properties by which it is characterized. The tool is no longer ready-to-hand but appears as a bare object, as "Being-just-present-at-hand" (*BT*; *SZ*, §16, 73). Nevertheless, a tool of a specific sort can, in principle, be replaced with another one of the same kind. Because the *telos* of the tool is external to its own being, such a replacement will not affect the purpose of the activity of which it is a part. When understood in terms of such an external *telos*, tools come into view as part of a more comprehensive structure of intelligibility – "a region," as Heidegger puts it.[5] A thing,

---

3 For an overview of the relation between *Zeug* and art in Heidegger's philosophy, see Harold Alderman, "The Work of Art and Other Things," in Edward G. Ballard and Charles E. Scott (eds.), *Martin Heidegger in Europe and America* (The Hague: Martinus Nijhoff, 1973), 157–169.

4 This is not to say that Heidegger, in the 1920s, fails to address how language forms a precondition for human experience at large. Rather, Gadamer pursues a line of argumentation that is suggested by the early Heidegger's claim that "discourse is . . . constitutive for the Being of the 'there'" (*BT*; *SZ*, §34, 165) but deliberately foregrounded after the so-called *Kehre*. For a discussion of the role of language in Heidegger's philosophy, see Cristina Lafont, *Heidegger, Language, and World-Disclosure*, trans. Graham Harman (Cambridge: Cambridge University Press, 2000), and *The Linguistic Turn in Hermeneutic Philosophy*, trans. José Medina (Cambridge, Mass.: MIT Press, 1999).

5 While explaining this point in *Being and Time*, Heidegger claims that "[w]ith anything encountered as ready-to-hand there is always an involvement in [*bei*] a region [*Gegend*]. To the totality of involvements which makes up the Being of the ready-to-hand within-the-world, there belongs a spatial involvement which has the character of a region. By reason of such an involvement, the ready-to-hand becomes something we can come across and ascertain as having form and direction" (*BT*; *SZ*, §24, 111).

such as a hammer, can only appear (as meaningful) against the background of a tool-totality, including wood and nails, as well as such tasks as the making of chairs, tables, or bookshelves. What makes Heidegger's analysis of the tool-structure an indispensable part of his "destruction" of the Cartesian understanding of world-hood, hence also a project of great importance for Gadamer's hermeneutics, is the need to illustrate that our relation to beings in the world cannot be adequately grasped so long as we take as our starting-point the picture of a mind, on the one hand, and the sphere of merely present-at-hand objects of cognition, on the other. Our relation to the world is always already organized in terms of pre-theoretical patterns of coping and interaction.

Focusing on the relation between a "work of work" and a work of art, Gadamer turns to Heidegger's idea that both the function of tools (that which they are made for, their "in-order-to") and their final purpose (their "for-the-sake-of-which") are external to their being. Here Gadamer finds a way to distinguish art from things in general – or, more precisely, from other things that are brought forth and that must therefore be seen as products of human will and intentionality – without involving a reference to aesthetic subjectivity. While the aim (*telos*) of the tool is external to its own being, art is not in this way a means to an end. It is, emphatically, its own end. Upon encountering works of art one cannot, Gadamer insists, "ask what purpose they serve" (*TM*, 477; *WM*, 481). Works of art are desirable for their own sake "and not, like the useful, for the sake of something else" (ibid.). As such, a work of art is dwelling within itself.[6] Even though a work of art, like a tool, is deliberately brought forth by human beings, its aim (or its

---

6 Another version of this argument is found in Gadamer's discussion of the sign. According to Gadamer, the sign is, by definition, a sign *for* something; its function is to refer to something other than itself (*TM*, 152; *WM*, 157). If it is the nature of the sign to call for our attention, then our attention is invoked only in order to be steered away from the sign's own being there (and over to the entity to which it refers). In the case that the sign makes us dwell on its own being, rather than point away from itself, it fails as a sign or is not properly grasped in its being as a sign. As Gadamer notes, "[s]howing points away from itself. We cannot show anything to the person who looks at the act of showing itself, like the dog that looks at the pointing hand." "The Play of Art" (1977), *RB*, 128; "Das Spiel der Kunst," *GW*, vol. VIII, 91. Following Gadamer, this means that there is typically "something schematic and abstract about [signs], because they point not to themselves but to what is not present" (*TM*, 152; *WM*, 157). The work of art, on the other hand, does not point away from itself. Even if the work might be seen as a kind of sign – as is the case with a monument (Gadamer's own example, *TM*, 149; *WM*, 154) – it does not refer to something which is not there. Rather, the work of art brings to attention its own existence as such.

telos) is intrinsically related to its own being there. The work is characterized by its autotelic structure.

By drawing a distinction between the kind of being that does not have its *telos* as part of its own existence and the kind of being that has its *telos* as an intrinsic part of its being, Gadamer, again, refers to the *Nicomachean Ethics*. Within Gadamer's own environment, Aristotle's work had, as mentioned, gained new relevance through Heidegger's teaching and in particular his seminar on Book VI of the *Nicomachean Ethics*. In this seminar, which Gadamer recalls as a formative intellectual experience,[7] Heidegger, who was at the time preoccupied with a study of Aristotle's notion of being, focuses on the distinction between *poiesis* and *praxis*. According to Aristotle, *poiesis* is an activity that relates to things (objects). *Praxis*, on the other hand, is an activity that involves other human beings.[8] When relating to things, productivity is not an end in itself; it is only a means to achieve some other end. When *Dasein* engages in intersubjective interaction, however, the situation is different: *praxis* does not strive for the realization of external ends, but is sustainable in its own right.[9]

In Chapter 1, we encountered the idea of an autoteleological structure in a context that differs from Aristotle's. In Gadamer's reading, Kant's conception of the ideal of beauty allows for a structure of this kind. What particularly interests Gadamer and makes him ascribe such great importance to the ideal of beauty is that here Kant, first, considers the experience of art in terms of an immanent *telos*, its being an aim in itself rather than a means to an end, and that he, second, relates this to the idea of a dialogical experience. Hence Kant ends up describing what Gadamer takes to be a non-subjectivist version of aesthetic autonomy. In wanting to develop a phenomenological account of art, Gadamer returns to the notion of autoteleology but without explicitly distinguishing between its Aristotelian and its

---

7 Gadamer recalls this seminar in his *Selbstdarstellung* of 1975: "Das Wichtigste aber lernte ich von Heidegger. Da war vor allem das erste Seminar, an dem ich teilnahm. 1923, noch in Freiburg, über das sechste Buch der Nikomachischen Ethik." "Selbstdarstellung Hans-Georg Gadamer," *WM*, vol. II, 485.

8 Aristotle, *The Nicomachean Ethics*, trans. W. D. Ross, *The Works of Aristotle* (Oxford: Oxford University Press, 1963), vol. IX, 1139b.

9 As such, it has what Jacques Taminiaux designates a "self-referential character." See Jacques Taminiaux, "The Reappropriation of the Nicomachean Ethics," in *Heidegger and the Project of Fundamental Ontology*, ed. and trans. Michael Gendre (Albany, N.Y.: SUNY Press, 1991), 124; "La réappropriation de l'*Ethique à Nicomaque*," in *Lectures de l'ontologie fondamentale. Essais sur Heidegger* (Grenoble: Jérôme Millon, 1989), 165.

Kantian legacy. Gadamer is not interested in the philosophical roots of the concept, but rather in its ontological possibilities. Distinguished by its autotelic being, art no longer appears as a thing that, in addition to its status as a thing, is characterized by the complementary property of beauty (which aesthetic consciousness traces back to the feelings induced in us upon the disinterested contemplation of the formal qualities of the work). The autotelic structure of art does not depend on an attitude that we adopt in order to approach the world aesthetically. Nor is it a value-predicate that we project onto things that are, in themselves, present-at-hand. The autotelic structure of the work is intrinsic to the manner in which it originally presents itself to us.

From the point of view of its dwelling in itself, art, ontologically speaking, turns out to be constituted in a way that differs from the being of both nature and man-made entities such as tools or equipment. Brought forth, yet dwelling in itself, art is reducible to neither. In accordance with Heidegger's suggestion that "*Art* is the origin [*Ursprung*] of the work and of the artist" (*OWA*, 57; *UdK*, 56, emphasis added), Gadamer claims that art is "its own origin ['ein eigener Ursprung']" (*TM*, 120; *WM*, 126). This is how Gadamer moves from a notion of aesthetic autonomy, based on subjective feeling, to a notion of the autoteleology of art, based on the work's ontological features, hence taking a first step beyond the paradigm of Kant and aesthetic consciousness. He manages to draw a distinction between art and things of "inferior aesthetic value" but without appealing to aesthetic subjectivity and the free play of the cognitive faculties. However, if Gadamer, by stressing the autoteleological nature of art, gets beyond a subjectivist understanding of autonomy, the next question is how he connects this with the cognitive dimension of art. For, as we saw in the previous chapter, Gadamer argues that in order to overcome the twin picture of Cartesian epistemology and aesthetic consciousness, we need not only to challenge its subjectivist notion of aesthetic autonomy, but also, by the same token, to develop a notion of truth, knowledge, and reason that is comprehensive enough to account for the experience of art and beauty.

Truth and beauty

In Chapter 1, we saw that Gadamer sets out to overcome the limitations of subjective aesthetics by allowing for a relative continuity between art and truth (truth as self-understanding). Kant's notion of the ideal of beauty hints at such a possibility, Gadamer argues, but, owing to the limitations of the critical project, i.e., its being a transcendental investigation into the validity of pure, aesthetic judging, does not fully provide it. What, then, does Gadamer mean by truth in this context? And how is the notion of truth related to the auto-teleological structure of art?

In Gadamer's view, as in Heidegger's, our modern understanding of truth has been dominated by the idea of a correspondence or adequation between (linguistic) representation, on the one hand, and matters of fact or states of affairs in the world, on the other. In an essay from 1957, "What is Truth?", Gadamer states this very clearly by claiming that predominantly "[t]he truth of speech is determined by the adequation of speech to the thing, i.e., as adequation of the presentation through speech to the presented fact."[10] If the truth of art were to be conceived along the lines of such an adequation-model, then art would be assessed in terms of its ability to present us with a faithful representation of a non-aesthetic reality. Within the framework of post-romantic aesthetics, such an understanding of art may, admittedly, appear both far-fetched and naïve. However, historically speaking, the idea of an "adequation" between work and world has been influential nonetheless. In Giorgio Vasari's classical study *The Lives of the Painters, Sculptors and Architects* (1550), for example, the history of visual art appears as a progressive development towards the ideal of a perfect representation of nature[11] – as a matter of making and matching, as Arthur Danto at one point puts it.[12]

According to Gadamer, the perception of the relation between work and world in terms of a model of adequation amounts to an understanding of art as an *Abbild* or a copy. The copy is rooted in its likeness to the original (*TM*, 138; *WM*, 143). In the case of aesthetic representation, what is copied would be a human action, an object, or

10 Gadamer, "What is Truth?", trans. Brice. R. Wachterhauser, in Wachterhauser (ed.), *Hermeneutics and Truth* (Evanston: Northwestern University Press, 1994), 36 (trans. modified); "Was ist Wahrheit?", *GW*, vol. II, 47.

11 See for instance Vasari's claim that Giotto's greatness consisted in his becoming "such a good imitator of Nature that he entirely abandoned the rude Byzantine manner," or his claim that a later painter, Masaccio di St. Giovanni, should be praised for "his constant endeavor . . . to make his figures life-like and real, as much like Nature as possible." Giorgio Vasari, *The Lives of the Painters, Sculptors and Architects*, ed. William Gaunt, trans. A. B. Hinds (London: Dent & Sons, 1963), vol. I, 66 and 264.

12 Arthur Danto, *After the End of Art: Contemporary Art and the Pale of History* (Princeton: Princeton University Press, 1997), 48.

the harmony of nature at large. If understood as a copy, the work of art would be appreciated in terms of its referential assignments, for it applies to every copy that it "tries to be nothing but the reproduction of something and has its only function in identifying it" (ibid.). Because it depends entirely on the original, the *telos* of the copy is external to its own being. It is, in other words, impossible to regard the relationship between work and world in terms of mere adequation without, concomitantly, compromising the autotelic being of art. Hence, to the extent that one remains within a representationalist model, there is no way in which art, determined in terms of its autoteleological being, can be granted cognitive content.

The wish to get beyond the representationalist paradigm in aesthetics was a decisive part of the romantic turn towards creative genius. The work of art, it was claimed, does not simply represent or copy what is already present, but discloses a new dimension of being. Yet, in Gadamer's analysis, the romantic aesthetics of genius remains caught up in a problematic subjectivism. Within this model, the work's capacity for disclosure is explained in light of artistic subjectivity. Hence the question Gadamer faces is that of whether it would be possible to retain the romantic notion that art is disclosive rather than imitative of nature, without thereby endorsing the reference to aesthetic subjectivity. Is there a way to salvage the idea of aesthetic expression (as opposed to mere reproduction) without buying into the subjectivism of aesthetic consciousness? In Gadamer's view, such a possibility is suggested by the very etymology of the term "beauty."

Initially, Gadamer claims, "beauty" did "not mean the fulfillment of a specific ideal of the beautiful, whether classical or baroque."[13] Beauty, rather, defined art as art, i.e., as something that "stands out from everything that is purposively established and utilized."[14] There is, he further claims, an etymological affinity between the predicate *schön* (beautiful) and the verb *scheinen* (to shine). The beautiful illuminates that which was previously left in darkness. This capacity of the work, Gadamer continues, cannot be understood in terms of the subjective conditions of aesthetic production. Rather, it depends on the relation between the process of illumination and the being (there) of what is thus illuminated. Understood in terms of the work's capacity for illumination, it is characteristic of beauty that "by making something else

---

13 "Intuition and Vividness," *RB*, 161; "Anschauung und Anschaulichkeit," *GW*, vol. VIII, 193.
14 Ibid.

visible, it is visible itself, and it is not visible in any other way than by making something else visible" (*TM*, 482f.; *WM*, 486).

Gadamer concludes from this that, with regard to art, no absolute distinction can be drawn between presentation and imitation. Referring, again, to ancient Greek philosophy, he develops the notion of an imitation that is laden with productive force. The Greek notion of *mimesis*, Gadamer finds, implies that "Imitation and representation are not merely repetition . . . but a 'bringing forth'" (*TM*, 114; *WM*, 120). Within the Greek paradigm, to imitate means to make present, and in this process of making present "the presentation remains essentially connected with what is represented – indeed, belongs to it" (*TM*, 139; *WM*, 143). The relation between presentation and the presented is understood in terms of an emanation, and "what emanates is an overflow. What it flows from does not thereby become less" (*TM*, 140; *WM*, 145). With regard to aesthetic presentation, Gadamer therefore speaks of an *"increase in being* ['Zuwachs an Sein']" (ibid.). Artistic presentation is not just one among several possible ways of relating to beings but differs *qualitatively* from other (non-artistic) modes of presentation. As Gadamer puts it, the work of art lets what it presents be in "the there more authentically ['eigentlicher ins Da gekommen']" (*TM*, 114; *WM*, 120).

Proceeding to develop his own hermeneutic philosophy of art, Gadamer is ready at this point to leave behind the conceptual resources of Kant and the romantics. Now it is Heideggerian phenomenology that plays the major part. The vocabulary of subjectivity, genius, and pure, aesthetic judging is replaced with the conceptual landmarks of Heideggerian phenomenology: *"Dasein,"* "being," and the difference between "being" and "beings." Moreover, the very emphasis on the link between the Greek concept of beauty and the idea of an emanation echoes Heidegger's use of the term *Ursprung* – as in *Der Ursprung des Kunstwerkes* (*The Origin of the Work of Art*). The title of Heidegger's essay not only promises an investigation into the origin of the work, but suggests, additionally, that art, in its being, is comparable to a source or a well – that it is an emanation. The spontaneity involved in aesthetic production is de-subjectivized and led back to the work of art itself. Gadamer points to the affinity with Heidegger's notion of *Ursprung* by suggesting that "The idea of emanation in Neoplatonism implies more than the physical movement of flowing out. The primary image, rather, is that of a source [*Quelle*]" (*TM*, 423; *WM*, 427, trans. modified).

In accordance with Heidegger's ontology in the period around the publication of *Being and Time*, Gadamer holds that to present itself as itself is an essential dimension of being. It is, if we follow Heidegger, what ultimately makes something a phenomenon in the first place (*BT*; *SZ*, §7, 28). In Heidegger's account, the very term "phenomenon" actually means to present itself: "The Greek expression . . . to which the term 'phenomenon' goes back . . . signifies 'to show itself,'" so that, concomitantly, it points to "that which shows itself, the manifest ['das Sichzeigende, das Offenbare']" (ibid.). Gadamer fully accepts this way of thinking and makes it a central premise in his own approach to art. The work of art, in his understanding, is distinguished in terms of its capacity to allow being to present itself (as self-presenting). "The specific mode of the work of art's presence," he claims, "is the coming-to-presentation of being ['Zur-Darstellung-Kommen des Seins']" (*TM*, 159; *WM*, 165). Dense and convoluted as it is, this passage marks the final farewell to the framework of Kant and aesthetic consciousness. The work's capacity to let beings be in their self-presenting being comprises the core of Gadamer's philosophy of art: art is the expression of the self-presentation of being.

If it is the essence of being to present itself, and if art expresses the self-presentation of being, then it seems that art stands in a special relation to being as such. In the work of art, being presents itself in its own being; art allows what it presents "to be for the first time fully what it is" (*TM*, 143; *WM*, 148). Art allows whatever is truly to be, or, alternatively, to be in truth. On encountering the work of art, we no longer approach the presented in terms of subjective means–ends thinking, but appreciate it in its own right. Moreover, such an appreciation can take place only in the form of artistic expression. In the work of art, Gadamer insists, "a truth is experienced that we *cannot attain in any other way*" (*TM*, xxiif.; *WM*, 2, emphasis added).

However, if Gadamer ascribes to art the potential for a kind of truth that transcends the notion of truth as adequation, how, then, does he envision the relationship between this kind of truth, on the one hand, and a more traditional notion of truth as adequation, on the other?

Transcending the Cartesian framework of modern philosophy

From the early 1920s onwards, Heidegger had criticized the notion of truth as correspondence or adequacy. He traces this notion back to Aristotle. This Greek philosopher, Heidegger claims, has "not only ... assigned truth to the judgment as its primordial locus ['ursprünglichen Ort'] but has set going the definition of 'truth' as 'agreement' [*Übereinstimmung*]" (*BT; SZ,* §44, 214). Although the Aristotelian notion of truth remains important throughout the development of Western thought, it is given a new and distinctively modern twist in Descartes' idea that the subject rationally establishes the norms of epistemic adequacy whereby a given representation or content is judged to be true. In Descartes' philosophy the best-known of such norms is perceptual clarity and distinctness.[15] Gadamer continues Heidegger's critique of this tradition.[16] Modern philosophy, he claims, identifies truth with the pacing-out of a "path of knowledge so consciously that it is always possible to retrace one's steps."[17] Ever since Descartes, he continues, "the rule of certainty has been considered the authentic ethos of modern science, only that which satisfied the ideal of certainty satisfied the conditions of truth."[18] This line of thinking extends beyond the domain of science proper. Constituting the "essence of modern science," the idea of truth as certainty "defines our whole life."[19] In alignment with the later Heidegger's critique of an instrumentalist understanding of rationality, Gadamer claims that the concept of truth as methodologically achievable – that is, in his view, the scientific concept of truth – is itself technological. "Science itself is technology," as he puts it.[20]

Forty years after the publication of *Truth and Method*, Gadamer's critique of science and its "technological" basis appears exaggerated. While reflecting on his philosophical development, Gadamer later grants that the image of natural science he had in mind when writing *Truth and Method* "was quite one-sided."[21] In the next chapter, I return to Gadamer's interpretation of scientific reason and his approach to Descartes, Kant, and enlightenment thinking in general. In the present context, however, it suffices to emphasize how Gadamer, in his analysis of the relationship between art and truth, presupposes that modern philosophy, in reducing truth to certainty, fails to realize that in order for there to be objects to be represented, a world in which objects present themselves must be disclosed in the first place. In his

---

15 According to Descartes, it applies that "whatever method of proof I use, I am always brought back to the fact that it is only what I clearly and distinctly perceive that completely convinces me." *Meditations*, in *The Philosophical Writings*, vol. II, 47.
16 "What is Truth?", 36; "Was ist Wahrheit?", 47.   17 Ibid., 37; ibid., 48.   18 Ibid.
19 Ibid.   20 Ibid., 38; ibid., 48.
21 Gadamer, "Reflections on my Philosophical Journey," *LLP,* 40.

account, the real problem of truth – the problem that post-Cartesian philosophy completely overlooks – is not whether a given (linguistic) representation really corresponds to some matter of fact. The real problem, rather, is "whether everything is so presented that it can be presented in speech."[22] For, in order to be presented in speech and to be given a propositional representation, phenomena must be present to us; they must be uncovered or disclosed in the first place.

Gadamer follows Heidegger in returning to the Greek concept of *aletheia* – truth as un-concealment or disclosure (*Unverholenheit* or *Unverborgenheit*). The understanding of truth as disclosure is, Heidegger argues, "the most primordial phenomenon of truth ['das ursprüng- lichste Phänomen der Wahrheit']" (*BT; SZ*, §44, 220). Furthermore, truth as disclosure (T1) is an ontological condition for truth as ade- quation (T2). Gadamer adopts this conception and claims that "Heidegger's question about the essence of truth first really went beyond the problem area of subjectivity."[23] For Heidegger, the uncovering of phenomena is not made possible by a subject's repre- sentational capacities. Rather, the notion of truth as disclosure points to the limitations of a subject-oriented understanding of truth. It pre- sents us with the idea of truth as a clearing in being, a space of intel- ligibility that is presupposed in all propositional synthesizing (and representation in general) but as something that cannot, as such, be understood as discursively structured.

How, then, does Gadamer situate the truth of art in relation to the notion of truth as *aletheia* (T1)? We have already seen that Gadamer takes the truth of art to be about the self-presentation (being) of beings (phenomena). Aesthetic presentation is a "coming-to-presen- tation of being ['Zur-Darstellung-Kommen des Seins']," as he puts it. This "coming-to-presentation of being" is precisely the kind of dis- closure that Heidegger characterizes as the most basic phenomenon of truth (T1). In the work of art, Gadamer thus claims, reality is "raised up" into "its truth" (*TM*, 113; *WM*, 118). Claiming that art "raises reality up into its truth," Gadamer does not wish to aestheticize truth (at the level of T1); that is, he is not suggesting that every phe- nomenon, in order for us to represent it, must be aesthetically uncovered. Rather, Gadamer proposes that the very way in which being presents (or discloses) itself to us is made manifest – symbolically expressed – in the work of art. Art does not disclose an object or an

22 "What is Truth?", 39; "Was ist Wahrheit?", 50. 23 Ibid., 43f.; ibid., 54.

entity in the world. It discloses the self-presentation of being. Hence, the work's disclosure, rather than itself being a precondition for predicative judgment and knowledge (T2), makes these preconditions present or manifest to us.

Language, truth, and art

In Chapter 1, we saw how Gadamer, in his reading of the *Critique of Judgment*, criticizes Hegel's idea of great art coming to a historical end. Yet, in working out his notion of the truth of art, Gadamer strives to create a higher synthesis of Heideggerian and Hegelian thinking.[24] While his engagement with the aesthetic tradition is indebted to Hegel's critique of Kant and the romantics, his account of the truth of art draws heavily on Heidegger's ontology and its insistence on the worldliness of *Dasein*. This insistence on the worldliness of *Dasein* allows Gadamer to re-inscribe the notion of art's disclosure of being into an ethical and political horizon – that is, to retrieve it as the disclosure of a historical world. As we saw in Chapter 1, this is a line of thinking that Gadamer traces back to Hegel's lectures on fine art – it is in fact what makes him claim that Hegel's aesthetics is superior to that of Kant and aesthetic consciousness.

Like Heidegger, Gadamer claims that the worldliness of *Dasein* must be contrasted with an existence that is played out within a mere environment (*Umwelt*). The term "environment" designates "all the conditions on which a living creature depends" (*TM*, 444; *WM*, 447). *Dasein*, however, is dependent not only on the satisfaction of natural needs; it is also characterized by a capacity for freedom, the ability to raise oneself above the environment. For man, "rising above the environment means *rising to 'world'* itself" (*TM*, 444f.; *WM*, 448). Human worldliness involves the ability to take a certain stance towards the environment, to approach it with a free and distanced orientation (ibid.). Such a free and distanced orientation is made possible through language. Language is the medium of freedom in the sense that it permits a reflective stance towards the given. Indeed, it is only through language that such a reflection is possible in the first place. In Gadamer's words, "what really opens up the whole of our world

---

24 Gadamer discusses the affinities between Hegel's and Heidegger's philosophies – and "the relationship both have to the speculative spirit of the German language" – in "Hegel and Heidegger," *HD*, 112ff.; "Hegel und Heidegger," *HDi*, 109ff.

orientation [*Weltverhaltens*] is language" (*TM*, 449; *WM*, 453). World and language are mutually dependent for their intelligibility. The verbal world in which we live is "not a barrier that prevents knowledge of being-in-itself but fundamentally embraces everything in which our insight can be enlarged and deepened" (*TM*, 447; *WM*, 450f.). As linguistically constituted, the world is inherently shared. It is "the common ground [*Boden*], trodden by none and recognized by all" (*TM*, 446; *WM*, 450). In being socialized into a language we are, at the same time, socialized into a world. To the extent that language cannot be mine only, this applies to the world as well. The intersubjective dimension of the world includes more than just the horizon of the present. As opposed to a mere environment, the world is made up of the historically mediated ideas and traditions that the linguistic community carries with it. Language cannot be separated from the being to which it lends expression; it has "no independent life apart from the world that comes to language within it" (*TM*, 443; *WM*, 447).

When understood in terms of a historically mediated world, language establishes the field of intelligibility within which judgments can be passed. As a totality, language is a condition for truth at the level of predication. Yet this also has consequences for our conception of truth at the level of correspondence (T2). If truth – as a correspondence between judgment and world – is itself made possible by *Dasein*'s being in the world, then it follows that as a quasi-monadic unity, "[t]here can be no proposition [*Aussage*] that is purely and simply true."[25] If the truth is in the whole (the world as a totality of meaning), then the individual proposition is not, in itself, a bearer of truth or falsity. Every proposition is conditioned by the totality of language, and thus it follows that "every proposition has presuppositions that it does not express."[26]

How, then, is this dimension of truth at the level of T2 related to the truth of art? While bringing about the self-presentation of being, art "is only encountered in a form that resists pure conceptualization."[27] It is, as Gadamer puts it, "an invitation to intuition ['was zu nichts als zum Anschauen einlädt']."[28] But if this is the case – if this

---

25 "What is Truth?", 41; "Was ist Wahrheit?", 52.   26 Ibid., 42; ibid., 52.
27 "The Relevance of the Beautiful" (1974), *RB*, 37; "Die Aktualität des Schönen," *GW*, vol. VIII, 128.
28 "Intuition and Vividness," *RB*, 161; "Anschauung und Anschaulichkeit," *GW*, vol. VIII, 193.

intuition presents the ontological pre-conditions of truth (T2), and if these preconditions are intrinsically connected to a linguistic totality – then it follows that the intuition of the work is simply a *Welt-anschauung*. This, exactly, is Gadamer's claim – and the point at which he senses an affinity between Hegel and Heidegger. Art, Gadamer insists, is "to be characterized as intuition, indeed, as a world view, *Welt-Anschauung*."[29] Prior to all "conceptual-scientific knowledge, the way in which we look upon the world, and upon our whole being-in-the-world, takes shape in art."[30] Understood in terms of the self-disclosure of being, the work of art expresses the pre-predicative horizon of meaning, the common ground on which our predicative and conceptual activities are based. It manifests what Heidegger calls the "outlook"[31] of a culture and what Hegel would speak of as its spirit or absolute. As such, the work of art symbolically presents the comprehensive field of meaning that is a precondition for the truth of assertoric judgment. Its truth is, as Gadamer argues, "the truth of our own world – the religious and moral world in which we live" (*TM*, 128; *WM*, 133). If philosophy, as in aesthetic consciousness, cuts itself off from taking a "moral or religious stance" towards art (*TM*, 85; *WM*, 91), it does, concomitantly, cut itself off from art as such. This is the conclusion of Gadamer's overcoming of the ills of modern philosophy: he links art to a notion of truth as world-disclosure that is prior to, yet has consequences for *Dasein*'s epistemic orientations. I discuss the epistemological ramifications of Gadamer's turn to the world-disclosive truth of art in Chapters 4 and 6. Before we proceed that far, however, I would like to ask how this contribution fares when judged, historically and systematically, as a theory of art.

Essentialism and historicity

In his deduction of the a priori conditions for a dimension of validity in pure, aesthetic judging, Kant had turned towards aesthetic subjectivity and the idea of a free play between the cognitive faculties of imagination and understanding. In Kant's third Critique, however, natural beauty plays the leading part. Aesthetic consciousness leaves

29 Ibid., 164; ibid., 195.   30 Ibid., 164; ibid., 196.
31 Upon approaching the Greek temple (taken in this context to be a work of art), Heidegger claims that "in its standing there, [it] first gives to things their look and to men their outlook on themselves" (*OWA*, 43; *UdK*, 39).

behind the interest in taste and natural beauty and turns, instead, to art. However, in undertaking such a turn to art, aesthetic consciousness remains faithful to the Kantian paradigm. Hence aesthetic consciousness ends up misunderstanding Kant; it defends a problematic notion of aesthetic immediacy, pure aesthetic presence, and a turn to aesthetic subjectivity. By defining art as "the truth about our world," Gadamer takes into account the historical aspect of art. Yet he does not wish completely to relativize the category of art, that is, to dissolve it into a myriad different aesthetic conceptions. On the contrary, he seeks to arrive at an understanding that addresses not only one particular period or kind of art, but art as such. In overcoming aesthetic consciousness, he does at the same time want to retain its aspiration to define art as art, i.e., to provide a notion of art that is comprehensive enough to "cover both what art is today and what it has been in the past."[32] How, then, can Gadamer defend the historical nature of art while at the same time producing a definition that accounts for both modern art and the works of the pre-modern or classical era?

For Hegel and the Hegelians, the term "classical" refers to ancient Greek art. Gadamer, by contrast, uses this notion to cover pre-modern art as such (and, later on, even to characterize the way in which great art traverses history). Classical art, he claims, was "not primarily understood as art,"[33] but in terms of didactic and edifying purposes. Embodying the *Mitte* of a given society, classical art erected a measure of meaningfulness; it expressed the ethical, political, and religious expectations in light of which shared practices gained significance. Lending voice to the moral horizon of the community, its truth was more fundamental than the choices and preferences of the individual subject. While it expressed the pre-predicative foundation that keeps a given "we" together, classical art called for no justification by the disinterested critic. Rather, its intelligibility relied on "a continuity of meaning which links the work of art with the existing world" (*TM*, 134; *WM*, 138). To contest the validity of such a work would at the same time be to contest the moral consciousness of the community. Hence pre-modern art is distinguished by the fact that its "obligatoriness [*Verbindlichkeit*]" was self-evident (*TM*, 118; *WM*, 123).[34]

32 "The Relevance of the Beautiful," *RB*, 19; "Die Aktualität des Schönen," *GW*, vol. VIII, 110.
33 Ibid.
34 While distinguishing between a work of art that serves integrative purposes in an organic society and one that may be traced back to the creativity of individual genius, Gadamer seems to presuppose that the pre-modern work presented the universal

Such an entwining of art and morality cannot be found in the modern age. In modernity the free artist creates without a commission and occasion. He or she is distinguished by the independence of the creative activity and thus acquires the characteristic social features of an "outsider whose style of life cannot be measured by the standards of public morality" (*TM*, 87; *WM*, 93). It is not just the artist who appears as an outsider. More importantly, art has lost its capacity to present, as binding, the standards of public morality. The work is cut off from its broader ethical, political, and religious contexts and no longer offers a self-evident sense of integration. If art, in previous eras, "occupied a legitimate place in the world, [so that] it was clearly able to effect an integration ['eine selbstverständliche Integration'] between community, society, and the Church on the one hand and the self-understanding of the creative artist on the other,"[35] then the modern situation is one in which "this self-evident integration, and the universally shared understanding of the artist's role that accompanies it, no longer exists."[36] The work of art has become "aesthetic"; it has become a work of art in the modern sense of the term: a work of art only. As such, it does indeed call for justification, and Gadamer understands this call, emerging at the time when aesthetics is established as an autonomous, philosophical discipline, as evoking "our situation of extreme modernity ['die Situation unserer zugespitzten Moderne']."[37]

Hermeneutics, no doubt, represents one possible response to our "situation of extreme modernity." Moreover, we may assume that Gadamer believes that his hermeneutic account of art responds more adequately to this situation than previous systems of aesthetic thinking were able to – and, more so, in particular, than the aesthetic consciousness was capable of doing. Nonetheless, Gadamer's notion of

voice of its society. This, however, is far from evident. For even though the classical work of art may have expressed a view of the world – as may, one should add, the modern work, too – this is not necessarily a view that was universally shared. Even Hegel realized this. In Hegel, ethical life is never reducible to a completely organic and unified code of practices, but is always conflictual (*zerrissen*). Gadamer, however, does not address this aspect of the pre-modern condition. He simply asserts, without further argumentation, that the pre-modern work embodies and enforces the unitary values of a given historical world. This is, as we shall see, an assertion that diminishes the relevance of Gadamer's philosophy of art – both with regard to the pre-modern work and with regard to modern culture.

35 "The Relevance of the Beautiful," *RB*, 6; "Die Aktualität des Schönen," *GW*, vol. VIII, 97.
36 Ibid. 37 Ibid., 10; ibid., 101.

the world-disclosive truth of art remains intimately connected to the "classical" work. "The real [*wirkliche*] experience of art," he claims, "does not experience art as art" (*TM*, 573, *WM*, vol. II, 472). When conceived as art only, the work cannot disclose the shared ethical-political standards of a given, historical world. It is not original in the sense of transcending every call for justification.

Gadamer's account of modern art gives rise to a number of questions. Given the historical development of art, how are we to understand the insistence on its world-disclosive truth? Is Gadamer suggesting that art in modernity has lost its capacity for world-disclosure? Although such a conclusion appears to follow from Gadamer's account of art and the way in which his description of world-disclosive truth corresponds to his understanding of classical art, we know already that he is critical of the thesis, developed by Hegel, of the death of great art in the post-romantic era. In addition to the systematic argument he offers against Hegel's end-of-art thesis (as retrieved in Chapter 1), Gadamer now provides a historical argument. We cannot, he claims, "talk about great art as simply belonging to the past, any more than we can talk about modern art only becoming 'pure' art through the rejection of all significant content."[38] For if we were to view modern art solely in terms of its claim for justification, then this would imply a clear-cut break between the pre-modern and the modern period. This, in Gadamer's view, would be misguided. While he admits that the situation of art has undergone substantial changes, Gadamer rejects the idea of an absolute break between the classical and the modern era. Even modern art, he argues, makes manifest the deeper ethical-political totality – the mythical foundation, as he sometimes puts it – of its society. For Gadamer, this continuity rests with the fact that not just classical but also modern art lends voice to its historical horizon. It may not do this in a way that is direct and unmediated (as in the pre-modern era), but the artist, even in relating negatively to his or her own community, nonetheless thematizes and brings to light the pre-predicative world-view of his or her historical world. Hence to regard the modern work in isolation from its larger, cultural surroundings is to misunderstand its meaning – a misunderstanding that Gadamer, as we have seen, traces back to aesthetic consciousness.

Now, few aestheticians would deny the existence of a relative continuity between classical and modern ("aesthetic") art, a continuity

---

38 Ibid., 19; ibid., 110.

that is visible not only from a bird's-eye view of the history of art, but also on the level of concrete works. An obvious example here is the nineteenth-century poet Charles Baudelaire, who explores a condition of hypermodernity – the crowds, the *flâneur*, the *bohême*, the cast-iron constructions, and the increasing sense of alienation in the new metropolis – through the classical form of the sonnet.[39] To the extent that modern art forms a new beginning, it only emerges, as Gadamer points out, against a more comprehensive historical background. However, to hold that there is a relative continuity between so-called classical and so-called modern art does not mean that one is forced to accept Gadamer's particular interpretation of the nature of this continuity, namely that it consists in the work's ability to represent an authoritative symbolic expression of the absolutes of a given culture. Thus the following concern persists: is it really possible to argue that the work of art embodies the ethical-political standards of a given society and at the same time reject the restrictions that both Hegel and the romantics had put on this conception? Indeed, insofar as art is understood in terms of its world-disclosive capacity, it is difficult to see how Gadamer can fully account for the intrinsic qualities of modern art.

It is helpful to address this problem in light of a concrete example, namely Gadamer's reading of Paul Celan. Gadamer deals with Celan's poetry in a series of essays. The most influential of these, "Who am I and Who are You?" (1973), is an interpretation of the lyrical sequence *Breath-crystal (Atemkristall)*.[40] Within twentieth-century poetics, Celan is commonly viewed as the modernist poet par excellence. Such an interpretation of Celan's work is offered by Adorno. In accordance with his claims about the constitutive enigma of modernist art, which we briefly encountered towards the end of the last chapter, Adorno situates Celan within a tradition in which art insists upon its own autonomy. In Adorno's view, this insistence is not, as Gadamer suggests, the result of abstraction or false self-understanding, but rather represents a genuine response to a society that is experienced as

---

39 The modernist sensitivity of Baudelaire's prose is emphasized in Walter Benjamin's *Charles Baudelaire: A Lyric Poet in the Era of High Capitalism*, trans. Harry Zohn (London: NLB, 1968); *Charles Baudelaire. Ein Lyriker im Zeitalter des Hochkapitalismus*, in Benjamin, *Gesammelte Schriften*, vol. I.2, 509–690.

40 Hans-Georg Gadamer, *Gadamer on Celan*, ed. and trans. Richard Heinemann and Bruce Krajewski (Albany, N.Y.: SUNY Press, 1997); *Wer bin Ich und wer bist Du?* (Frankfurt am Main: Suhrkamp Verlag, 1995).

increasingly false, corrupt, and perverted. As modern, the work is bound to reflect its own conditions, claims Adorno. It must, as he puts it, "incorporate its own decline; as the critique of the spirit of domination it is the spirit that is able to turn against itself."[41] In Adorno's reading, Celan responds to this challenge in a most uncompromising manner. Having lived through the horrors of the Second World War, he sees no alternative but to cultivate an expression that, in Adorno's words, "is permeated by the shame of art in the face of suffering that escapes both experience and sublimation."[42] His language withdraws from culture and ordinary communication and, at the end of the day, even from the category of art itself. Celan's poetry, Adorno insists, "imitate[s] a language beneath the helpless language of human beings, indeed beneath all organic language: It is that of the dead speaking of stones and stars."[43] The language of the dead is the very last resort when life as well as death is deprived of meaning.

Gadamer, however, sees nothing of this in Celan's work. Regardless of the experiences conveyed in Celan's poems, in Gadamer's view language "is always the language of conversation."[44] Accordingly, Celan's work does not reflect the feeling that language fails the poet, but the experience – echoing the later Heidegger's claim that language is the house of Being – that "The covering of words is like a roof over us."[45] Language, "the covering of words," "secure[s] the familiar."[46] In the familiar covering of words, the I encounters the you of the poetic text. The I and the you are unified in a harmonious whole. In Gadamer's reading, Celan's hermetic, paratactic, and fragmentary form gives way to the experience of a unified and coherent meaning. The question that Gadamer does not address, however, is whether Celan's poetry can really be read in terms of a hermeneutically harmonizing model without thereby being deprived of its most essential character.

If one seeks to defend Gadamer's conception of art one could argue, against the universalist aspiration that he starts out with, that even if the notion of art as "the truth about our world – the religious and moral world in which we live" misses fundamental aspects of modernist art, his philosophy is well suited to describe the nature of pre-modern (classical) art. However, this is not the case. By basing his

---

41 *Aesthetic Theory*, 320; *Ästhetische Theorie*, 474.   42 Ibid., 322; ibid., 477.   43 Ibid.
44 "Letter to Dallmayr," trans. Richard Palmer and Diane Michelfelder, in Palmer and Michelfelder (eds.), *Dialogue and Deconstruction*, 99.
45 "Who am I and Who are You?," *Gadamer on Celan*, 81; *Wer bin Ich und wer bist Du?*, 29.
46 Ibid.

notion of art on the idea of an ethical-political world-disclosure, Gadamer not only provides too narrow an account of modern art, but also defends a rather static understanding of classical culture. Approaching (classical) art in terms of its ability to disclose a common, organic horizon of meaning, Gadamer fails to account for aspects of these works that do not fit into his harmonizing model. Once again, it is helpful to illuminate this point with the aid of some concrete examples.

We have already seen how Gadamer elaborates his critique of romantic aesthetics by contrasting the modern notion of the symbol with the allegorical expression. Gadamer takes allegory to be a mode of representation that "rests on firm traditions and always has a fixed, stateable meaning which does not resist rational comprehension through the concept [but is closely related to] the rationalization of the mythical" (TM, 79; WM, 85). Given Gadamer's emphasis on the ethical-political world-disclosure of art, he simply cannot consider other possible ways of recounting the historical aspects of the allegory without being forced to dismiss its importance to art. He cannot, for instance, account for the aspects of allegory that someone like Walter Benjamin is interested in (even though Gadamer actually refers to Benjamin in his discussion of allegory, TM, xxxi; WM, vol. II, 441, footnote). Like Gadamer, Benjamin seeks to rescue allegory from its devaluation throughout the romantic era. And, like Gadamer, he is interested in the way in which "[f]or over a hundred years the philosophy of art has been subject to the tyranny of a usurper who came to power in the chaos which followed in the wake of romanticism."[47] Again, like Gadamer, Benjamin claims that the (quasi-)romantic notion of the symbol soon leads to a devaluation of the allegorical expression. However, in Benjamin's view such a devaluation fails to realize how allegory, and in particular baroque allegory, represents a response to the genuinely modern experience of a loss of binding ethical-political values. Allegory, Benjamin claims, is "in the realm of thoughts, what ruins are in the realm of things."[48] It is, he continues, "common practice in the literature of the baroque to pile up fragments ceaselessly, without any strict idea of a goal, and, in the unremitting expectation of a miracle, to take the repetition of stereotypes

---

47 Walter Benjamin, *The Origin of the German Tragic Drama*, trans. J. Osborne (London: NLB, 1977), 159; *Ursprung des deutschen Trauerspiels*, in Benjamin, *Gesammelte Schriften*, vol. I.1, 336. 48 Ibid., 178; ibid., 354.

for a process of intensification."[49] In Benjamin's reading, allegory appears as an aesthetic form that counters the idea of the "pre-aesthetic" artwork as a disclosure of a common world in Gadamer's sense of the term. My point here is not to pass any final verdict on which of these models leaves us with the best account of allegory, but simply to emphasize that given Gadamer's understanding of art in terms of its organic, communal, and collective features, he fails to consider how allegory, as a rhetorical trope, also articulates experiences that we have later come to identify as typically modern in that they no longer reflect an integrating web of shared values and practices.

Another example, while not taken from the realm of fine art in the narrow sense of the word, may further elucidate my point. In Chapter 1, we saw how Gadamer traces the ethical-political aspect of taste back to Gracián and early modern humanism. On Gadamer's reading, Gracián cultivates the ideal of a humanistic *Bildung* (*TM*, 35; *WM*, 41). The concept of good taste is intrinsically related to that of a good society. What Gadamer does not take into account, however, is how Gracián's notion of taste is saturated by a more pessimistic stance. If taste, in his work, includes a dimension of knowledge, then this is not only a dimension of practical knowing, referring ultimately to the idea of the good society, but also an insight into the fundamental groundlessness of human existence.

What motivates Gracián's turn to taste and judgment is not only the dream of a good society, but also the idea that we are, in his words, "stuck in the mud from which [we were] formed" so that there is nothing to do but to go forwards and try to "escape as best as [one] can."[50] We need people who are capable of passing apt judgments – heroes, as Gracián calls them – simply because we need to see how one may at all endure the dreary conditions of human life. The hero does not uncover an intrinsic organic meaning in society or social life, but affirms the groundlessness of it all. This is the Gracián who so fascinated Nietzsche and Schopenhauer, his German translator. In Gracián's view, the human condition is intrinsically tragic: "We climb the ladder of life, and the rungs – the days – disappear one after another, the moment we move our feet. There is no way to climb down, nothing to do but go forward."[51] This is an aspect of Gracián's

49 Ibid.
50 Baltasar Gracián, *A Pocket Mirror for Heroes*, trans. Christopher Maurer (New York: Doubleday, 1996), 70.
51 Ibid., 77.

aphorisms that Gadamer completely overlooks and, moreover, one that he must overlook to avoid overthrowing the consistency of his overall argument.

As shown by these examples, Gadamer's approach to the history of art is threatened by an overemphasis on the ethical-political world-disclosure of the work. In attempting to overcome the subjectivation of art in aesthetic consciousness, Gadamer lets himself be guided by a very peculiar notion of the work's ability to manifest the ethical-political foundation of a given, historical world. His endeavor to work out a concept of art that is comprehensive enough to "cover both what art is today and what it has been in the past" ends up hypostatizing, as the paradigm of art as such, a work that reflects a set of ethical-political values that transcend the scope of critical reflection and judgment.

Beyond subjectivism: play and ecstatic self-forgetfulness

Gadamer's hypostatization of the work of art that transcends the scope of critical reflection and judging is not limited to his understanding of art (his answer to the question of what a work of art is and how it is distinguished from other man-made objects), but also shapes his understanding of the relationship between work and recipient, which is perceived as a kind of play (*Spiel*).

We have seen that the concept of play was an important part of the aesthetic tradition that Gadamer criticizes. In the *Critique of Judgment*, Kant argues that the aesthetic feeling is induced by the unconstrained co-ordination of imagination and understanding, a free play that Dieter Henrich compares to "a dance of two partners who harmonize in their movements without influencing each other."[52] This idea is further developed in Schiller's utopian notion of aesthetic education. Here the play-drive ("der Spieltrieb") refers to the harmonious relation between form-drive ("der Formtrieb") and sense-drive ("der sinnliche Trieb"). In the play-drive, feelings and passions ("Empfindungen und Affekten") are brought "into harmony with the ideas of reason."[53] Schiller ascribes to this harmony an ethical and political significance. In his view, it is only an aesthetic state that can make society real (*wirklich*): "[t]aste alone brings harmony into society, because it fosters harmony in the individual. All other forms of

---

52 "Kant's Explanation of Aesthetic Judgment," in Henrich, *Aesthetic Judgment*, 52.
53 *On the Aesthetic Education of Man*, Fourteenth Letter, 99 (English); 98 (German).

perception divide man, because they are founded either upon the sensuous or upon the spiritual part of his being."[54] In spite of the differences between Kant's and Schiller's aesthetics,[55] they both appeal to the concept of play in order to elucidate a particular relation between imagination and understanding, or, better still, a particular structure between freedom and necessity. Play, as Schiller puts it, is neither subjectively nor objectively contingent, and yet imposes no kind of constraints from within or from without.[56] It is this idea of a structure that cannot be expressed in the form of general laws, but that is nevertheless not contingent or accidental, that Gadamer adopts. Although he dismisses the idea that aesthetic experience is anchored in the free play of the cognitive faculties, he is determined to retain the idea of a free and spontaneous, yet organized, structure.

In turning to Kant's notion of free play, Gadamer follows his teacher Heidegger and his attempt to rescue Kant from his nineteenth-century critics. In Chapter 1, we saw how Gadamer's reading of Kant's third Critique represents a revision of Heidegger's rejection of modern aesthetics as the element in which art dies. Nonetheless, the idea of free play – or, rather, the idea of the disinterestedness by which free play is conditioned – is a notion in which Heidegger takes a certain interest. It is the point, so to speak, where he is willing to modify his massive critique of the modern philosophy of art. Lecturing on Nietzsche's revolt against subjective aesthetics, Heidegger discusses how Schopenhauer mistook Kantian disinterestedness for "sheer apathetic drift" (*N*, 108; *Ni*, 108). He insists that in Kant's work "interest" does not signify that something is meaningful and significant for us, so that, concomitantly, an attitude of *dis*interesteness would imply a neglect of this significance or meaning. Rather, the term "interest" invokes an effort to gain something "for oneself as a possession, to have disposition and control over it" (*N*, 109; *Ni*, 108). In Heidegger's reading, to take an interest in the object amounts to adopting an attitude in which we approach the object as a mere means and not as something that is valuable in its own right. Against this background, the notion of *dis*interestedness need not signify sheer neglect. Rather, with Kant's conception of disinterestedness, "the

---

54 Ibid., Twenty-seventh Letter, 215 (English); 214 (German).
55 For a discussion of these differences, see Frederick Beiser, *Schiller as Philosopher: A Re-Examination* (Oxford: Clarendon Press, 2005), 13–46.
56 *On the Aesthetic Education of Man*, Fifteenth Letter, 103f. (English); 102f. (German).

essential relation to the object itself comes into play . . . for the first time the object comes to the fore as pure object and . . . such a coming forward into appearance is the beautiful" (*N*, 110; *Ni*, 110). In appreciating the phenomenon as it is – that is, for Heidegger as well as for Gadamer, in the way it presents itself to us in its being – *Dasein* must display a willingness to allow the object to disclose itself as itself. If this experience is characterized by passivity, then it is not passivity of the kind that Schopenhauer had in mind. It is, to borrow a distinction from Gadamer's discussion of the ideal of beauty, a lack of interest in the object qua means or instrument, but not a lack of interest in the object as such. At stake is a passivity that allows being to manifest itself as itself – that is, allows art to stand forth in its autotelic being. Disinterestedness, in other words, is not only *negatively* determined, as an absence of interest, but also entails a *positive* dimension, a particular openness or sensitivity towards the experience conveyed by art and beauty.

We have already seen that Gadamer fails to acknowledge the hermeneutic potential of Kant's notion of natural beauty. This – his retrieval of the notion of play – is the point at which it becomes clear why a Kantian notion of disinterestedness is not enough to satisfy him. That is, disinterestedness, in the sense developed by Kant, may well be a necessary condition for aesthetic experience. However, it is not a sufficient condition. In recasting the notion of play, Gadamer's aim is not only to describe, phenomenologically, a non-pragmatic relation to being (which he has already done with his distinction between work and *Zeug*), but also to show how the play-like nature of the experience of art sets aside or even drives out the reflective capacity of the recipient altogether. This is a move that by far transcends the mindset of Kantian Idealism, and that, as we will see, has repercussions not just for Gadamer's understanding of art but also for his conception of hermeneutic reason.

According to Kant, the free, yet regular, movement of play characterizes a certain state of mind evoked by the (disinterested) contemplation of beauty. Gadamer, by contrast, claims that play is not related to subjectivity at all. "When we speak of play in reference to the experience of art," he professes, "this means neither the orientation nor even the state of mind of the creator or those enjoying the work of art, nor the freedom of a subjectivity engaged in play" (*TM*, 101; *WM*, 107). In asserting the irreducibility of play to "the mood ['die Stimmung'] or the mental state ['geistige Verfassung'] of those who play" (*TM*, 106; *WM*, 112), Gadamer appeals to the resources of ordinary language. Although we theoretically might be "accustomed to relating phenomena such as playing to the sphere of subjectivity" (*TM*, 104; *WM*, 110), a closer examination of the ordinary use of the term "play" and its variants in "playing," "playfulness," and so on and so forth, reveals the limitations of this perspective. "*Something* is playing ['*etwas* spielt'] somewhere or at some time," we say; "*something* happens ['*etwas* spielt sich ab']," or "*something* is going on ['*etwas* [ist] im Spiele']" (*TM*, 104; *WM*, 109, emphasis added). Such a use of the term "play" indicates the trans-subjective nature of playing. Playing cannot be explained in terms of autonomous subjectivity. When we speak, for instance, of the play of the waves, the play of forces, or the play of light, we do not refer to the mental or emotional state of the observer. Rather, we refer to the structure of the waves or the light itself. This structure is not self-identical over time, but "renews itself in constant repetition" (*TM*, 103; *WM*, 109). What is repeated is a certain pattern that cannot be rendered in terms of laws or determinate propositions, but that is realized only in freedom. In accordance with the autotelic structure of the artwork, play "has no [external] goal that brings it to an end" (ibid.). Its aim consists in the maintenance of the movement itself.

Drawing on the work of the Dutch anthropologist Johan Huizinga – the author of the study *Homo Ludens* (1938), which was widely read in northern Europe at the time – Gadamer argues that play, far from being reducible to a specific aesthetic dimension of subjectivity, is related to human culture as such. Play expresses a dimension of life that transcends the constraints of reproduction and natural needs. It is related to our most fundamental quest for existential meaning. Hence there is, Huizinga argues, a continuous relationship between the activity of playing and the anthropological structure of religious celebration:

> Primitive society performs its sacred rites, its sacrifices, consecration and mysteries, all of which serve to guarantee the well-being of the world, in a spirit of pure play truly understood. Now, in myth and ritual the great instinctive forces of civilized life have their origin: law and order, commerce and profit, craft and art, poetry, wisdom and science. All are rooted in the primeval soil of play.[57]

According to Gadamer, the analogy with religious rites and festivals uncovers an important phenomenological aspect of play. When

---

57 Johan Huizinga, *Homo Ludens: A Study of the Play Element in Culture* (Boston: The Beacon Press, 1955), 5.

understood in terms of the festival, it appears that play is made possible by a particular form of seriousness. In playing, Gadamer argues, the "purposive relations ['alle Zweckbezüge'] that determine active and caring existence have not simply disappeared, but are curiously suspended" (*TM*, 102; *WM*, 107). Play itself is characterized by "sacred seriousness ['heiliger Ernst']" (ibid.), that is, by a willingness to be directed by the rules or rhythms of the game itself. Accordingly, "the player himself knows that play is only play and that it exists in a world determined by the seriousness of purposes. But he does not know this in such a way that, as a player, he actually *intends* this relation to seriousness" (ibid.). The player, in other words, must forget that what he is engaged in is only play: the participation must be immediate, and the player cannot question or criticize the rules or the playing as such.

As an activity in which we participate by making its goals our own, play is prior to the reflective self-determination of the individual player. In playing, we submit to a totality of meaning that transcends the scope of reflective subjectivity. Play fulfills its purpose if, and only if, the player lets go of his claim to autonomous self-determination. Like the religious ceremony, play properly presupposes that "the player loses himself in play ['der Spielende im Spielen aufgeht']" (*TM*, 102; *WM*, 107f.). Play takes place without the full control of the players; the "to-and-fro motion" of the game "follows of itself" (*TM*, 104; *WM*, 110). As such a to-and-fro movement, play absorbs the player into its movement; it "draws him into its domination and fills him with its spirit," as Gadamer puts it (*TM*, 109; *WM*, 115). In the act of playing, spontaneity and freedom are not understood in terms of subjectivity. Neither the individual player nor the sum of players are, strictly speaking, playing the leading part. Rather, "the actual subject of play is ... *play itself*" (*TM*, 104; *WM*, 109f., emphasis added). It is play, and not players, that must be accorded originality.

In Gadamer's view, this is what makes the model of play a particularly promising starting-point for an account of the experience of art. The work of art, Gadamer argues, is "*not* an object that stands over against a subject" (*TM*, 102; *WM*, 108, emphasis added). Understood in light of play, the work of art is "original" in the sense that it is ontologically prior to the individual recipient. Hence, in order to relate fully to the work one must be willing to be completely "carried away [*hingerissen*]" (*TM*, 125; *WM*, 130). One must be ready to forget oneself and be absorbed by the truth of the work. In this, the ontological structure of play reflects the being of art. For, as we have seen, "[t]he 'subject' of the experience of art, that which remains and endures, is not the subjectivity of the person who experiences it, but the work itself" (*TM*, 102; *WM*, 108). In presenting an authority that is self-evident, the world-disclosive truth of art is more original than the individual critic or interpreter; it evades every reference to artist as well as critical recipient, and only to the extent that we realize this are we able to respond properly or, as Gadamer would say, authentically, to art.

Overcoming aesthetic consciousness?

By stressing the autotelic being, the world-disclosive truth, and the play-like ontology of art, Gadamer wants to get beyond the subjectivist framework of Kant and aesthetic consciousness. As we have already seen, the notion of world-disclosive truth leaves Gadamer poorly equipped to deal with the history of art. Moreover, we have seen that Gadamer casts the work–recipient relationship in terms of the notion of play. The next question to be addressed is thus to what extent the turn towards play serves to redeem Gadamer's original intention of over-coming aesthetic consciousness and its notion of aesthetic immediacy. To answer this question it is helpful to return, once again, to Hegel. As we have seen, it is Hegel who delivers the premises for Gadamer's critique of Kant's cultivation of natural beauty. It is Hegel who initially criticizes the paradigm of romantic aesthetics. And, finally, it is Hegel who, in spite of the Heideggerian framework of Gadamer's thinking, influences the historical and ethical-political accent of his under-standing of the world-disclosive truth of art.

Both Gadamer and Hegel worry that post-Kantian aesthetics relies on a subjectivist notion of aesthetic autonomy and that, as a conse-quence, it promotes an unsound emphasis on aesthetic immediacy. In facing this twin problem, Gadamer, like Hegel, assumes that the solution to the subjectivism problem (i.e., the claim that art is set off from the demands of cognition and truth) contains the solu-tion to the immediacy problem as well (i.e., the notion of art as given to consciousness in terms of its pure, aesthetic qualities). With regard to the problems of subjectivism and immediacy, what is needed is a willingness to take into account the comprehensive, cultural sphere of meaning and practice that has been left out of aesthetics since Kant.

In this context, Gadamer again refers to Hegel's critique, in the *Phenomenology of Spirit*, of the beautiful soul. He also, albeit indirectly, refers to Hegel's discussion of sense-certainty.[58] The figure of sense-certainty asserts that the objectivity of experience rests with the fact that it is given to the mind in an ineffable "here and now" – a moment that does not involve any conceptual work or intellectual synthesis. This is a position that claims, to quote Hegel, that "In *ap*prehending . . . , we must refrain from trying to *com*prehend . . . ['von dem Auffassen das Begreifen abzuhalten']" (*PS*, 58; *PhG*, 82). Sense-certainty traces the objectivity of experience back to its emphatic *mine-ness*, identifying objective truth with subjective certainty. Hegel's point is that such a mine-ness cannot be stated or made known. By emphasizing the ineffability of experience, the knowledge invoked is threatened by being mine only – sheer *meinen*. What allegedly was the most objective aspect of perception, its immediacy, may turn out to be sheer arbitrariness (as Hegel and Gadamer also claim is the case with regard to natural beauty). Rather than something that comes in addition to truth, mediation is an essential aspect of it. In criticizing the figure of sense-certainty, Hegel thus rejects the understanding of truth in terms of a relatedness to an ineffable dimension of being, a dimension that is unmediated by language. As Terry Pinkard puts it, "[i]f you can't *say* it or *show* it, you don't *know* it."[59]

As we have seen, Gadamer draws on this discussion in his critique of aesthetic consciousness. This, I have argued, is the most promising aspect of his critique of romantic aesthetics. Against a model that privileges subjective immediacy as being prior to, more original than, and independent of language and understanding, Gadamer claims that art, rightly understood, is detached from all subjective meaning ('[a]bgelöst von allem Meinen').[60] The focus on the immediacy of the aesthetic reduces the meaning of the work to a pure *meinen*, to nothing but subjective meaning. Artistic beauty, however, should not be perceived in this manner. Instead, we ought to realize that art is a cultural phenomenon that always has a dimension of meaning – that it

58 Whereas Robert Stern sees the discussion of sense-certainty as a general critique of the idea of conceptually unmediated knowledge, Pinkard suggests a closer connection between the discussion of sense-certainty and the critique of the unhappy consciousness as "the way in which the skeptic must live his life." See Robert Stern, *Hegel and the Phenomenology of Spirit* (London: Routledge, 2002), 43–45, and Terry Pinkard, *Hegel's Phenomenology: The Sociality of Reason* (Cambridge: Cambridge University Press, 1996), 69.
59 Pinkard, *Hegel's Phenomenology*, 27.
60 "On the Contribution of Poetry to the Search for Truth" (1971), *RB*, 107, trans. modified; "Über den Beitrag der Dichtkunst bei der Suche nach der Wahrheit," *GW*, vol. VIII, 72.

speaks to us, as Gadamer puts it, in a meaningful way. Art articulates the larger horizon of our historical culture. Thus conceived, it must be granted a dimension of truth, although not *conceptual* truth. It is a truth, Hegel would insist, that, unlike propositional truth, is sensuously mediated: the truth of an intuition – an intuition of the world. What we face here is a hermeneutic truth in the sense of its being a world-view that is expressive of who we are, the truth about our own historical tradition.

In spite of their criticism of romantic aesthetics, both Hegel and Gadamer recognize that the romantics were the first to develop a philosophy of art proper (the standpoint of art, as opposed to the standpoint of taste). They were also – although this is not recognized by Hegel and Gadamer – among the first, within the modern era, to offer a historical retrieval of the development of art (here I am not thinking of Winckelmann's cultivation of Greek sculpture that so impressed Hegel, but of the Schlegel brothers' studies of medieval art, of Shakespeare, and of the history of tragedy, to mention only a few examples). Yet, even if one acknowledges that Hegel and Gadamer have a somewhat biased perception of romantic aesthetics, one must recognize two principal differences between a romantic and a Hegelian conception. First, the romantics (the Schlegels in particular) conducted research in the history of art in addition to developing their aesthetics. That is, in their view, the history of art could only provide useful examples of more general philosophical points. The history of art was seen as important, and yet a significant, systematic role in their philosophical accounts of aesthetics was not conferred upon it. With Hegel, however, this changes. The history of art is not some kind of pastime activity that we engage with in addition to the task of arriving at its philosophical definition. Unless we can give an account of how and why art changes throughout the ages, we have no proper understanding of the essence of art. The systematic and the historical are essentially two sides of the same coin. Art is, in essence, a historical phenomenon. Second, and closely related to the first point, is the fact that unlike the romantics, Hegel, in reflecting upon the historicity of art, at the same time gives an account of the conditions of possibility (the necessary and sufficient conditions) of having a philosophy of art in the first place. Great art, he thinks, can only be determined philosophically (in accordance with its concept or essence) when each and every historical possibility is realized. Only when great art has come to its historical end can we know, philosophically, what art is. That is, in the earlier periods, we are familiar with art, to be sure. However, the essence of great art – of that which is common throughout the changes and vicissitudes of art history – can only be determined when its historical development has been brought to an end and the philosopher can catalogue its basic forms and historical expressions without him- or herself being part of this development.

Gadamer adopts the first of Hegel's two points vis-à-vis the romantics: that art (but also spirit in general) is historically mediated. This is why he refers to himself as a Hegelian philosopher and claims that it is only Hegel's philosophy that puts modern hermeneutics back on track. After Hegel – or, rather, after Hegel is read properly (Dilthey and the historical school read Hegel, but not properly, Gadamer claims)[61] – the meaning of the work of art cannot possibly be bound up with the original intentionality of creative genius. Now the meaning of the work is tied up with its mediation in tradition at large. As for Hegel's second point, the end-of-art thesis (and the claim that only such a thesis can authorize a non-partisan philosophical account of art), Gadamer, as we saw in Chapter 1, is quick to back off. He seeks to appropriate the idea of the historical mediation of art but without accepting that the historical development of great art has come to an end. Gadamer's rejection of this idea is of a systematic, rather than an empirical, nature. His claim is not that Hegel was wrong in locating the end of art in early nineteenth-century culture, but that the very idea of an end of great art contradicts the general, hermeneutic gist of Hegel's philosophy and, moreover, is untenable on systematic grounds.

According to Gadamer, there is no end to the history of great art. To think that there is, is not just intellectual hubris – it is to miss the very point of the sensuous nature of art, its being an intuition in and through tradition. As such, art lives historically; it offers itself to ever new interpretations, and its meaning gets progressively richer and ever more concrete. It is not, as Hegel thought, up to the post-historical philosopher to conceptualize the essence of art. Art, as it were, follows the play-like dialectics of tradition itself. The meaning of art gets realized in an ongoing, ever-enveloping repetition, yet not a repetition that is self-identical, but one that allows for unity in difference.

Gadamer may well be right in criticizing the colossal ambitions involved in Hegel's effort to join a historical and a systematic account of

---

61 I return to Gadamer's discussion of Hegel and twentieth-century Hegelianism in Chapter 4.

great art by taking on the perspetive of its sublation into religion and philosophical thinking. Yet regardless of what one makes of Gadamer's critique of Hegel's end-of-art thesis, it is hard, upon comparing Hegel's and Gadamer's respective solutions to the problems of aesthetic consciousness, not to worry that by casting the experience of art in terms of the passivity and trans-reflective structure of play, Gadamer, unlike Hegel, simply introduces a new variety of aesthetic immediacy – and that he therefore in effect undermines his own effort to overcome aesthetic consciousness (in addition to, as we will see, creating a number of problems within his reflections on hermeneutic reason). For if Gadamer, in wanting to overcome both the subjectivization of art in aesthetic consciousness *and* its objectification in Hegel's philosophy, moves from a paradigm of aesthetic subjectivity to one of autoteleology and play, he still does not question the notion of an immediate (given) kind of truth or authority that resides beyond the community of taste and critical judging. Hence even though Gadamer, in his (Hegelian) critique of aesthetic consciousness, scorns the drive towards immediacy, he ends up claiming that the truth of art presents itself with a similar kind of immediacy – only that this immediacy is no longer connected to the way in which aesthetic forms are given to subjectivity, but to a world-disclosive truth. Hence whereas Hegel always insists, along the lines of a Kantian commitment to autonomy, on the relation between art and critical reason (judgment), Gadamer claims that a genuine artistic creation is "always distinguishable from the cultured society that is informed and terrorized by art criticism."[62] This desire for an immediate, world-disclosive truth-claim is, I take it, the inherently naïve romanticism of Gadamer's philosophy of art – the point at which his own critique of aesthetic consciousness backfires and we see a return of the very same element, namely a problematic orientation towards immediacy, that Gadamer initially set out to criticize.

Hegel, Heidegger, and the problems of subjectivism and immediacy

One could, at this point, deem Gadamer's failure to overcome aesthetic consciousness an unwanted, yet relatively innocent, aspect of his philosophy of art. However, this failure betrays a deeper problem,

---

62 "The Universality of the Hermeneutic Problem" (1966), *PH*, 5; "Die Universalität des hermeneutischen Problems," *WM*, vol. II, 221.

one that not only has to do with the issue of immediacy in aesthetics, but also influences his views on critical thinking as such. One way to address this problem would be to cast it in terms of a lack of fit between the Heideggerian and the Hegelian commitments in Gadamer's work.

In 1960, the year he published *Truth and Method*, Gadamer completed an essay called "The Truth of the Work of Art." This essay was originally produced to accompany the final edition of Heidegger's *The Origin of the Work of Art*. In this text, Gadamer – soon leaving behind the format of an introduction so as to pursue an independent analysis of art – addresses a wide range of questions within modern aesthetics, not least the problem that had caught his attention in *Truth and Method*, namely that of Hegel's thesis on the historical end of great art. The 1960 essay is interesting because Gadamer here discusses the cognitive content of art by comparing Heidegger's position to that of Hegel. Gadamer's relation to Heidegger is, as we have seen, ambivalent. Consequently, Gadamer's first philosophical work, *Plato's Dialectical Ethics*, the *Habilitationsschrift* that also shines through in his reading of Kant's *Critique of Judgment*, was written, as already noted, in an attempt to "emancipate" himself "from the style of Heidegger." But in this early text, Gadamer not only seeks to liberate himself from Heidegger's style of philosophizing. More importantly, he sets out to rehabilitate Plato, a thinker whom Heidegger blamed for the subsequent decline of Western philosophy. In Gadamer's view, Plato is not a metaphysical thinker. Plato, rather, questions the (metaphysical) idea of knowledge as a final result – as something we have or possess – relating it instead to the dialectical self-questioning that lives and thrives in genuine dialogical interaction.[63]

Along similar lines, Gadamer's study of Kant's *Critique of Judgment* initially distanced itself from the more monolithic nature of Heidegger's renunciation of modern aesthetics (excepting the brief reflections on disinterestedness in the Nietzsche lectures). In Gadamer's reading, Kant's aesthetics is not simply "the element in which art dies." It is also a work that offers philosophical resources of which hermeneutics, if historically responsive, ought to make use. By retrieving Kant's notion of the ideal of beauty, Gadamer arrives at an

---

63 In Chapter 4, I return to Gadamer's interpretation of *Philebus* and the way in which it deviates from Heidegger's reading of Plato. However, as we will see, Gadamer's work on the *Philebus*, in spite of its deviation from Heidegger's reading of Plato, draws heavily on Heidegger's call for a salvaging destruction of the tradition of philosophy.

understanding of art in terms of a reflective and intersubjectively mediated self-encounter. Art is granted a cognitive dimension, but without this leading, as in Hegel's aesthetics, to the idea of a sublation of the truth of art into religion and, ultimately, philosophical thought. As the years pass, it seems that Gadamer's need to distance himself from Heidegger gradually disappears. In line with this development, Gadamer's 1960 discussion of Heidegger offers no critical double-reading of the kind that characterizes his engagement with Kant. Instead, Gadamer is prepared to present Heidegger's philosophy of art as the ultimate solution to the problems and paradoxes he has uncovered in modern aesthetics.

In his lectures on the origins of the work of art, and in particular in the appendix to the final and printed version, Heidegger leaves unanswered the question of the affinity between his own philosophy and that of Hegel. Gadamer, however, is in no doubt about this affinity. The similarities between Hegel's and Heidegger's conceptions of art are, he argues, striking. "[T]he Hegelian definition of beauty," he explains, shares with Heidegger's own effort the fundamental transcendence of the antithesis between subject and object, and does *not* describe the Being of the work "in terms of the subjectivity of the subject."[64] Nevertheless, Gadamer finds that Heidegger transcends the limitations of modern aesthetics more convincingly than Hegel. Although Hegel, by regarding the work of art as the sensuous embodiment of Spirit, succeeds in overcoming Kant's subjectivization of aesthetics, it appears to Gadamer that "Hegel's description of the Being of the work of art *moves in this direction*" – that is, in the direction of subjectivism.[65] This is the case, Gadamer continues, because in Hegel's aesthetics it is "the sensuous manifestation of the Idea, conceived by self-conscious thought, that constitutes the work of art."[66]

The importance of this remark should not be underestimated. Gadamer here expands the field of aesthetic subjectivization to include the idea of spirit's self-encounter in the work of art. As opposed to the philosophical intuitions that animate his reading of Kant's ideal of beauty, Gadamer now claims that in order to overcome the dangerous process of subjectivization initiated by Kant and

---

64 "The Truth of the Work of Art" (1960), *HsW*, 104f.; "Die Wahrheit des Kunstwerkes," *HW*, 89, emphasis added.
65 Ibid., emphasis added. 66 Ibid.

aesthetic consciousness, art must encompass more than what can be explained in terms of the dialogical self-encounter of spirit. Our understanding of art in terms of an intersubjective spirit or world (*Welt*) must be completed with the idea of a non-reflective, non-subjective aspect of reality, namely what Heidegger captures with the mythic-poetical notion of the earth (*Erde*).[67] In Gadamer's reading, Heidegger's notion of the earth discloses a radically non-subjective aspect of reality. In the work of art, this aspect of reality is present in the artistic material, in the marble of the sculpture, the colors of the painting, and even the tones of a musical work.[68] What shows itself in the material dimension of the work is not the reflective power of a dialogical, historical spirit. Rather, "what comes forth in this way in the work is precisely its being *closed-off* and *closing-itself-off* ['*Verschlossensein und Sichverschließen*']."[69] The earth shows itself as itself only when it withdraws from our reflective capacities, and nowhere is this process

67 According to Gadamer, the introduction of a concept of this sort marks a break with the guiding focus of *Being and Time*. In *Being and Time*, Heidegger challenged the pivot of post-Cartesian philosophy – the idea of autonomous reason or consciousness – by analyzing *Dasein* as a "thrown projection." *Dasein* is always already given direction by a certain disposition or mood (*Stimmung*). Moods are radically non-subjective. As such, the insistence on the "thrownness" of human being threatens the idea of spirit's reflective self-possession (or autonomy). Yet Heidegger sets out, in the mid-1930s, further to shatter the categories of modern philosophy. The concept of the "earth" must be situated within this context. However, according to Gadamer, there is no way to get from the "hermeneutical limiting concept of disposition or moodfulness to a concept such as the earth" (*HsW*, 100; *HW*, 85). Hence, one may add, there can also not be any way, upon investigating the work of art, to get from the idea of a spirit's self-encounter in the work to the idea of the work's capacity also to exhibit the limitation of our hermeneutic resources through the conflict of "world" and "earth."
68 Yet that out of which the artwork is composed – the material – comes into real existence as something that transcends the realm of human intentionality and self-understanding only when it is brought into the work (*HsW*, 104; *HW*, 88). The material aspect of the work shows itself only when contrasted to or in conflict with human spirit. As Heidegger puts it, "[t]hat into which the work sets itself back and which it causes to come forth in this setting back of itself we called the earth . . . In setting up a world, the work sets forth the earth. This setting forth must be thought here in the strict sense of the word. The work moves the earth itself into the Open of a world and keeps it there. *The work lets the earth be an earth*" (*OWA*, 46; *UdK*, 43). When entering into the conflict with the "world," the "earth" is so to speak elevated to an ontologically higher level. For example "[t]he tones that constitute a musical masterwork are tones in a more real sense than all other sounds or tones. The colors of a painting are colors in a more genuine sense than even nature's wealth of colors. The temple column manifests the stone-like character of its Being more genuinely in rising upward and supporting the temple roof than it did as an unhewn block of stone" (*HsW*, 104; *HW*, 89).
69 Ibid., emphasis added.

of withdrawal more evident than when contrasted with the world of human intentionality and self-understanding in the work of art.

In his discussion of Kant in *Truth and Method*, Gadamer shows how the truth of art rests in its ability to open up a self-encounter of human spirit. In the 1960 essay on Heidegger, by contrast, such a solution is deemed inadequate. It is deemed too idealistic, or, as Gadamer puts it, a conception that still works in the direction of a subjectivist aesthetics. Inspired by the audacity of Heidegger's account of the ontology of art – of what he, like Heidegger, speaks of as its *origin* – Gadamer now suggests that in order to overcome the "spiritualistic metaphysics of German Idealism"[70] it is not sufficient to emphasize the work's capacity to open the possibility for spirit's self-recognition in a non-conceptual medium. What is needed, rather, is for us to recognize that art presents us with a non-spiritual, non-reflective aspect of reality: namely, the earth (*Erde*).

The objection could be made at this point that Gadamer's text is indeed an introduction to Heidegger's philosophy of art, and that Gadamer, in his own work, hardly uses the language of world and earth. However, even if the text did initially accompany the publication of Heidegger's *Origin of the Work of Art*, it does not, as mentioned, stick to the format of a mere introduction. Moreover, even if Gadamer himself, being well aware of the problems adhering to Heidegger's mytho-poetical vocabulary, does not appeal to the category of *Erde*, the very notion of play, signifying a point at which the critical-reflective subjectivity subjects itself to a sublime happening of Being, takes him precisely in this direction. That is, the notion of play represents Gadamer's own effort to avoid renewing the subject-centeredness that he and Heidegger had taken to represent the aesthetic legacy of German Idealism. While the 1960 essay cannot, when considered in isolation, provide the premises for an exhaustive discussion of Gadamer's philosophy of art, it nevertheless provides a lens through which it may be approached and certain problematic tendencies may be highlighted. For, given Gadamer's discussion of art in the essay on Heidegger as well as in *Truth and Method*, two very different conceptions begin to take shape. On the one hand, the work of art is interpreted by Gadamer as a product of spirit; it is understood in terms of what the work "says" – that is, in terms of a dialogical process of self-formation. It is precisely this conception that Gadamer, when

70 HsW, 99; HW, 85.

drafting the first part of *Truth and Method* in the early 1930s, finds anticipated in Kant's discussion of the ideal of beauty, and it is precisely this point that makes him suggest that upon turning to the work of art, Kant himself is less of a Kantian than one would expect, given the overall framework of the third Critique. On the other hand, however, Gadamer, towards the later parts of *Truth and Method* and in his 1960 essay on Heidegger, is not satisfied with such a humanistic, and potentially also subjectivist, understanding of art. He seeks something more radical, the idea of the artwork as an "event of being ['ein Seinsvorgang']" (*TM*, 144; *WM*, 148). An adequate philosophy of art, Gadamer claims – thus again expressing his indebtedness to Heidegger – "does not preach blind commitment out of nihilistic despair, but opens itself to a hitherto concealed experience that transcends thinking from the position of subjectivity, an experience that Heidegger calls *being* (*TM*, 100; *WM*, 105). However, it is impossible to see how the conception of the work as such an event of being can be harmonized with Gadamer's other claim, being more in line with his reading of Kant's *Critique of Judgment*, that hermeneutic reason, which "includes a reflective dimension from the very beginning,"[71] must be granted an all-encompassing scope. This is the problem to which I turn in Chapter 4.

---

71 "On the Problem of Self-Understanding" (1961), *PH*, 45; "Zur Problematik des Selbstverständnisses. Ein hermeneutischer Beitrag zur Frage der 'Entmythologisierung'," *GW*, vol. II, 121.

4

HISTORY, REFLECTION, AND SELF-DETERMINATION: CRITIQUING THE ENLIGHTENMENT AND HEGEL

In developing a notion of the world-disclosive truth of art, Gadamer repeatedly points out that his intention is not only to overcome aesthetic consciousness and articulate an ontological account of art, but also to "develop from this starting point a conception of knowledge and of truth that corresponds to the whole of our hermeneutic experience" (*TM*, xxiii; *WM*, 3). Hence the question emerges of how the problems of Gadamer's account of art – most notably the tension between the reflective-dialogical approach he sketches in his encounter with Kant and Plato and a more passive model of play and self-forgetfulness – affect his understanding of hermeneutic rationality.

In contrast to his writing on art and aesthetic experience, Gadamer's discussion of hermeneutic rationality has received ample attention within the Anglo-American and European traditions alike. From within an Anglo-American context, Richard Rorty, John McDowell, and Robert Brandom have appealed to Gadamer's attempt at overcoming a problematic Cartesian paradigm in philosophy by emphasizing our situatedness within a linguistically and historically mediated world. From within a European discourse, Jürgen Habermas and Karl-Otto Apel have celebrated Gadamer's turn towards a communication-oriented, dialogical paradigm. Yet some critics, especially within the German tradition, have worried that Gadamer, given his interest in the world-disclosive truth of art, ends up defending a position that, in the words of Ernst Tugendhat, lets "an ontologically inflated conception of art [become] a substitute for the question of the justification of norms," and that he, as a consequence, ends up advocating "an ideal of receptivity as against a critical, methodological approach," thereby forsaking the enlightenment ideals of reflection and autonomy.[1]

Against the claim that Gadamer simply rejects the enlightenment notion of reflective autonomy, I argue that, in developing his commitment to hermeneutic rationality, he seeks to rescue the self-critical capacity of thinking, albeit in a way that avoids the "false objectification inherent in the idealist conception of reflection."[2] He does so, first, by criticizing the enlightenment "prejudice against prejudice" and, second, by adopting a Hegelian notion of the reflexivity of historical reason. In approaching philosophical hermeneutics, the question is therefore not whether Gadamer is for or against the enlightenment paradigm of post-Cartesian philosophy. The important question, rather, is whether or not he can harmonize his critical-reflective intent with his desire to portray the world-disclosive event of art as paradigmatic for our relation to truth and knowledge at large. Gadamer ultimately fails to do this. This is due to a conflation in his work of the epistemic and the existential dimensions of self-reflection. As a consequence, Gadamer's notion of hermeneutic rationality ends up being torn between, on the one hand, a promising attempt to offer a non-subjectivist notion of critical reflection and, on the other, a problematic appeal to understanding as a sovereign and authoritative "event of being."

This chapter starts with a discussion of Gadamer's critique of the "the Cartesian basis" of the Enlightenment and its prejudice against prejudice. The next step is then to survey the reception of this part of Gadamer's work, and in particular the objections voiced by Apel, Habermas, and Tugendhat. These philosophers underestimate Gadamer's commitment to reflection and self-understanding. His aim is not to dispense with reflection as such, but to work out a notion of reflection that is critical and historically sensitive at the same time. Gadamer does so by drawing on Hegel's *Phenomenology of Spirit*. Yet if Gadamer is sympathetic to Hegel's historicization of reason, he nonetheless finds that Hegel does not go far enough. At the end of the day, Hegel dismisses the commitment to historicity so as to defend the idea of the tradition's transparency to itself in absolute spirit. Late

---

1 Ernst Tugendhat, "The Fusion of Horizons," in *Philosophische Aufsätze* (Frankfurt am Main: Suhrkamp Verlag, 1992), 430.
2 "On the Scope and Function of Hermeneutical Reflection" (1967), *PH*, 35; "Rhetorik, Hermeneutik und Ideologiekritik. Metakritische Erörterungen zu 'Wahrheit und Methode'," *WM*, vol. II, 245.

nineteenth-century theorists of the humanities, Gadamer argues, failed to see this. Instead of appropriating the promising historical strands of Hegel's notion of reflectivity, they turned to the quasi-Cartesian aspect of his philosophy. However useful it may be for the development of his own hermeneutic position, Gadamer's critique of Hegel's Cartesianism is not acceptable. Gadamer fails to see how Hegel's introduction of the standpoint of absolute spirit allows him to respond to the problem of normativity in understanding. This points to a deeper schism between Hegel and Gadamer. Whereas Hegel follows the Enlightenment in focusing on an epistemically oriented notion of self-understanding, including the self-understanding of historical reason, Gadamer develops an existential notion of self-understanding. He wants, in short, to transform the very notion of truth in understanding into a notion of authenticity. This is also why Gadamer moves the experience of art into the center of hermeneutics. In his model, artistic truth is the paradigm case of truth as authenticity. With this move, however, a tension makes itself felt between Gadamer's enlightenment aspirations and the anti-enlightenment currents of his work. Rather than whether he is for or against the Enlightenment, this is the real problem when engaging Gadamer's hermeneutic re-articulation of truth, rationality, and knowledge.

Prejudice against prejudice

Gadamer develops his notion of hermeneutic rationality in dialectical interaction with his critique of modern epistemology, that is, his rejection of the "Cartesian basis" of modern thinking. In ascribing to art a dimension of truth, Gadamer challenges the idea that reason authorizes its own activity in an act of "absolute self-construction" (*TM*, 277; *WM*, 281). Gadamer's discussion of the Enlightenment takes this criticism one step further. Again, Gadamer approaches past philosophy in terms of its embodiment as a *Gestalt* or general intellectual paradigm. "Enlightenment," as he applies the term, does not refer to a narrowly defined period in the history of philosophy, but to a larger set of presuppositions that tends to stifle our thinking about reason, truth, and knowledge. Furthermore, Gadamer yet again adopts the strategy of immanent criticism. His aim is not to critique the enlightenment paradigm from an external point of view, but to measure the notion of a completely autonomous, self-legislative reason against the Enlightenment's own commitment to self-reflection and criticism. Is the notion of a completely autonomous and self-legislative reason really the best way to conceptualize the nature of critical reflection and thinking? Or does the idea of a completely self-legislating reason itself presuppose a set of prejudices whose legitimacy enlightenment thinking systematically fails to address?

According to Gadamer, our being in the world is historical. Historicity is the most fundamental ontological condition of human life. As such, it is a pre-condition for critical thinking. The historical world in which we live constitutes the field of intelligibility, the totality in which critical reason orients itself and gains direction. When understood as such a totality, the world cannot be turned into an object of reflective inquiry. Critical thinking is simply not standing outside the world (*TM*, 301; *WM*, 307). Rather, it is conditioned by circumstances it cannot validate from a purely epistemic point of view. Unlike what the enlightenment philosophers took to be the case, reason is not "its own master but remains constantly dependent on the given circumstances in which it operates" (*TM*, 276; *WM*, 280f.). Reason is never fully autonomous or self-authorizing, but "exists for us only in concrete, historical terms" (*TM*, 276; *WM*, 280). It cannot assess its own historical framework from a point of view beyond this framework itself. Indeed, the very assumption that the historicity of reason is a problem that begs a theoretical solution is itself a misunderstanding. The historicity of reason, Gadamer argues, is without alternatives – not only as an empirical matter of fact, but also as a normative structure.

Gadamer fleshes out this point by analyzing the philosophical status of prejudices (*Vorurteile*). The Enlightenment, he argues, leaning on the work of Leo Strauss, views prejudice as the antithesis of critical reason, "the unambiguous polemical correlate of the very ambiguous word 'freedom'" (*TM*, 271; *WM*, 275, footnote). Prejudices are handed down by tradition and dogmatically accepted. Yet, according to Gadamer, this negative conception of prejudice is not the only one available. Initially, he claims, the term "prejudice" (*Vorurteil*) held no evaluative meaning, but simply meant "a judgment that is rendered before all the elements that determine a situation have been finally examined" (*TM*, 270; *WM*, 275). Upon further investigation, some prejudices would prove legitimate and others prove false. Prejudice as such was not something that could or should be avoided.

Against what he takes to be the epistemic foundationalism of the Enlightenment – its claim that "The only thing that gives a judgment dignity is its having a basis, a methodological justification" (*TM*, 271;

WM, 275)[3] – Gadamer advocates an ontological rehabilitation of prejudices. In his view, the scope of methodological justification is limited. The field of prejudices, on the other hand, co-exists with our life-world and is, as such, indefinite. We cannot dispense with the situatedness of reason, and therefore neither with the prejudices by which reason orients itself. Prejudices are "biases of our openness to the world. They are simply conditions whereby we experience some-thing – whereby what we encounter says something to us."[4] Hence, at the end of the day it is "not so much our judgments as it is our prejudices that constitute our being."[5] Prejudices make up an inher-ent part of our pre-reflective understanding of the world.

The fact that reason is necessarily historical should not be seen as an impediment to free thinking. It is, rather, a condition of possibility for it. According to Gadamer, this becomes clearer on examining the ordinary use of the term "situatedness" or "situation." In ordinary language, we "define the concept of 'situation' by saying that it rep-resents a standpoint that limits the possibility of vision" (*TM*, 302; *WM*, 307). As such, it is intrinsically related to the phenomenological notion of a horizon, the range of vision that includes everything that can be seen from a particular vantage-point. But even if the horizon constitutes the limit of our vision, we speak of the "possible expansion of horizon, of the opening up of new horizons, and so forth" (ibid.). It is intrinsic to our use of this concept that the horizon is flexible. In Gadamer's view, this is why the term "horizon," at least since Nietzsche and Husserl, has been such an important part of the philosophical vocabulary: it reflects the way in which situatedness and freedom are mutually dependent. If not situated within a given historical horizon, "freedom" would be but an empty concept. And, vice versa, were the horizon a fixed, delimiting framework, it would allow for no freedom at all. In the tradition from Nietzsche to Husserl, the term "horizon" points to the twofold determination of our finite being. On the one hand, the horizon is "that beyond which it is impossible to see" (*TM*,

---

3 It is worth noting in this context that, according to Gadamer, his critique of the quasi-Cartesian concept of *method* does not restrict the relevance or scope of *science*. In the very last and concluding paragraph of *Truth and Method* Gadamer claims that the fact that in striving for knowledge "the knower's own being comes into play certainly shows the limits of method, but *not* of science" (*TM*, 491; *WM*, 494, emphasis added).

4 "The Universality of the Hermeneutical Problem" (1966), *PH*, 9; "Die Universalität des hermeneutischen Problems," *WM*, vol. II, 224.

5 Ibid.

306; *WM*, 311). On the other hand, this "beyond," rather than having a fixed limit, is gradually altered and expanded. A horizon is "always in motion" (*TM*, 304; *WM*, 309); it is "something into which we move and that moves with us" (ibid.).

Given such an understanding of prejudices, Gadamer can go on to claim that the "global demand of the Enlightenment," the demand for the "overcoming of all prejudices," will ultimately "prove to be a prejudice" (*TM*, 276; *WM*, 280). Equally importantly, he can argue that at the end of the day this prejudice – the prejudice against prejudice – is the most harmful of prejudices, in that it prevents us from examining the influence of prejudices as such. As Gadamer puts it, "[a] person who believes he is free of prejudices, relying on the objectivity of his procedures and denying that he is himself conditioned by historical circumstances, experiences the power of the prejudices that unconsciously dominate him as a vis a tergo" (*TM*, 360; *WM*, 366). Contrary to what the Enlightenment took to be the case, the commitment to critical thinking does not require that we deny the situatedness of reason. What is rational is to acknowledge "man's finite, historical mode of being" (*TM*, 277; *WM*, 281).

According to Gadamer, philosophy should therefore rid itself of the idea of a completely autonomous and self-legislative reason. Instead, it must ask what it implies for our conception of truth and knowledge that our prejudices constitute a condition of possibility for experience as such. Addressing this question, hermeneutics does not culminate in the articulation of a method. Nor, however, does it exclude one. For, according to Gadamer, hermeneutics "seeks to discover and bring into consciousness something which [the] methodological dispute serves only to conceal or neglect, something that does not so much confine or limit modern science as precede it and make it possible" (*TM*, xxix; *WM*, vol. II, 439). Spelling out these enabling conditions, Gadamer's hermeneutics reflects the epistemological implications of the most fundamental ontological conditions of our historical being in the world.

Now, it is one thing to assert, as Gadamer does, the finitude of human existence, and hence also of critical thinking and reflection. It is something quite different, however, to claim, as Gadamer also does, that the enlightenment tradition, in its commitment to critical-reflective reason, is "abstract and revolutionary" (*TM*, 281; *WM*, 285), i.e., that it ignores the historical situatedness of human rationality. How, then, does Gadamer end up with such a picture of the Enlightenment?

In addressing the prejudice against prejudice, Gadamer primarily refers to Descartes.[6] However, Descartes does not engage in meta-critical reflection on the nature of the Enlightenment as a paradigm in the history of philosophy. For that we need to turn to Kant. Standing at the peak of the Enlightenment, Kant articulates its most fundamental principles. In Kant's view, the enlightenment spirit answers to the Horacian *sapere aude* – dare to know! This, in turn, is contrasted with dogmatic obedience. Enlightenment is the ability to think for oneself: "man's release from his self-incurred tutelage."[7] It is a response to every kind of "personal despotism or . . . avaricious or tyrannical oppression."[8] The Enlightenment is committed to the liberty of thought and speech. But this liberty is more than a formal right. On Kant's account, the *sapere aude* appears as an ethical-political vocation, a task to which we must perpetually commit ourselves. Citizenship proper, Kant claims, involves taking on the "propensity and vocation to free thinking."[9] Kant's understanding of the Enlightenment generates an important question with regard to Gadamer's critique. Does Kant's understanding of prejudice – of that with which a free and undogmatic reason is contrasted – really overlap with the concept of prejudice that Gadamer seeks to rehabilitate?

When reflecting on the conditions for an enlightened society, Kant is mainly concerned with religious dogmatism. He has, he explains, "placed the main point of enlightenment . . . chiefly in matters of religion because . . . rulers have no interest in playing the guardian with respect to the arts and sciences and also because religious incompetence is not only the most harmful but also most degrading of all."[10] Gadamer, however, has a different agenda and introduces the term "prejudice" in relation to the fore-structure (*Vorstruktur*) of understanding (*TM*, 269; *WM*, 274). This discussion refers explicitly

---

6 At this point, Ernst Cassirer offers a more plausible interpretation of the enlightenment notion of method, claiming that "The whole eighteenth century understands reason in this sense; not as a sound body of knowledge, principles, and truths, but as a kind of energy, a force which is fully comprehensible only in its agency and effects. What reason is, and what it can do, can never be known by its results but only by its functions [Ausübung und Auswirkung]." *The Philosophy of the Enlightenment*, 13; *Die Philosophie der Aufklärung*, 16.

7 "What is Enlightenment?" in Immanuel Kant, *On History*, ed. and trans. Lewis White Beck (London: Macmillan, 1963), 3; "Beantwortung der Frage: Was ist Aufklärung?" in *Was ist Aufklärung? Aufsätze zur Geschichte und Philosophie* (Göttingen: Vandenhoeck & Ruprecht, 1985), 55.

8 Ibid., 4; ibid., 56.   9 Ibid., 10; ibid., 61.   10 Ibid., 9; ibid., 61.

to the first part of Heidegger's *Being and Time*. In Heidegger's work, the idea of the fore-structure of understanding – i.e., that our understanding of the world orients itself in terms of a fore-having, a fore-sight, and a fore-conception (*BT*; *SZ*, §32, 150) – is a function of *Dasein*'s circumspective relation to its surroundings. As such, it accounts for the way in which the world is disclosed through pre-reflective practices, rather than theoretically sensitized orientations.

However, only a few pages later Gadamer deploys the term "prejudice" in order to address the philosophy of the Enlightenment. Here, the terms "fore-structure" and "prejudice" are used more or less synonymously. As indicated by Kant's enlightenment credo, though, the idea of prejudice, of that against which critical reason is directed, refers not to the deepest foundation of our acting and thinking, the complex web of know-how that makes up our life-world, but to the vast amount of ordinary beliefs and opinions that we have more or less passively adopted from the past, and whose validity we do not call into question. These beliefs and opinions may well be criticized, altered, or replaced, but without necessarily affecting the way in which the world is disclosed to us at a pre-reflective level. One might, for example, revise one's views on some hitherto unquestioned authority (be it that of king, pope, or clergymen), claiming that it must be based on rational grounds rather than dogmatic acceptance. This, however, does not necessarily involve altering one's pre-reflective knowledge of or familiarity with the world. What we revise when criticizing these prejudices is not the ontologically most fundamental aspects of our life-world. Because the Enlightenment, in attacking the way in which prejudices curb the freedom of reason, did not address the most basic (pre-reflective) aspects of the life-world, it is implausible to think of it as "abstract and revolutionary" in Gadamer's sense of the terms.

Arguably, Gadamer's claim in this context would be that one cannot categorically distinguish between the deep-structures of language, practice, and intersubjectivity and the ideas and structures that are handed down to us by tradition, history, and religion. But even though there may be, admittedly, a complex, dialectical relationship between these dimensions of the life-world, Gadamer is not right in playing down the difference between the Enlightenment's *epistemic* conception of uncritical beliefs and opinions and a much broader, *ontological* understanding of tradition and prejudices à la Heidegger.

The notion of prejudices that Gadamer wishes to rehabilitate is not the one that the enlightenment thinkers criticized. Gadamer, however, never makes this explicit. By overlooking the distinction between two different notions of prejudices, he fails to acknowledge how the continued relevance of the enlightenment tradition rests with the claim that the authority or validity of our beliefs cannot be related to the fact that these beliefs *de facto* have been handed down by tradition. Nor can it be grounded in a *de facto* public acceptance. According to Kant, the legitimacy of a given belief rests on its being based on rational grounds. This is precisely why the Enlightenment is defined by Kant as man's emergence from his self-incurred tutelage, where tutelage is understood as the inability to use one's own understanding without the guidance of another.[11] By evading this most fundamental idea of the Enlightenment, Gadamer offers a picture of this paradigm that is far more polemical than it would have had to be in order for him to make his point about the historicity of reason. Moreover, he ends up fueling the common misunderstanding that hermeneutics is fundamentally anti-Enlightenment in spirit.

Situatedness and normativity

The Anglophone reception of Gadamer's work has generally endorsed his critique of the post-Cartesian paradigm in philosophy. This is particularly true of Rorty's reading of Gadamer in *Philosophy and the Mirror of Nature*. Rorty, an avid reader of Heidegger, highlights *Truth and Method* as an example of a philosophy that has reached beyond the representationalist paradigm of Cartesian–Kantian philosophy.[12] Whereas the "Cartesian–Kantian pattern is to see traditional philosophy as an attempt to escape from history,"[13] Gadamer's hermeneutics substitutes "the notion of *Bildung* (education, self-formation) for that of 'knowledge' as the goal of thinking."[14] In Gadamer's

11 Ibid., 3; ibid., 55.
12 For Rorty's reading of Heidegger, see "Self-Creation and Affiliation: Proust, Nietzsche, and Heidegger," in *Contingency, Irony, and Solidarity* (Cambridge: Cambridge University Press, 1989), 96–121; "Heidegger, Contingency, and Pragmatism," "Wittgenstein, Heidegger, and the Reification of Language," and "Heidegger, Kundera, and Dickens," in *Essays on Heidegger and Others*. Philosophical Papers, vol. II (Cambridge: Cambridge University Press, 1991), 27–49, 50–65, 66–82; "Overcoming the Tradition: Heidegger and Dewey," in *Consequences of Pragmatism* (Hertfordshire: Harvester Wheatsheaf, 1991), 37–59.
13 Richard Rorty, *Philosophy and the Mirror of Nature* (Oxford: Basil Blackwell, 1980), 9.
14 Ibid., 359.

work, Rorty finds a position in which "getting the facts right . . . is merely propaedeutic to finding a new and more interesting way of expressing ourselves."[15] From the edifying, as opposed to the epistemological or the technological, point of view, he continues, "the way things are said is more important than the possession of truth."[16] This, basically, is what Rorty gets out of his encounter with *Truth and Method*. A more detailed analysis of Gadamer's critique of Descartes and the Enlightenment is not to be found in his work.[17]

The same can be said of John McDowell's references to Gadamer in *Mind and World*. Eager to overcome the "dualism of [conceptual] scheme and Given,"[18] McDowell refers to the Gadamerian notions of *Bildung* and effective history.[19] Yet he never pauses to ask, as he would most probably do when it comes to Sellars, Strawson, Quine, or Davidson, what these concepts actually mean and what kind of unclarities they might host or cover up. It is, for example, puzzling how McDowell, in appropriating Gadamer's distinction between a mere environment and a historical, human world (involving a free and distanced outlook on the environment),[20] fails to note that Gadamer himself borrows this notion from Heidegger – and thus also fails to ask to what extent such a distinction really can, without further argumentative labor, be imported into a philosophical context like his own.

Within a German context, however, the situation is different. Since the publication of *Truth and Method*, Gadamer's critique of the Enlightenment has generated a wide-spanning discussion. At stake is not only the enlightenment legacy, but also the general relevance of Gadamer's hermeneutics. In his review of *Truth and Method*, Habermas articulates this concern in an illuminating manner. According to Habermas, it is Gadamer's achievement to stress that language co-exists with a given life-form or horizon, without thereby inferring that different languages exist as closed or monadic units (the latter is

---

15 Ibid.   16 Ibid.
17 Rorty does, however, give an account of the various kinds of historical-hermeneutical work in "The Historiography of Philosophy: Four Genres," in *Philosophy in History*, ed. Richard Rorty, J. B. Schneewind, and Quentin Skinner (Cambridge: Cambridge University Press, 1984), 31–48.
18 John McDowell, *Mind and World* (Cambridge, Mass.: Harvard University Press, 1994), 4.
19 See ibid., 35f., 115–119, as well as McDowell's "Response to Rüdiger Bubner," in Nicholas H. Smith (ed.), *Reading McDowell: On "Mind and World"* (London: Routledge, 2002), 296f.
20 *Mind and World*, 115–119. See also the Afterword, 184f.

the view that Habermas at the time ascribed to the later Wittgenstein).[21] Gadamer, Habermas claims, maintains the unity of reason in the pluralism of languages. In Gadamer's hermeneutics, however, the unity of reason is grounded upon the normativity of a continuous and all-encompassing concept of tradition. Gadamer, Habermas worries, neglects the enlightenment notion that critical reason proves itself "in being able to reject the claim of tradition."[22] He focuses onesidedly on the ontological conditionedness of critical thought, thus denying reason "the power of reflection."[23] This, in short, is Habermas's critique of Gadamer in the years immediately after the publication of *Truth and Method*. Later, Habermas further refines and modifies his criticism. In particular, he develops an interest in Gadamer's turn to dialogue and practical reasoning. Nonetheless, he remains adamant that Gadamer's ontological orientation leaves him poorly equipped to articulate the distinction between *de facto* and *de jure* aspects of understanding. In Habermas's view, such a distinction is needed because our practices of communication may, as the result of asymmetric power-relations, be systematically distorted. Even though one may, as Habermas puts it, be sympathetic to Gadamer's "hermeneutic reservations . . . against monological self-certainty which merely arrogates to itself the title of critique,"[24] one should not be seduced by his willingness to let go of the enlightenment commitment to reflective reason and criticism.

Related concerns have been voiced by Karl-Otto Apel. According to Apel, Gadamer's ontological hermeneutics "made something like a normatively controlled progress in understanding appear totally inconceivable."[25] Against a position that, in his view, dissolves the question of normativity in interpretation, Apel maintains the

21 See Jürgen Habermas, "A Review of *Truth and Method*," trans. Fred. R. Dallmayr and Thomas McCarthy, in Gayle L. Ormiston and Alan D. Schrift (eds.), *The Hermeneutic Tradition: From Ast to Ricoeur* (Albany, N.Y.: SUNY Press, 1990), 216ff.; "Der hermeneutische Ansatz," in *Zur Logik der Sozialwissenschaften* (Frankfurt am Main: Suhrkamp Verlag, 1982), 275ff.
22 Ibid., 237; ibid., 305.
23 Ibid.
24 Jürgen Habermas, "The Hermeneutic Claim to Universality," trans. Joseph Bleicher, in *The Hermeneutic Tradition*, 270; "Der Universalitätsanspruch der Hermeneutik," in *Zur Logik der Sozialwissenschaften*, 366.
25 Karl-Otto Apel, "Regulative Ideas or Truth-Happening?: An Attempt to Answer the Question of the Conditions of the Possibility of Valid Understanding," trans. Ralf Sommermeier, *LLP*, 67.

possibility that some beliefs or interpretations legitimately, and on principled grounds, aspire to be more objectively valid than others. To insist upon a dimension of validity amounts, in Apel's words, to approaching Gadamer's hermeneutics with a "quasi-Kantian reservation."[26]

In calling for a dimension of normativity in understanding, Apel refers not only to Kant, but also to the later Heidegger. Apel claims that throughout the 1960s, Heidegger significantly revises his concept of truth as world-disclosure. Responding to Ernst Tugendhat's criticism of the concept of a world-disclosive truth – Tugendhat had criticized Heidegger for universalizing world-disclosive truth[27] – Heidegger claims that although a hermeneutic world-disclosure is a necessary condition for truth, it is not, strictly speaking, sufficient. In addition to truth as world-disclosure, one needs a conception of validity: in Apel's view, Heidegger here "does nothing less than revoke that thesis which he had held with growing determination since *Sein und Zeit*: namely, that the more original and the only significant conception of truth is the unconcealment of beings on the ground of the *disclosedness of being-there*, that is, the *opening of Being*."[28] Gadamer, he continues, fails to realize this. Hence he fails to see that hermeneutics, in following Heidegger's ontological turn, must be able to secure the validity of our beliefs by appealing to rationally grounded procedures of justification.

However, although Apel claims that Gadamer overlooks this shift in Heidegger's thinking – thereby also implying that his own transcendentally oriented hermeneutics (and not Gadamer's ontological hermeneutics) represents the true successor to Heidegger's philosophy – he does not ask why such an overlooking occurs in the first place. Tugendhat, on the other hand, addresses this question. In his review of Gadamer's *Philosophical Hermeneutics*, Tugendhat argues that in order to arrive at a hermeneutic position like that of Gadamer, you simply "start with Heidegger's conception of truth, but disregard his ontology and then replace both the existentialism of his earlier philosophy and the mysticism of his later writings by a profound sense for the humanist tradition."[29] Tugendhat finds this move highly

---

26 Ibid.
27 See Ernst Tugendhat, "Heidegger's Idea of Truth," trans. Christopher Macann, in Christopher Macann (ed.), *Martin Heidegger: Critical Assessments* (London: Routledge, 1992), vol. III, 79–92.
28 "Regulative Ideas or Truth-Happening?" 72.
29 Tugendhat, "The Fusion of Horizons," 426.

problematic. He worries that Gadamer fails to realize that for Heidegger the "understanding of the entire philosophical tradition since the pre-Socratics was . . . a necessary precondition for tackling the philosophical questions themselves."[30] For Gadamer, "what the master thought of as a means [namely the study of tradition], soon became an end in itself."[31] Eminent historical texts are no longer critically assessed. The idea of a reflective relation to the past is overshadowed by the celebration of historical self-appropriation. In Tugendhat's view, this is an anti-enlightenment tendency in Gadamer's philosophy.

I have already argued that Gadamer's understanding of the Enlightenment is too negative. Furthermore, I have been criticizing his notion of the world-disclosive truth of art. Hence one would perhaps expect an unconditional affirmation of Apel's, Habermas's, and Tugendhat's lines of criticism. Such an expectation, however, would be premature. In spite of valuable insights, these criticisms miss an important point: the fact that Gadamer himself offers a one-sided account of the enlightenment paradigm does not necessarily mean that his own hermeneutics should be conceived of as being in outright opposition to the enlightenment project. Even though Gadamer follows Heidegger in criticizing the Cartesian reduction of truth to certainty, and even though he grounds the understanding of truth as adequation (T1) in a notion of truth as hermeneutic world-disclosure (T2), Gadamer insists that he does not want to leave out the concept of reflection from his understanding of truth. He attempts to reformulate the idea of a critical reflection in a manner that prevents it from falling prey to subjectivism. The idea of a reflective consciousness, he claims, cannot be understood in terms of an isolated epistemic cogito, but is intrinsically related to the historical unfolding of tradition. This is Gadamer's concept of a "wirkungsgeschichtliches Bewußtsein" – an aspect of his thinking that Heidegger could never accept.[32] At stake is the idea that although consciousness finds itself situated within a comprehensive historical context, a totality that cannot, as such, be subject to critical reflection, it is not deprived of the possibility of critically

---

30 Ibid., 429.   31 Ibid.
32 In an interview from 1993, Gadamer claims that "man kann wohl sagen, daß dies für Heidegger eine der größten Herausforderungen meiner ganzen Arbeit war, daß ich hier den Begriff des Bewußtseins gebrauchte." Carsten Dutt, *Hermeneutik. Ästhetik. Praktische Philosophie. Hans-Georg Gadamer im Gespräch* (Heidelberg: Carl Winter, 1993), 22.

approaching and interrogating the norms and principles that dominate in a given historical situation.[33]

This aspect of Gadamer's thinking shows that he by no means desires to go against the tenors of the Enlightenment. For if, like Habermas and Apel, one takes the Enlightenment to involve the commitment to a self-critique of reason, then Gadamer, in retaining a concept of reflective consciousness, does not wish to oppose the enlightenment spirit. Rather, he takes it to the point where it – as critical, reflective, and self-authorizing – is forced to question its most fundamental presupposition: the idea of a completely autonomous and self-responsive reason that is able to transcend its own historical situatedness. This is why Gadamer can claim that "What Kant calls Enlightenment in truth corresponds to what hermeneutics has in view."[34]

Gadamer argues that a thorough investigation into the validity of our prejudices must also question the uncritical faith in the reflective powers of an isolated, epistemic subjectivity. Qua enlightened and responsive, individual reason should not perceive itself as completely autonomous, but reflect its situatedness within a historical tradition whose movements it cannot fully control and to which it contributes through hermeneutic work and historical queries. As Gadamer himself puts it:

> It is extremely astonishing . . . that philosophical hermeneutics . . . [is] being discussed under the title 'critique of enlightenment' and not with reference to the idealist concept of the 'completed enlightenment' which was coined by Fichte. For what matters to us can only be the question whether a completed enlightenment which would dissolve all human predisposition and societal prejudices is an intelligible claim.[35]

Hegel and the historicity of reason

In line with his critique of the Enlightenment, Gadamer seeks to carve out a notion of reason that is comprehensive enough to accept its situatedness in history. Yet, in doing so, he does not start from scratch. Instead, he can lean on the philosopher from whom the very idea of the historicity of reason is first taken, that is, he can turn to Hegel and his "idea of hermeneutics" (*TM*, 169; *WM*, 174).

---

33 Gadamer's critiques of Kant, aesthetic consciousness, and Hegel offer three examples of such reflection.
34 "Reply to David Detmer," *LLP*, 287.   35 Ibid.

Hegel, surely, wanted to get beyond the enlightenment paradigm. Yet he never rejected the notion of critical-reflective reason. This is precisely the kind of position Gadamer needs. How, then, does Hegel, in Gadamer's view, develop his hermeneutic rearticulation of the enlightenment commitments in philosophy? He does so by forging a link between self-understanding and understanding of the past. On Gadamer's reading, the Enlightenment had not paid sufficient attention to the historicity of reason, but focused on an abstract, methodological notion of normativity borrowed from the physical sciences. Hegel, by contrast, claims that only by understanding the past can we understand ourselves. The historical horizon is not to be bracketed in the name of objectivity or critical reflection. Rather, the very capacity for objectivity and critical reflection rests with the ability to account for our own historical situation as the outcome of the gradual development of a tradition that itself transcends the particularities of the cultural horizon in which the reflecting I is situated. When the present appears as dialectically mediated with the past, tradition is no longer identified with unreflected prejudices. Critical reason now realizes the productivity involved in tradition. In approaching a given problem or subject matter, reason takes into account the historical development of the horizon in which this problem or subject matter occurs as meaningful in the first place. Furthermore, reason reflects on the prejudices of the present by coming to terms with the hermeneutic horizon of cultures that are temporally distant from our own.

The continuity of tradition enables us to engage in a dialogical relationship with the past. This dialogue is not about understanding the past as an object to be studied by a detached historical consciousness, but about developing the shared historical self-understanding that tradition ultimately is. The insistence on the continuity of tradition is crucial to Gadamer's rearticulation of the enlightenment commitment to self-reflection in terms of the resources provided by Hegelian hermeneutics. As Gadamer puts it, Hegel had realized that "All self-knowledge arises from what is historically pre-given, what . . . we call 'substance,' because it underlies all subjective intentions [*Meinen*] and actions" (*TM*, 302; *WM*, 307). With Hegel, the objectivity of reason is no longer wedded to a capacity to abstract from its situatedness within a given, historical horizon. The ideal of a formal, methodological reason is left behind. Integration is what matters. In its Hegelian version, hermeneutics is all about acknowledging the past as a tradition by which we are formed and through which our philosophizing gets its ultimate shape and orientation. Given such a point of view, philosophy does not believe itself to start without pre-suppositions. Nor does it legitimize itself by reference to procedural rationality. Or, rather, to the extent that philosophy does proceed along these or similar lines, as Gadamer criticizes enlightenment philosophy for doing, it misunderstands its mandate. By overlooking its own historicity, reason fails to question its most fundamental pre-suppositions. Only when philosophy acknowledges its own historical presuppositions is it philosophy proper. According to Gadamer, Hegel was the first to realize this – hence also the first to realize the true philosophical potential of the enlightenment commitment to self-criticism and reflection.

Gadamer presents his own hermeneutics as fundamentally Hegel-ian in spirit. "[I]ts task," as he puts it, "is to retrace the path of Hegel's phenomenology of mind until we discover in all that is subjective the substantiality that determines it" (ibid.). The substantive in the sub-jective, the historical in what appears trans-historical, the notion of tradition as a continuous, circular back-and-forth movement between understanding ourselves and understanding history – this is what philosophical hermeneutics, just like dialectical phenomenology, brings to light.

However, if Gadamer's effort to overcome a naïve and ahistorical notion of reflection culminates in the wish to develop a Hegelian hermeneutics, he is not, for that reason, uncritically adopting every aspect of Hegel's work. Hegel, to be sure, had shown that self-understanding involves an understanding of historical context. Moreover, he had shown that this is only made possible by the deeper continuity of an integrating tradition. Yet in Gadamer's view, Hegel fails to give an adequate account of what this self-understanding amounts to – he fails, as it were, to transform the enlightenment impulse in a sufficiently radical way.[36]

In the course of the previous chapters, we have seen that Gadamer approaches Hegel's aesthetics with a rather ambivalent attitude. Basing his critique of Kant and aesthetic consciousness on a set of

---

36 Interestingly, Habermas addresses a similar problem in a recent essay, "From Kant to Hegel and Back Again: The Move Towards Detranscendentalization," in *Truth and Justi-fication*, trans. Barbara Fultner (Cambridge, Mass.: MIT Press, 2005), 175–213; "Wege der Detranszendentalisierung. Von Kant zu Hegel und zurück," in *Wahrheit und Rechtfertigung. Philosophische Aufsätze* (Frankfurt am Main: Suhrkamp Verlag, 1999), 186–229.

Hegelian worries, he nonetheless refuses to adopt Hegel's idea that we can only know, philosophically, what art is when great art is brought to its historical end and thinking (conceptual work) takes over as the most adequate register for the self-expression of spirit. While accepting Hegel's critique of the modern subjectivization of aesthetics, Gadamer does not want to go all the way with Hegel's own alternative. What holds him back is, again, the idea of spirit's full understanding of itself at the end of its development in history. Gadamer's claim – both with regard to Hegel's philosophy of art and with regard to his thinking in general – is that although Hegel, with his notion of the historicity of reason, takes a valuable step beyond the Cartesian–Kantian paradigm in philosophy, he still remains a prisoner of the very paradigm that he criticizes. While expounding this point, Gadamer's critique forks into two argumentative branches: first, a comparison of Platonic dialogue and Hegelian dialectics, and, second, a review of previous, hermeneutic efforts at rescuing the relevance of Hegel's phenomenology, most importantly those of Wilhelm Dilthey and the historical school. In order to come to terms with the full complexity of Gadamer's critique of Hegel – hence also with his relationship with enlightenment philosophy in general – both these points will have to be considered.

Dialogue and dialectics

Following the argument sketched out in his discussion of Kantian and Hegelian aesthetics – the claim that even though Hegel ascribes to art a dimension of historical truth, it is Kant who first realizes the true dialogical potential of art – Gadamer's critique of Hegel's Cartesian orientation is developed with reference to Socratic–Platonic dialectics.

Initially, the contrasting of Hegelian and Platonic dialectics may appear a surprising move. Greek philosophy, no doubt, was important for Hegel.[37] But why see the critique of Hegel in terms of a contrast with the Socratic–Platonic way of doing philosophy? Two factors may help in answering this question, both having to do with Gadamer's intellectual environment in the early 1930s. First, it is important to know that when Gadamer, in order to develop a historically sensitive

---

37 See John Glenn Gray, *Hegel and Greek Thought* (San Francisco: Harper & Row, 1969) and, for a different kind of approach, Michael Forster, *Hegel and Skepticism* (Boston: Harvard University Press, 1989).

hermeneutics, turns to Hegel, he is, as we saw with regard to his critique of Hegel's aesthetics, well aware of Heidegger's reluctant attitude to this nineteenth-century philosopher. In a lecture from 1958, Heidegger summarizes his critique by suggesting that Hegel completes the *telos* of Platonic philosophy.[38] In Heidegger's understanding, Hegel, in doing so, draws on the modern, Cartesian notion of self-reflection. In Hegel's system, the absolute is understood as the self-identity of spirit. The second important factor is the influence exercised by the Greek scholar Julius Stenzel.[39] In contrast to Heidegger's up-front rejection of the Plato–Descartes–Hegel tradition, Stenzel emphasizes how Platonic philosophy yields an alternative to the model of self-reflection that had prevailed within the German tradition since the Enlightenment.[40]

Like Julius Stenzel, Gadamer, from his early studies of Plato, is much more positive in his attitude to Plato than Heidegger ever was. Like Heidegger, however, he emphasizes, against Stenzel, the philosophical affinities between Plato and Hegel. In this way, Gadamer develops his own original take on the Plato–Hegel relation. Against both Stenzel and Heidegger, Gadamer refuses to read Hegel simply as a representative of enlightenment thinking gone wrong and insists upon deploying the resources of ancient dialectics to illuminate the strengths as well as weaknesses of Hegel's *Phenomenology of Spirit*.[41] Only thus – by overcoming the weaknesses while maintaining the strengths – can Gadamer succeed in providing a hermeneutics that

38 Martin Heidegger, "Hegel and the Greeks," trans. Robert Metcalf, in *Pathmarks*, ed. William McNeill (Cambridge: Cambridge University Press, 1998), 323–336; "Hegel und die Griechen," *Wegmarken*, GA, vol. IX, 427–444. See also Martin Heidegger, *Hegel's Concept of Experience* (*1942–43*), trans. John Glenn Gray (New York: Harper & Row, 1989); *Hegels Begriff der Erfahrung, Holzwege*, GA, vol. V.

39 As Gadamer puts it: "Among the German Plato scholars at that time it was Julius Stenzel whose work pointed in a direction similar to my own," "Reflections on my Philosophical Journey," *LLP*, 9.

40 In Gadamer's words, "Taking note of the aporiae of self-consciousness in which both idealism and its critics found themselves trapped, Stenzel observed in the Greeks the 'restraining of subjectivity'." Ibid. Gadamer also discusses Stenzel's work in a review article from 1929, "Julius Stenzel, *Metaphysik des Altertums*," *GW*, vol. V, 294–299.

41 See "Hegel and the Dialectic of the Ancient Philosophers," *HD*, 5–35; "Hegel und die antike Dialektik," *HDi*, 7–30. There is no contradiction between this claim and the suggestion that "Hegel has consciously taken up the model of Greek dialectics. Hence whoever wants to learn from the Greeks has always already been learning from Hegel first" (*TM*, 460; *WM*, 464, trans. modified). Both these claims underline how Gadamer emphasizes the intellectual kinship between Hegel and the Greeks.

"retraces[s] the path of Hegel's phenomenology of mind." How, then, does Gadamer, drawing on the resources of Socratic–Platonic dialogue, develop his critique of Hegel's dialectics?

In *Plato's Dialectical Ethics*, Gadamer brings out the importance of dialogue in Plato's early works, and the *Philebus* in particular. We have already seen, in Chapter 1, how Gadamer praises Socrates for practicing philosophy as an ongoing intersubjective exchange, rather than a set of doctrines and arguments. Plato is "no Platonist," as Gadamer puts it. The dialogical aspect of Plato's philosophy is not some kind of literary decorum, but is essentially tied up with his conception of truth, rationality, and knowledge. Philosophy is an ongoing dialogical exercise. As such, it is motivated by a willingness to recognize the rationality of the other – it is driven by the *docta ignorantia*. In Gadamer's words, "knowledge of our own ignorance is what human wisdom is ['Sie ist das Wissen des Nichtwissens']."[42]

While focusing on the Socratic *docta ignorantia*, Gadamer notes an affinity between Socratic dialogue and the Hegelian dialectics of history. In Socratic dialogue, the conversation is maintained by the interlocutors' capacity to gain knowledge as agreement on a given problem or subject matter, although this agreement, to the extent that it involves a positive claim to knowledge, most often proves to be parochial and in need of further, discursive work. At stake, as Gadamer reads it, is an ongoing progress towards increased universality, a perpetual effort to reach a dialectical sublation of two opposing standpoints into a more universal third. According to Gadamer, Hegel's phenomenology is motivated by a similar dynamic. Even though Socrates, in the early Platonic dialogues, develops his position through discussion with someone else (whereas the shapes of Hegelian consciousness develop through the self-criticism of spirit), it is nonetheless the case that spirit, in the *Phenomenology*, proceeds through gradually overcoming that which is alien. The very self that is engaged in the process matures through considering and integrating the point of view of the other. This is the central philosophical intuition of Hegelian dialectics: that it "transforms what stands opposed to it into its own" (*HD*, 107; *HDi*, 105). In this sense, Hegel, too, is a dialogical thinker, and it is the force of his thinking to move the dialectics of dialogue from the level of interpersonal conversation to the level of history and tradition.

---

42 "On the Origins of Philosophical Hermeneutics," *Philosophical Apprenticeships*, 185; "Selbstdarstellung Hans-Georg Gadamer," *WM*, vol. II, 501.

Yet Gadamer also finds Hegel's philosophy to be permeated by a less dialogical ethos. For in developing the idea of a continuous, dialectical relationship between past and present, Hegel, echoing the end-of-art thesis that Gadamer has already been criticizing, defends the idea of spirit reaching the end of its education in history. At this point, spirit has gained complete self-understanding. The immediacy of each historical period (its "in itself") is sublated into a reflective philosophical criticism (its "for itself"), and, ultimately, into the full transparency involved in spirit's self-relation at the point of gaining absolute knowledge. At stake is a self that is not merely a self "but the identity of the self with itself" (*PS*, 489; *PhG*, 587). Furthermore, Hegel takes this identity to be "complete and immediate" (ibid.). To Gadamer, who remains fascinated by the Socratic notion of knowledge as an ongoing self-questioning, this is the most problematic strand of Hegel's otherwise promising understanding of the historicity of reason.[43] Like Heidegger and Stenzel, Gadamer traces this element back to a Cartesian or broader enlightenment legacy in modern thinking.[44] In Hegel's work, the commitment to dialogical dialectics culminates in what Gadamer takes to be an objectification of thought, "a method which was finally raised to the level of self-consciousness in Descartes and which assumes its ultimate form in Hegel's logical panmethodism" (*HD*, 111; *HDi*, 108).[45]

The idea that Hegel should be some kind of quasi-Cartesian or naïve enlightenment philosopher may at first seem absurd. Throughout his philosophical trajectory, Hegel positions himself as a fierce critic of Descartes. Descartes, Hegel claims, arrives at his famous cogito argument by defending an untenable form of philosophical idealism – a direction of thought that, as Hegel puts it, "proceeds from what is inward; according to it everything is in thought, mind itself is all content."[46] In

---

43 Gadamer explains: "The first person who wrote a history of philosophy . . . was also the last to do so – Hegel. And in Hegel, history was cancelled and fulfilled [*aufgehoben*] in the presence of absolute spirit." "Reflections on my Philosophical Journey," *LLP*, 35.

44 "Hegels Idee der Phänomenologie [liegt] in der cartesianischen Linie," (*HD*, 35; *HDi*, 31, see also *HD*, 111; *HDi*, 108).

45 Hence there is no contradiction between Gadamer's 1960s tracing of Socratic elements in Hegel's thought and his earlier claim that the understanding of philosophy as an ongoing dialogical exercise is lost after Plato. After Plato, Gadamer had claimed in 1931, "philosophizing is no longer the carrying out of a shared philosophical process" (*PDE*, 5; *PdE*, 8).

46 *Lectures on the History of Philosophy*, vol. III, 163; *Vorlesungen über die Geschichte der Philosophie*, vol. III, 67.

emphasizing the historical development of thinking and philosophy, of spirit's realizing itself in the historical world, Hegel wishes to escape the potential abstractions of Cartesian thought. Nonetheless – and this is where Gadamer finds textual support for his reading – Hegel is determined to maintain the possibility of an absolute self-reflection of spirit. The mutual determination of self-reflection and autonomy is for Hegel an a priori of modern thinking.[47] Yet self-reflection ought not to be cast as subjective, i.e., it ought not to be cast in a way that simply reproduces the threat of idealism that worries him with regard to Descartes' philosophy. According to Hegel, the self-reflection of spirit is mediated by history, and it is intersubjective through and through.[48] Hegel is thus entertaining a historicized notion of self-reflection, one that takes the certainty of the reflecting self, its recognizing itself as itself, to be the result of an intersubjectively mediated, historical process.

Although Hegel criticizes Descartes' abstract (idealistic) notion of self-reflection, he does not question the idea of a complete and self-grounding self-reflection as such.[49] This is the point at which Gadamer directs his criticism. Like Hegel, Gadamer finds that modern philosophy begins with Descartes' notion of absolute self-reflection.[50]

---

47 Along these lines, Hegel, in the lectures on the history of philosophy, retrieves the emergence of Cartesian philosophy as the homecoming of modern spirit: "Here, we may say, we are at home, and like the mariner after a long voyage in a tempestuous sea, we may now hail the sight of land." Ibid., 217; ibid., 120.

48 As Pinkard puts it: "If modern 'absolute spirit' . . . is that set of practices in which the self-renewing task of 'absolute knowing' developed at the end of the *Phenomenology* is carried out, then by the Hegelian account of 'absolute spirit' and modern life, the task of modern philosophy . . . will be to construct and evaluate those accounts of who we are and to continue to skeptically ask if – as the human community has done in the past – we aren't just fooling ourselves again. Taken in this way, Hegelianism would be what Hegel intended it to be: not a finished 'system' done once and for all in Prussia in the 1820s, but an ongoing series of dialectical reflections on the possibilities available to the human community such that we can see what kind of self-identities are open to us and how we might in turn account for the people that we would be." *Hegel's Phenomenology*, 343. In this reading, we get a notion of absolute spirit that does indeed stand much closer to the early Gadamer, with his emphasis on dialogic-Socratic reason, than Gadamer himself would acknowledge. In this context, though, I will not explore this affinity, but focus on the criticism put forward by Gadamer and the consequences of his reading of Hegel for his hermeneutic philosophy.

49 This aspect of Hegel's thinking (and of German Idealism in general) is given a more positive interpretation in Robert Pippin, *Hegel's Idealism: The Satisfaction of Self-Consciousness* (Cambridge: Cambridge University Press, 1989), part II, 91–162.

50 " . . . the Cartesian characterization of consciousness as self-consciousness continued to provide the background for all modern thought." "Man and Language" (1966), *PH*, 61; "Mensch und Sprache," *WM*, vol. II, 148.

Unlike Hegel, however, Gadamer argues that the Cartesian paradigm in philosophy is one in which "reflection is granted a false power ['falsche Macht']."[51] This is an important formulation. By claiming that absolute reflection is granted "false power," rather than being plainly inadequate, Gadamer makes it clear that he does not want to put the dialogical-dialectical Hegel up against the very idea of reflection as such. Instead, he sets out to distinguish between the promising and the less promising aspects of Hegel's notion of self-reflection. His point is in other words not that we need to scrap the notion of self-reflection altogether, but that the very notion of an *absolute* self-reflection (or self-understanding) needs to be subjected to further questioning and scrutiny.[52] Hegel, Gadamer worries, fails to do this. Hence he also fails to overcome the problems of the enlightenment paradigm in a fully adequate and hermeneutically mature manner.

Whereas Stenzel stages a radical contrast between Plato and Hegel, and whereas Heidegger deems Hegel the problematic end-point of a decay that started with Platonic philosophy, Gadamer deploys his notion of Socratic–Platonic dialogue as a lens through which the hermeneutic resources of Hegel's work can be illuminated. His aim is not to leave Hegel behind so as to issue a call for a return to Plato (like Stenzel did). Nor does he intend to produce a sweeping narrative of the forgetfulness of Being in Western philosophy (like Heidegger had been doing). Rather, he attempts to point out an internal, systematic problem with Hegel's thinking – a problem that, in his view, will have to be solved if hermeneutics is to adopt the Hegelian insistence on the continuity of historical spirit (integration) and its dimension of self-understanding, hence successfully overcoming the naïvety of the enlightenment paradigm in philosophy.[53]

In Gadamer's view, the very idea that self-transparency constitutes the highest mode of being is at odds with the historical thrust of

---

51 "On the Scope and Function of Hermeneutical Reflection," *PH*, 33; "Rhetorik, Hermeneutik und Ideologiekritik," *WM*, vol. II, 244.

52 For a more detailed discussion of Gadamer's critique of the enlightenment notion of reflection, see my "Between Enlightenment and Romanticism: Some Problems and Challenges in Gadamer's Hermeneutics," in *The Journal of the History of Philosophy*, vol. 46, no. 2 (2008), 285–306.

53 For an alternative reading of the limits of Hegel's hermeneutics, see Andreas Arndt, "Fortschritt im Begriff. Hegels Aufhebung der Hermeneutik in seinen Vorlesungen zur Geschichte der Philosophie," in *Hegel-Jahrbuch 1997. Hegel und die Geschichte der Philosophie*, ed. Andreas Arndt, Karol Bal, and Henning Ottmann (Berlin: Akademie Verlag, 1998), 108–115.

Hegel's thought. It represents the point at which historical reason ceases to be historical. The hermeneutic force of Hegel's thinking – "the inclusion of history within the framework of philosophy's questioning" – is threatened by a model in which spirit, in retrieving its progressive development in history, realizes that the dialectical development of history finally culminates in the scheme of a trans-historical logic. This is the basic outline of Gadamer's critique of Hegel: he endorses Hegel's idea that our relation to history involves a dimension of self-reflection (self-understanding) that is best understood as a continuous process of integration. Yet, because he is committed to a Socratic ideal of knowledge as an ongoing process, Gadamer rejects the idea that this process can or should ever be brought to a final standstill. Hence Gadamer determines the task of hermeneutics as that of filling "the place vacated by Hegel's absolute knowledge" (*TM*, 230; *WM*, 234). Reading Plato through Hegel, Gadamer moves from the self-understanding at stake in interpersonal dialogue to the self-understanding at stake in our engagement with tradition. Reading Hegel through Plato, he insists that this self-understanding is never brought to completion, but is and remains an ongoing hermeneutic challenge. Only this way, he finds, is it possible to maintain the notion of the historicity of reason in a fully adequate and consistent manner.

Dilthey and nineteenth-century Hegelian hermeneutics

If Stenzel and Heidegger had espoused a critical attitude towards philosophical Hegelianism, this was not entirely groundless. In Gadamer's view, post-Hegelian philosophy fails to take up the hermeneutically most promising aspects of the *Phenomenology of Spirit* (i.e., the emphasis on self-understanding and integration) and turns instead to the elements of his philosophy that Gadamer criticizes (i.e., his latent Cartesianism, his failure to break loose from a naïve enlightenment paradigm). This, Gadamer claims, in particular applies to nineteenth-century hermeneutics and philosophy of the human sciences – that is, the theorizing of Ranke, Droysen, and Dilthey. It is their adoption of Hegel and the Enlightenment that makes it imperative for Gadamer to distance himself from the Cartesian elements in Hegel's thought.

At first, this might seem an unexpected point to make on Gadamer's part. With Ranke, Droysen, and the historical school the general Hegelian climate of late nineteenth-century German culture seems to be brought to an end. Any attempt at a priori writing of history now appears a thing of the past. A priori writing of history, it is claimed, fails to take into account how history is not just the playing-field of necessity, but also the arena of freedom (*TM*, 204; *WM*, 207f.). Indeed, as recounted by Gadamer, virulent anti-Hegelianism was the intellectual birth certificate of the historical school (*TM*, 200; *WM*, 204). Yet Gadamer finds the historical school to be a lot more Hegelian than it was ever prepared to admit. Although the historicists criticized a priori constructions of history, both Ranke and Droysen presuppose "the full self-transparency of being" (*TM*, 211; *WM*, 215). That is, they both presuppose that the scientific historian, like the philosopher of absolute knowledge, encounters world-history as an objective entity, fully accessible for its reconstructive work.

With Ranke and Droysen, the Hegelian legacy continues at the level of a philosophical subconscious, a hermeneutic return of the repressed, so to speak. With Dilthey, however, the Hegelianism of post-romantic hermeneutics is brought to the fore. Dilthey, to be sure, was one of the first to appreciate the philosophical implications of Hegel's early, theological writings.[54] In addition to this, he draws on the philosophy of Friedrich Schleiermacher, to whom he dedicated an extensive, intellectual monograph.[55] Dilthey endeavors to combine the romantic focus on individuality, methodology, and historical reconstruction with a Hegelian attentiveness to the continuity of tradition in the multi-plicity of historical world-views.[56] Gadamer, however, argues that Dil-they manages to synthesize these opposing intellectual positions only by adopting the least promising aspect – the unhermeneutic, Cartesian streak – of Hegel's thinking (*TM*, 476; *WM*, 480).

Gadamer's critique of Dilthey is somewhat crude. However, for our purposes, it is not necessary to go into the details of Gadamer's

---

54 Wilhelm Dilthey, *Die Jugendgeschichte Hegels. Die Jugendgeschichte Hegels und andere Abhandlungen zur Geschichte des Deutschen Idealismus*, ed. Herman Nohl, *Gesammelte Schriften*, vol. IV (Göttingen: Vandenhoeck & Ruprecht, 1990).

55 Wilhelm Dilthey, *Leben Schleiermachers. Erster Band*, ed. Martin Redeker, *Gesammelte Schriften*, vol. XIII (Göttingen: Vandenhoeck & Ruprecht, 1970); *Leben Schleiermachers. Zweiter Band*, ed. Martin Redeker, *Gesammelte Schriften*, vol. XIV (Göttingen: Vandenhoeck & Ruprecht, 1966). I return to Schleiermacher's philosophy in Chapters 5 and 6.

56 Thus he challenges the view, still prevalent today, of there being an unbridgeable gap between romanticism and Hegelian philosophy. Such a view is found, for example, in Bohrer, *Die Kritik der Romantik*. For a balanced discussion of Hegel and the romantics, see Pöggeler, "Hegels Kritik der Romantik".

reading, but it suffices to see how Gadamer positions Dilthey with regard to Hegel.[57] He claims that while Dilthey's turn to the category of life (*Leben*) remains tied up with the aesthetic metaphysics of the romantics, this position is elevated to that of an absolute self-reflection of historical spirit (*TM*, 230; *WM*, 234). According to Gadamer, Dilthey is a Hegelian philosopher insofar as he turns the notion of absolute self-reflection into the guiding principle of hermeneutic philosophy. If Dilthey criticized the a-priorism of conceptual speculation, "he did not hesitate about the inner infinity of the mind" (*TM*, 232; *WM*, 236). In Gadamer's assessment, the problem is therefore not that Dilthey's hermeneutics is Hegelian per se, but that it is Hegelian in the wrong way – i.e., not in the way that Gadamer himself proposes. For Gadamer, the challenge facing any philosopher interested in post-Hegelian hermeneutics is therefore not whether hermeneutics should be construed as being for or against Hegel, but that of using the hermeneutically relevant aspects of Hegel's phenomenology against the problematic Hegelian strands of twentieth-century hermeneutics and philosophies of the human sciences. This is so because, in spite of the problems Gadamer detects in Hegel's historical justification of philosophy, he finds it "overwhelmingly superior to all later attempts" (*HDi*, 104; *HD*, 103).[58]

Hegel's philosophy of history

So far, we have looked at Gadamer's critique of Hegel and the Enlightenment and his attempt at reworking the enlightenment challenge of self-reflection and self-understanding into a philosophical theory that remains faithful to Hegel's insight into the historicity of reason and the importance of hermeneutic integration. What we have not done, however, is ask whether Gadamer's reading of Hegel – his critique, and also his hermeneutic appropriation – is philosophically sound, or whether, like his reading of Kant and the

---

57 For a comprehensive discussion of Dilthey's hermeneutics and philosophy of the human sciences, see, again, Makkreel's *Dilthey*. See also Jos de Mul, *The Tragedy of Finitude: Dilthey's Hermeneutics of Life*, trans. Tony Burrett (New Haven: Yale University Press, 2004).

58 Hence it is problematic to claim, as Robert Pippin does, that Hegel is Gadamer's "principal opponent." Robert Pippin, "Gadamer's Hegel," in Jeff Malpas, Ulrich Arnswald, and Jens Kertscher (eds.), *Gadamer's Century: Essays in Honor of Hans-Georg Gadamer* (Cambridge, Mass.: MIT, 2002), 218.

Enlightenment, it is colored by Gadamer's own prejudices. In Gadamer's hermeneutic scheme, the promising aspects of Hegel's dialectics are held up not only against a problematic, enlightenment paradigm, but also against the problematic, non-hermeneutic strands of Hegel's own philosophy that were to be reinforced within post-Hegelian philosophy of history and interpretation. At stake is a dichotomy in which dialogue, the historicity of reason, and the notion of a continuous, historical integration is played out against the understanding of reason as being its own master, i.e., as being able to transcend its situatedness in history and reach some kind of ahistorical truth or self-understanding. Facing these alternatives, Gadamer subscribes to the notion of understanding as self-understanding and the idea of an integration between past and present. To what extent, though, is it right to read Hegel's claim about the self-identity of historical spirit in post-enlightenment philosophy as a case of naïve enlightenment thinking (rather than an integral part of what Gadamer speaks of as Hegel's hermeneutic philosophy)?

According to Hegel, spirit reconstructs its own development in history as a process of self-understanding. The continuity of its development in and through different historical *Gestalten* is detectable only from the vantage-point of its culmination in absolute self-knowledge. The standpoint of enlightened modernity, i.e., of Hegel's own time, is brought to self-awareness through a genetic retrieval of the history of spirit. The epistemic, ethical, political, and aesthetic standards of this period are the outcomes of a process in which spirit learns from the aporia it has been facing and the problems it has worked through. Hence the position of the phenomenologist is at one and the same time non-contingent (it is the necessary culmination of a development that lends itself to rational reconstruction) and deeply historical (it is developed *and* justified with reference to the learning process of the tradition). By providing such an account of spirit's education in history, Hegel wishes to get beyond the limits of subjective idealism and its Cartesian legacy without lapsing into historicist relativism.[59] That is, he

---

59 For Hegel's critique of subjective idealism, see Ludwig Siep, *Hegels Fichtekritik und die Wissenschaftslehre von 1804* (Freiburg/Munich: Karl Alber Verlag, 1970). After Herder's reflections on the problem of relativism in the mid-1770s this was perceived as a genuine, philosophical problem. On Hegel's knowledge of Herder, see Frederick Beiser, in "Hegel's Historicism," in Beiser (ed.), *The Cambridge Companion to Hegel* (Cambridge: Cambridge University Press, 1993), 275. Hegel refers to Herder's *Ideen*, although not the problem of relativism in particular, in *ILHP*, 10; *EiGP*, 13.

wants, at one and the same time, to claim that spirit, at the end of its *Bildung*, is situated within a given historical horizon *and* that it can offer a rational justification of its own point of view that is universally valid rather than simply the product of one particular culture or life-world.

While it retrieves its development in history, reason obtains an ever increasing degree of self-understanding. When it conceptually grasps its progress in history (as externalized, concretely expressed, and mediated by its other), spirit at the same time moves from being indeterminate to being determinate, from being un-free to gaining freedom and self-determination. Being *in* the process of a developing history, the full dynamic of this movement is cognitively beyond reach. Only when this process of learning is brought to its completion in modernity is philosophical reason able to see through the leaps and gaps of history and grasp conceptually what drives it forward and what, when perceived in light of the overall development, remains historical cul-de-sacs.

To insist upon the progressive continuity in history is to insist upon the possibility of objectively ordering the given historical facts. And objectively ordering historical facts means that we have to highlight some and leave others aside. Ordering is always done from a given point of view. Throughout the maturing of spirit in tradition, reason's range of vision and understanding is always provincial. It strives, to be sure, to establish a certain order among what at first appears to be random facts. It tends to insist, furthermore, on the universality of its conceptualizations. Yet it sometimes realizes the inconsistency or limitedness of its point of view and leaves it behind for new, possibly more universal, standpoints. It is precisely because he insists that the standpoint of reason is always a function of a local life-world context that Hegel holds that the *Phenomenology of Spirit* can only be written at the point at which spirit has reached total reflective clarity. Such a point of view is achieved as a result of historical development, allowing the philosopher to assess the competing and potentially provincial interpretations and extracting from each what emerges as true and lasting within the dialectical scheme.

Contrary to what Gadamer claims, then, Hegel does not retain a notion of the reflective self-understanding of spirit because he naïvely adopts a Cartesian or enlightenment idea of the self-transparency of consciousness. Nor is the point of view of absolute reason forced upon the historical material. In Hegel's model, it is reason's development in history that allows it to abstract itself from and take a reflective stand in relation to the life-world context in which it finds itself situated and the past from which it results. The notion of reason's transparency to itself, of a reason that is able to construct meaning and continuity in the diversity of historical facts, is in other words wedded to the hermeneutic problem that Hegel addresses in the *Phenomenology of Spirit*, namely, the tension between the historical situatedness of thought and the philosophical need for a universally valid account of reason. This is the first problem with regard to Gadamer's reading of Hegel: he fails to see how Hegel's alleged Cartesianism, his notion of reflection, is not external – it is not artificially added, as it were – to his notion of the historicity of reason, but grows organically out of it. The second problem with it is related to Hegel's notion of historical work – i.e., to his perception of practical hermeneutic engagement with the historical tradition in which the interpreter is situated.

Although Gadamer rehabilitates the notion of *Bildung* as historical self-understanding, he never confronts Hegel's discussion of interpretative, historical work. Hegel, admittedly, does not provide a systematic account of this issue. Yet the fact that Hegel does not offer any substantial, systematic account of historical research is not as such a legitimate reason for not considering the reflections that he actually does provide. The most comprehensive discussion of historical work is found in his *Introduction to the Philosophy of World History* and in the many introductions to his lectures on the history of philosophy given at the University of Berlin throughout the 1820s.

In the introduction to the lectures on world history, Hegel insists that "history must be apprehended accurately [*getreu*]."[60] Even within such a realm as political history, Hegel maintains the importance of retrieving a notion of objectivity (*ILHP*, 190; *EiGP*, 261). However, Hegel's commitment to critical standards and methodological reflections does not apply to actual history only, but also to our approach to intellectual history, philosophy included – i.e., to an area that interests Gadamer in *Truth and Method*.

Hegel emphasizes that in thinking, especially in speculative thinking, understanding differs from merely grasping the grammatical meaning of words and assimilating that meaning. Furthermore, he claims, confirming the general drive of Gadamer's reading, that

---

60 G. W. F. Hegel, *Lectures on the Philosophy of World History: Introduction*, trans. H. B. Nisbet (Cambridge: Cambridge University Press, 1984), 29; *Die Vernunft in der Geschichte*, ed. Johannes Hoffmeister (Hamburg: Felix Meiner, 1955), 31.

although the history of philosophy seems at first "to be a thing of the past and to lie outside our real present life" (*ILHP*, 9; *EiGP*, 12), this simply masks a deeper continuity enabled by the fact that "what we *are* we are at the same time in history" (ibid.). This continuity is nothing but the tradition, which is "not the becoming of things alien to us, but our own becoming, the becoming of *our* philosophy" (*ILHP*, 11; *EiGP*, 14).

However, in spite of this deeper continuity between past and present, Hegel explicitly warns against models that apply or interpret the past in terms of the concerns of the present. He insists that in our dealing with past philosophers we must not "saddle them with arguments and assertions which were not made or thought of at all, even if they could be correctly derived from the principle or thought of this . . . philosophy" (*ILHP*, 45; *EiGP*, 66). We should, in short, "not look behind the old philosophies for more than what is there" (ibid.). In order to avoid this, Hegel insists that the historian of philosophy "must adhere strictly, historically, precisely, to the very own words of his author[s], not draw conclusions from them and so make something different of them" (*ILHP*, 47; *EiGP*, 69). While developing his thoughts on the history of philosophy, Hegel is in other words aware of the potential problems that rest with the discrepancy between the over-determinacy of the speculative categories, on the one hand, and the indeterminacy of historical facts and expressions, on the other. This is important with regard to Gadamer's reading of Hegel. For if Hegel, in the *Phenomenology of Spirit*, provides a notion of understanding as self-understanding and stresses the necessity of integration, then he also emphasizes that such a self-understanding is only possible to the extent that the interpreter aspires to an understanding of the other on his or her own terms and as situated within a given cultural and historical context. This is a kind of reflection that seems altogether absent in Gadamer's account of Hegel's philosophy in particular and of hermeneutic reason more generally. If Gadamer were to give full justice to the hermeneutic relevance of Hegel's philosophy – and its capacity to combine enlightenment reflection with an acknowledgement of the historicity of thought – he would have had to provide a detailed discussion of this aspect of Hegel's notion of historical work.

Epistemic and existential commitments in hermeneutics

Hegel asks how, in historical understanding, we can ever get beyond the limitations of our own horizon, or rather, in light of what absolute criteria our judgments within history can be assessed. He responds by saying that no such standpoint is available when spirit is on the way to self-understanding. Only when spirit has reached identity with itself in absolute knowledge is such a standpoint available to it. Gadamer, by contrast, insists that there is no such thing as a standpoint beyond our concrete and historical interpretations or a possibility to abstract from (which is not the same as to reject) the interpreter's situatedness within a particular life-world. Nonetheless, Gadamer maintains that interpretation of the past is not arbitrary. Interpretation obtains direction and continuity from the interpreter being embedded within a continuous tradition. Gadamer, as we have seen, captures this continuity with the term "wirkungsgeschichtliches Bewußtsein," the idea of a tradition that, like Hegel's spirit, is more comprehensive than the consciousness of the individual interpreter. Again like Hegel's notion of spirit, Gadamer's notion of historically effected consciousness refers to the idea of tradition becoming ever more concrete and richer in its articulations through the interpretative work of later generations. Yet unlike Hegel, Gadamer insists that this process never reaches a final culmination. Like true Socratic dialogue, cultural transmission is a process that only lives as it dynamically changes and is underway. Because Gadamer insists that we are, emphatically, finite historical beings, all hermeneutic activity implies adding to tradition by applying it in ever new, historical contexts.

While engaging with a given text or tradition, we are, Gadamer claims, at the same time shaped by tradition itself. The self-understanding gained through the encounter with history changes the outlook of the interpreter. To strive towards a final comprehension of the rational meaning of history is simply to misunderstand the nature of philosophical hermeneutics. The meaning of historical texts (for Gadamer the past is generally addressed in terms of a written tradition) depends on a fusion of horizons between work and interpreter. Essentially linked to application – a process in which the meaning of the text gets realized in ever new contexts – every interpretation adds something new. Or, as Gadamer puts it in a passage quoted earlier on, "understanding, as it occurs in the human sciences, is essentially historical ... in them a text is understood only *if it is understood in a different way*" (*TM*, 309; *WM*, 314, emphasis added, see also *TM*, 297; *WM*, 302). Given the importance of *applicatio*, interpretation of history – and of ourselves – can never be brought to an end. Alternatively, as Gadamer expresses it, to be historical "means that knowledge of oneself can never be complete" (*TM*, 302; *WM*, 307). This is not, as the enlightenment philosopher would think, due "to a deficiency in reflection but to the essence of the historical being that we are" (ibid.).

Gadamer claims that there is indeed continuity in tradition but that this continuity is not predicated upon a model of absolute self-understanding. He seeks to articulate a notion of a consciousness – hermeneutic consciousness, as he calls it[61] – that never knows itself completely (it is forever referred to historical work) but that, all the same, remains assured of the continuity and normative power of its own tradition. For Hegel, anything like this would be a contradiction in terms.[62] In his work, there is an intrinsic relation between self-understanding and the idea of a continuity of tradition that enables the phenomenological process of integration, learning, and *Bildung*. Absolute spirit is the result of a process in which each shape of consciousness grows out of – and renders explicit – the problems of the previous figure, yet Hegel, as a philosopher theorizing about this movement, must tease out and conceptually articulate the idea of a continuity between the various shapes of consciousness.

Even though he argues that his hermeneutics represents a critical continuation of Hegel's philosophy of history – a continuation through which Gadamer distinguishes himself from the problematic Hegelian influences that he detects in Dilthey and the historical school – Gadamer cannot find support for his claim that this hermeneutic side of Hegel's philosophy can be set apart from the Cartesian strands of his thinking, nor for his claim that Hegel's real hermeneutics is all about self-understanding and integration (in the sense of abolishing the distinction between interpretation and application). Furthermore, what Gadamer himself presents as a hermeneutically reworked Hegelianism proves to be a position that, when assessed from a Hegelian point of view, does not hold. Why, then, does

---

61 This is Gadamer's very own contribution to philosophy: it is his way to maneuver between the Cartesian legacy in modern philosophy, on the one hand, and Heidegger's rejection of the notion of consciousness altogether, on the other.

62 As Walter Jaeschke puts it, "[i]f the meaning of history is defined as the realization of a specific goal, this history necessarily comes to an end when this goal is achieved – unless one determines this goal in such a way that it is unfulfillable, and thus history leads into an infinite progress. But nothing is more alien to Hegel than this." Walter Jaeschke, "World History and the History of the Absolute Spirit," in Robert L. Perkins (ed.), *History and System: Hegel's Philosophy of History* (Albany, N.Y.: SUNY Press, 1984), 114.

Gadamer, in his effort to get beyond the perceived limitations of romantic hermeneutics, want to align himself with Hegel? In the final part of this chapter, I want to claim that this follows from a misreading of Hegel's notion of self-understanding, or, rather, from the lack of capacity to account for the difference between the epistemic and the existential dimensions of self-understanding in history.

By stressing his indebtedness to Hegel, Gadamer grants historical authority to his own philosophical project. He does not, as it were, invent a brand new hermeneutics, but ferrets out and explicates the promises of a Hegelian philosophy that had been misinterpreted by the tradition. For a thinker who claims that truth is mediated in and through the gradual unfolding of tradition, such a project of legitimation is of the utmost importance. Moreover, this strategy of interpretation not only characterizes Gadamer's reading of Hegel, but also, as we have seen, his interpretation of Kant's third Critique (Kant grasped the hermeneutic nature of art but, due to the restrictions of the transcendental project, he was forced to leave this behind). Nonetheless, when considering the critique of the Enlightenment and of Hegel, one cannot help noticing that Gadamer's hermeneutics – given its Heideggerian orientation – responds to a problem that differs substantially from that of Hegel. Hegel had been asking how it could be possible to conceive of reason as historically situated without thereby ending up in the relativist dead-end of naïve historicism. Gadamer's hermeneutics, by contrast, responds to what he, in the 1930s, experienced as a wave of unwanted, aesthetic humanism. Aesthetic humanism fails to see that art can convey truth. Gadamer wishes to provide an alternative to this model, and this is what initially triggered the work that we today know as *Truth and Method*: the desire to show that art has a truth and authority of its own.

When worrying about the predominance of aesthetic consciousness, Gadamer is not concerned with art in a narrow sense of the term but with historical culture in a much broader meaning of the term. Standing in the shade of the enlightenment rejection of the normativity of tradition, we are about to turn the tradition into a museum. Tradition is either rejected as irrelevant to our present orientations or admired in terms of its pure aesthetic qualities. In either case, the past has ceased to matter as a source of normativity and meaning. Wanting to amend this situation, Gadamer emphasizes that self-understanding involves historical interpretation. However, the self-understanding at stake here is not an intersubjective, historicized notion of spirit's gradual progress in history. Genuine historical self-understanding is not, as it was for Hegel, about grasping the historical sources of normativity and practice, so as to be able to acknowledge them as ours *or* criticize them as unwanted prejudices. For Gadamer, what is at stake is not simply a historical-phenomenological account and systematic evaluation of norms and values, but a deeper, more existential engagement with the past. In understanding the past, we reach a more profound understanding of ourselves: we understand ourselves, our being in the world, as emphatically historical. To the extent that truth is involved in this process, it is not conceived in terms of validity or objective standards, but as the achievement of a more authentic existence.

This aspect of Gadamer's hermeneutics is made even clearer when one takes into account his retrieval of the classical. In modernity, Gadamer argues, the term 'classical' is reduced "to a mere stylistic concept" (*TM*, 285; *WM*, 290). Partly due to Hegel – who identified classical art with the period of the ancient Greeks and saw in classical art the work of a bygone level of spirit – the idea of the classical has lost its normative force. It is reduced to a concept of a period (and even Gadamer, as we have seen, frequently uses the term "classical" as interchangeable with the period of pre-modern art). As such the classical is defined by that which comes before it as well as that which comes after. Yet, in this case, Gadamer claims, "historical conscious-ness . . . includes more than it admits of itself" (*TM*, 287; *WM*, 292). For the very notion of a humanistic education embodies the idea of the classical as a normative, rather than simply a period-specific, con-cept. Here, the classical is, as Gadamer puts it, "more than a concept of a period or of a historical style, and yet it nevertheless does not try to be the concept of a suprahistorical value ['übergeschichtlicher Wertgedanke']" (ibid.). As part of a liberal education, the classical refers to a distinctive mode of being historical: the idea that something is preserved because it perpetually "allows something true to come into being" (ibid.). Hence the aspect of the classical that interests Gadamer is primarily the idea of an authority that is preserved and handed down prior to all historical reflection (*TM*, 287).[63]

---

63 In German: "Klassisch ist, was der historischen Kritik gegenüber standhält, weil seine geschichtliche Herrschaft, die verpflichtende Macht seiner sich überliefernden und bewahrenden Geltung, aller historischen Reflexion schon vorausliegt und sich in ihr durchhält" (*WM*, 292).

As it applied to the great work of art, the classical does not need to prove its authority. Recognizing the classical, we apprehend it as a text whose authority does not depend on our (individual) acceptance. Its authority is always already proved because the horizon of the work extends into and forms the beliefs and practices in terms of which we understand ourselves. The classical opens a historical reality to which consciousness belongs (*zugehört*) and is subordinate (*untersteht*) (*TM*, 288; *WM*, 292f.). The idea of such subordination – no longer characteristic only of our encounter with sublime art, but also with, say, the great historical works of philosophy – would have been alien to a philosopher like Hegel. What is more, however, it shatters the very concept of a dialogical acknowledgment by which Gadamer's critique of Hegel was initially motivated. Whereas the interpersonal dialogue was understood by Gadamer in terms of the parties' mutual right, or rather obligation, to question the given conception of a subject matter, such an emphasis on mutuality can hardly be found in his understanding of the classical. It is, so to speak, we who are interrogated by the classical work.[64] The classical is distinguished by the ability to erect a standard whose validity does not call for critical validation. Responding adequately to this standard, we simply "listen." The claim of the classical rests in its positing of a kind of authority which does not have to prove itself to us *as* an authority.[65]

Gadamer argues that when authentically relating to our own being we realize – along the lines of the experience of art – that it is not we who question the past, but we who are being questioned by the past. We are being questioned not only with respect to our understanding of this particular text or artwork, but also with regard to our relation to tradition as such – that is, with regard to our existence as historical beings. If authentically experienced, the works of the past address us with an imperative like that of Rilke's "Archaïscher Torso Apollos": "Thou must alter thy life."[66] The great works of the tradition beg neither criticism nor philological or historical research but

---

64 "Aesthetics and Hermeneutics" (1964), *PH*, 104; "Ästhetik und Hermeneutik," *GW*, vol. VIII, 8.

65 In *Truth and Method*, Gadamer speaks of the self-evident "obligatoriness [*Verbindlichkeit*]" of classical works (*TM*, 118; *WM*, 123). See also "The Relevance of the Beautiful," *RB*, 19; "Die Aktualität des Schönen," *GW*, vol. VIII, 110.

66 "Aesthetics and Hermeneutics," *PH*, 104; "Ästhetik und Hermeneutik," *GW*, vol. VIII, 8. For Rilke's poem, see Rainer Maria Rilke, *New Poems*, ed. and trans. Edward Snow (New York: North Point Press, 2001), 183; *Die Gedichte* (Frankfurt am Main: Insel Verlag, 1992), 503.

self-examination – self-examination because we live in a culture that is no longer able to respond adequately to its own historicity. Hence the challenge we face, living under the twin specter of aesthetic consciousness and the enlightenment rejection of the normativity of the past, is once again to be able authentically to take on our historical being in the world. This problem – at least in the form that we find it articulated in Gadamer's philosophy – was not part of Hegel's reworking of enlightenment philosophy. Instead, it is a problem that Gadamer inherits from Heidegger, although Gadamer, as we have seen, also criticizes certain elements of his teacher's philosophizing.

Now, there is nothing wrong, per se, in wanting to go beyond the restrictions of a Heideggerian framework by appealing to the resources of Hegel's phenomenology. In Gadamer's case, however, it seems that in his effort to grant historical legitimacy to his own hermeneutics of integration and carve out, against the enlightenment prejudice against prejudices, a hermeneutics of historical reflection and self-understanding, he overlooks the differences between a historical-epistemic and a historical-existential notion of self-understanding. For in spite of the differences between enlightenment thinking and Hegelian hermeneutics, with regard to this particular distinction, it seems clear that Hegel does indeed belong within the same framework as the Enlightenment – even though his emphasis is not on working out an ahistorical notion of reason, but on the retrieval of rationality and self-understanding in history. Hence Gadamer's hermeneutics cannot, as it sets out to do, fill the philosophical space vacated by Hegel's notion of spirit's identity with itself in absolute knowledge. In his craving for an existentially apt approach to historical understanding, Gadamer simply evades the underlying problem of Hegel's philosophy of history, namely the possibility of combining a notion of the historicity of reason with the question of validity in understanding. This, in my view, is a pity, because the task that Gadamer initially set himself – namely, that of developing a critical, post-Hegelian hermeneutics – would be of great value and relevance within the landscape of contemporary philosophy,[67] and it is, moreover, a project that would stake out a promising course for

67 I am thinking for example of John McDowell's reading of Hegel in *Mind and World*. See also Richard Bernstein, "McDowell's Domesticated Hegelianism," in Smith, *Reading McDowell*, 9–24. Yet another example is Robert Brandom's reading of Hegel in *Tales of the Mighty Dead* (Cambridge, Mass.: Harvard University Press, 2002), 178–234.

the critical, yet sympathetic, adaptation of enlightenment thinking that Gadamer also recommends.

The problem with Gadamer's misreading of Hegel and the Enlightenment is not only that he gets them both wrong. By linking Hegel's notion of absolute spirit with a problematic Cartesian–enlightenment philosophy of reflection, and by systematically failing to address Hegel's own reflection on historical work, Gadamer overlooks how Hegel himself never fails to address the perhaps most pressing problem bequeathed to us by the Enlightenment: the potential conflict between the situatedness of reason and the need for a rational justification of epistemic, ethical, and aesthetic norms. Having rejected Hegel's notion of absolute spirit as an instance of bad, unreflected Cartesianism – rather than understanding it as a response to a genuine problem in the philosophy of history and the humanities at large – Gadamer fails to recognize that this is a question of great importance for hermeneutics. Precisely because Gadamer is not (as Habermas, Apel, and Tugendhat seem to argue) against the Enlightenment, but seeks to give it a historical twist, this is a problem that should have been taken more seriously.

Because he does not address the complexity of Hegel's hermeneutic legacy, Gadamer fails to keep open the space of discourse that Hegel and his generation were the first to brand as philosophically relevant and pressing: the question of validity in understanding. Only by dealing with this problem are we able to discuss possible – Hegelian and non-Hegelian – solutions to it. In order to do so, it is not necessary to reject Gadamer's philosophy. What is needed, rather, is a willingness to see Gadamer's hermeneutics as an extension of the enlightenment project while at the same time questioning his sublation of the epistemological question of self-understanding into an existential one. In addressing this issue, it will be helpful to contrast Gadamer's position with the hermeneutic theories of a nineteenth-century philosopher who has so far been left out of the discussion, namely Friedrich Schleiermacher.

5

SCHLEIERMACHER'S CRITICAL THEORY OF INTERPRETATION

Until Heidegger and Gadamer, hermeneutics focused on the practical, philological challenges we encounter in engaging with the texts of the past. Gadamer, however, has surprisingly little to say about this issue. As far as he is concerned, what matters is the way in which we relate (or fail to relate) authentically to tradition and keep alive the world-disclosing and existentially challenging truths of the great historical works. For Gadamer, hermeneutics is at the same time a theory of *Dasein*'s historical being in the world and a theory of its experiencing and understanding itself in light of the truth of the texts and artworks of the past.

In this chapter, I turn to the problem of the practical interpretation of texts that are temporally or culturally distant from the interpreter. No part of Gadamer's work could prove a better touchstone for an assessment of his interpretatory program than his reading of the nineteenth-century philosopher Friedrich Daniel Ernst Schleiermacher and his critical theory of interpretation. This, it seems, would be the place where Gadamer could test and discuss the boundaries of his own philosophical hermeneutics. Yet such an encounter never takes place. In *Truth and Method*, Gadamer dismisses Schleiermacher as the philosopher who seals the fate of modern hermeneutics by ushering it into a problematic, romantic dead-end, heavily infested with the problems adhering to the aesthetics of genius and methodological ideals of a Cartesian stamp. As it is, Gadamer never enters into a fair discussion of Schleiermacher's philosophy of interpretation, but leaves the reader with a systematically distorted picture of his notion of individuality and an equally misconstrued retrieval of his call for a critical method in understanding. Gadamer's reading is not expressive of a dialogical attitude of the kind that he himself locates at the heart of the hermeneutic project, but presents us with an untenable straw-man that allows the ontological turn in hermeneutics to emerge as a superior alternative to the outlook of early nineteenth-century theory of interpretation.

As it develops in the period of German Idealism, Schleiermacher's hermeneutics does not represent a naïve, positivistic theory of the kind that Gadamer ascribes to him. Instead, it is Schleiermacher's achievement to have developed a set of critical-philological reflections on the practical challenge of understanding others, be they culturally and temporally close to or distant from the interpreter. As such, the concerns of early nineteenth-century hermeneutics are different from, but not incompatible with, the ones addressed in *Truth and Method*. And as we will see in this and the concluding chapter, Schleiermacher's hermeneutics suggests a way of getting beyond some of the problems that adhere to Gadamer's ontological turn.

My discussion of these issues begins with a brief exposition of Gadamer's approach to early nineteenth-century theories of understanding and continues by dealing more specifically with his critique of Schleiermacher in *Truth and Method*, focusing on the concept of individuality and the notion of a method in interpretation. I then point out the problems with Gadamer's reading of Schleiermacher's notion of individuality and, subsequently, discuss the limitations of his critique of a hermeneutic method. Gadamer's modification of his critique, throughout the late 1960s and early 1970s, is put under scrutiny next. While allowing for some important philological corrections, philosophically speaking this revision remains of a merely cosmetic nature. Why, then, does Gadamer systematically misread this part of nineteenth-century hermeneutics? This question is answered by reference to his political humanism and his call for existentially challenging rather than historically accurate interpretations. The problems inherent in this dimension of Gadamer's work, which are often overlooked in the secondary literature, should trigger a return to the hermeneutic legacy of German Idealism and its focus on critical standards in interpretation, rather than *Dasein*'s existential appropriation of its own historicity. In their orientation towards questions of validity, Schleiermacher and his generation plot a way to reinsert a notion of objectivity into hermeneutics.

The universality-claim of nineteenth-century hermeneutics

Friedrich Schleiermacher is perhaps best known for his romantic re-conceptualization of Protestant theology. In such works as *On Religion: Speeches to its Cultured Despisers* (1799) and *Christmas Eve* (1806), he offers a phenomenological account of religious experience in terms of individuality, intuition, and feeling. These topics are then further explored in *The Christian Faith* (1822), his major work within the philosophy of religion.[1] However, the reflections on religion constitute just one of Schleiermacher's intellectual commitments. He also contributed to the fields of aesthetics, epistemology, and ethics. A strong interest in the politics of education led Schleiermacher to take an active part in the foundation of the University of Berlin in 1809, where he taught, along with Hegel, until his death in 1834.[2]

In Halle, Schleiermacher studied with Eberhard, who was a leading figure of the Leibnizian and Wolffian reaction against Kant.[3] Schleiermacher was influenced by Kant and Fichte's enlightenment commitment, yet critical of its potential subjectivism.[4] He also took a

---

1 These works are all translated into English: *Christmas Eve*, trans. Terrence N. Tice (San Francisco: EM Texts, 1991); *On Religion: Speeches to its Cultured Despisers*, trans. Richard Crouter (Cambridge: Cambridge University Press, 1988); *The Christian Faith*, vols. I and II, various translators (New York: Harper & Row, 1963).

2 For an account of Schleiermacher's position at the University of Berlin, and of his relations with Hegel in this period, see Gunter Scholtz, "Schleiermachers Theorie der modernen Kultur mit vergleichendem Blick auf Hegel," in *Kunsterfahrung und Kulturpolitik im Berlin Hegels, Hegel-Studien*, vol. XXII, ed. Otto Pöggeler and Annemarie Gethmann-Siefert (Bonn: Bouvier, 1983). For a study of the relationship between Schleiermacher's and Hegel's philosophies of religion, see Walter Jaeschke, "Paralipomena Hegeliana zur Wirkungsgeschichte Schleiermachers," in Hermann Fischer *et al.*, *Schleiermacher-Archiv*, Band I, Teilband 2, Internationaler Schleiermacher-Kongreß 1984, ed. Kurt-Victor Selge (Berlin: Walter de Gruyter, 1985), 1157–1171.

3 See Frederick Beiser, *The Fate of Reason* (Cambridge, Mass.: Harvard University Press, 1987), 219f.

4 Heinz Kimmerle offers an overview of Schleiermacher's reading of Kant and Fichte in "Das Verhältnis Schleiermachers zum transzendentalen Idealismus," *Kant-Studien*, vol. 51, nos. 1–4, 1959–60, 410–426. See also "Exzerpt aus Immanuel Kant: Über den Gemeinspruch: Das mag in der Theorie richtig sein, taugt aber nicht für die Praxis" (1793), *KGA*, Erste Abteilung. Schriften und Entwürfe, vol. XIV, *Kleine Schriften 1786–1833*, ed. Matthias Wolfes und Michael Pietsch, 19–25 and "Notizen zu Kant: Kritik der praktischen Vernunft" (1789), *KGA*, Erste Abteilung. Schriften und Entwürfe, vol. I, *Jugendschriften 1787–1796*, ed. Günter Meckenstock, 129–135.

strong interest in classical philosophy and, together with Friedrich
Schlegel, set out to translate the entire work of Plato.[5] However,
Schlegel withdrew from the project at an early stage, and Schleier-
macher translated some of the dialogues on his own. Although
Schleiermacher's translations proved controversial, they were soon
praised as congenial to the spirit of Plato's work.[6]

   Schleiermacher lectured on the problems of hermeneutics in the
period between 1805 and 1833. Apart from two academy lectures
from 1829, he never completed a major work on this issue.[7] Nevertheless, the lecture notes, the student annotations, and his engagement with the problems of interpretation in such texts as *Dialektik*
and *Ästhetik*, provide us with the most coherent articulation of the
early nineteenth-century philosophy of understanding.[8]

5 For a discussion of Schleiermacher's position within the early romantic movement,
   see Kurt Nowak, *Schleiermacher und die Frühromantik. Eine literaturgeschichtliche Studie
   zum romantischen Religionsverständnis und Menschenbild am Ende des 18. Jahrhunderts
   in Deutschland* (Göttingen: Vandenhoeck & Ruprecht, 1986), 107–118 and
   Schleiermacher. Leben, Werk und Wirkung (Göttingen: Vandenhoeck & Ruprecht,
   2001), 79–97.
6 On the basis of his work on Plato, Werner Jaeger even describes Schleiermacher as
   the Winckelmann of Greek philosophy. See Werner Jaeger, *Humanistische Reden und
   Vorträge* (Berlin: Walter de Gruyter, 1960), 129. For an account of the reception of
   Schleiermacher's translations of Plato as well as the general principles of translation
   that he employs, see Hermann Patsch, *Alle Menschen sind Künstler. Friedrich Schleiermachers poetische Versuche*, Schleiermacher-Archiv, vol. II, ed. H. Fischer, H.-J. Birkner, G.
   Ebeling, H. Kimmerle, and K.-V. Selge (Berlin: Walter de Gruyter, 1986), 68–76. I
   return to Schleiermacher's philosophy of translation in Chapter 6.
7 The title *Hermeneutics* does not, in other words, refer to a single work by Schleiermacher, but to a series of unpublished manuscripts. These are now available in three
   different critical editions. First, Schleiermacher's friend and student Friedrich Lücke
   put together an edition of Schleiermacher's hermeneutics. Here the lacunas in
   Schleiermacher's manuscripts were filled in on the basis of student notes. It is this
   version of Schleiermacher's hermeneutics that was known to Dilthey, and also to
   Gadamer when he conceived his first critique of Schleiermacher. The second critical
   edition, compiled by Gadamer's student Heinz Kimmerle, appeared under the title
   Hermeneutik. Nach den Handschriften (Heidelberg: Carl Winter, 1974). Finally, Manfred
   Frank published a critical edition of Schleiermacher's hermeneutics in 1977. Largely
   based on Lücke's version of *Hermeneutik*, this edition is entitled *Hermeneutik und Kritik*
   (Frankfurt am Main: Suhrkamp Verlag, 1993).
8 This does not mean that Schleiermacher was the only early nineteenth-century thinker
   who explored the problems of understanding and interpretation. For a comprehensive
   study of romantic hermeneutics, see Reinhold Rieger, *Interpretation und Wissen. Zur
   philosophischen Begründung der Hermeneutik bei Friedrich Schleiermacher und ihrem geschichtlichen Hintergrund*, Schleiermacher-Archiv, vol. VI, ed. H. Fischer, H.-J. Birkner, G. Ebeling,
   and K.-V. Selge (Berlin: Walter de Gruyter, 1988). I return to this point at the beginning of Chapter 6.

In Gadamer's work, Schleiermacher is presented as the figure who fatally imports the romantic conceptions of genius and aesthetic individuality to the realm of hermeneutics. That said, however, one should not forget why Gadamer takes such a strong interest in Schleiermacher's hermeneutics in the first place. Only if there exists at least a minimal, yet non-trivial, affinity between Schleiermacher's and Gadamer's ideas of understanding is it worthwhile for Gadamer critically to engage with the trajectory of early nineteenth-century hermeneutics. Gadamer finds such a moment of affinity in Schleiermacher's universalizing of the hermeneutic problem. Earlier hermeneuticians such as Ast, Wolf, Ernesti, and Morus had been working within the fields of Biblical studies and ancient Greek literature.[9] In Schleiermacher's view, this approach to hermeneutics rests on little but "a collection of observations" (*HC*, 6; *HuK*, 75). It involves no reflected account of the conditions of possibility for validity in interpretation and fails to "fulfill any scientific demands" (*HC*, 6; *HuK*, 76). What is needed is a move from the limited focus of *hermeneutica specialis* to a philosophical account of *hermeneutica generalis*: a theory of the conditions of possibility for validity in understanding that is rooted in reflections on the conditions of possibility for understanding as such.[10] According to Schleiermacher, a critical hermeneutics must be based on a general theory of language. Indeed, in its written or spoken form, language is "the only presupposition in hermeneutics and everything that is to be found, including the other objective and subjective presuppositions, must be discovered in language" (*HK*, 50; *HKi*, 38). This is a view that Gadamer shares, and he quotes these lines as the motto of the third part of *Truth and Method*, that is, the part entitled "The Ontological Shift of Hermeneutics Guided by Language."

9 Friedrich Ast articulates his view on ancient Greek literature in *Grundlinien der Grammatik, Hermeneutik und Kritik* and *Grundriss der Philologie*. Wolf's most influential text in this regard is *Vorlesungen über die Encyklopädie der Altertumswissenschaft*. For an overview of Ast's and Wolf's theories (and their impact on Schleiermacher), see Wach, *Das Verstehen.*, vol. I, 31–62 (Ast) and 62–82 (Wolf).

10 For an overview of Schleiermacher's notion of universal hermeneutics, see Paul Ricoeur, "Schleiermacher's Hermeneutics," *The Monist*, vol. 60, no. 2, 1977, 183f. Schleiermacher's claim that he is the first to articulate a universal hermeneutics is, however, questionable. The idea of a *hermeneutia generalis* reaches far beyond Schleiermacher, and it seems that his idea of his general hermeneutics being "new" only betrays his lack of knowledge of the older hermeneutic tradition. See Werner Alexander, *Hermeneutica Generalis. Zur Konzeption und Entwicklung der allgemeinen Verstehenslehre im 17. und 18. Jahrhundert* (Stuttgart: M&P, Verlag für Wissenschaft und Forschung, 1993), 3ff.

Yet, according to Gadamer, Schleiermacher never redeems the promises of his path-breaking universalizing of hermeneutics. For that we need to go to Hegel, that is, to the (in Gadamer's view) more promising aspects of his phenomenological method, namely, his insight into the historical aspects of thought and language and his emphasis on the continuity of historical mediation. In Gadamer's retrieval of modern hermeneutics, Schleiermacher remains a child of the era of German Idealism, and his hermeneutics is beset with the twin problems of positivism and romanticism. As a consequence, his claim about the universality of language is constrained by "very perceptible limits" (*TM*, 197; *WM*, 200). These limits, Gadamer continues, are particularly evident in Schleiermacher's notion of individuality and his outline of a method in interpretation.

Individuality and feeling in interpretation

In his hermeneutics, Schleiermacher is not interested in the problem of self-understanding and authentic historical existence. What draws his attention is the problem of understanding others – be they others who are close to the interpreter, or, more often, those who are temporally or culturally distant from his or her own horizon of experience. Consequently, hermeneutics, in Schleiermacher's work, is not conceived in terms of an ongoing integrating tradition in which the interpreter is situated and through which he or she understands him- or herself (as Gadamer takes it to be the case in Hegel's *Phenomenology of Spirit*). In dealing, mainly, with works from the ancient Greek and Hebrew periods, the problem he addresses is how the critical reader can make sense of words and propositions at a time when their original context of understanding is long gone and the interpreter can assume no direct access to the customary application that the author once took for granted.

Given such an orientation, a critical-reflective hermeneutics – that is, hermeneutics as a *Kunstlehre* – is distinguished from the unreflected (*laxere*) interpretative practices that typically characterize our everyday communication. The unreflected, more lax practice functions as though understanding were not a problem, as though it "results as a matter of course" (*HC*, 21; *HuK*, 92). It expresses its aim negatively, in an almost tautological maxim: "misunderstanding should be avoided" (ibid.). The proper or more strict (*strengere*) hermeneutical practice, by contrast, reflects the idea that "misunderstanding results as a matter of course" (*HC*, 22; *HuK*, 92). In the stricter hermeneutic practice, the interpreter does not presuppose a direct access to the meaning of the text. Rather, he or she anticipates, in the best possible manner, the risks of misunderstanding. According to the stricter hermeneutic practice, understanding must, as Schleiermacher puts it, be deliberately "desired and sought at every point" (ibid.), and this is only achieved through reflection on the nature of language and symbolic performance in general, as well as knowledge of the linguistic and cultural resources that were at the author's disposal. On a general level, symbolic performance is constituted by the interplay between a common reservoir of grammatical rules and semantic possibilities, and the individual application of these conventional resources. Even though "every person is on the one hand a location in which a given language forms itself in an individual manner, on the other their discourse can only be understood via the totality of the language" (*HC*, 8; *HuK*, 78). As a theory of the conditions of possibility for validity in understanding, hermeneutics must respond to this situation by offering both "understanding by reference to language and understanding by reference to the one who speaks ['Verstehen in der Sprache und Verstehen im Sprechenden']" (*HK*, 68; *HKi*, 56). These two standards, attending to the linguistic and cultural resources the speaker has at his or her disposal, as well as his or her individual application of these shared resources, make up the methodological core of Schleiermacher's critical hermeneutics.

Schleiermacher calls the reflection on the common resources of language grammatical interpretation. Grammatical interpretation investigates the relation between the particular text and the "language area" in which it emerges (*HC*, 90; *HuK*, 167).[11] Reflection on how language forms itself in an individual expression is the task of technical or psychological interpretation.[12] Technical interpretation

---

11 Grammatical interpretation is guided by two principles. Whereas the first claims that everything "in a given utterance which requires a more precise determination may only be determined from the language area [*Sprachgebiet*] which is common to the author and his original audience" (*HC*, 30; *HuK*, 101), the second maintains that the "sense of every word in a given location must be determined according to its being-together [*Zusammensein*] with those that surround it" (*HC*, 44; *HuK*, 116). In other words, the first principle brings to attention the place of the given language-use within its most comprehensive context, the second focuses on the relation of a word or a passage to its immediate surroundings. Manfred Frank offers a clear account of these two sides of grammatical interpretation (and the way in which they are related to Schleiermacher's conception of language in general) in *Das individuelle Allgemeine*, 266ff.

12 The idea of a technical interpretation is further elaborated in ibid., 315ff.

concentrates on how the individual "collaborates in the language" (*HC*, 91; *HuK*, 167) and aims at a "complete understanding of style" – i.e., of "the treatment of the language" (*HC*, 91; *HuK*, 168).[13] Gadamer finds Schleiermacher's conception of grammatical interpretation a "brilliant" contribution to hermeneutics (*TM*, 186; *WM*, 190). Nonetheless, he claims that it is technical or psychological interpretation that makes up "Schleiermacher's particular contribution" (*TM*, 187; *WM*, 191). Thus he feels entitled to ignore the grammatical aspect of Schleiermacher's theory.

Because he focuses exclusively on the notion of technical interpretation, which he takes to be in line with the aestheticist attitude of post-Kantian romanticism, Gadamer finds that in Schleiermacher's hermeneutics a text is not "to be understood in terms of its subject matter but as an aesthetic construct, as a work of art or 'artistic thought'" (ibid.). Allegedly, early nineteeth-century hermeneutics approaches the texts as an expression of unconscious production, and the task of the interpreter is to bring to consciousness what was not conscious in the process of creation. As Gadamer puts it – in a quotation that makes it clear how he immediately situates Schleiermacher within the paradigm of aesthetic consciousness and its culture of immediacy – romantic hermeneutics strives towards "a placing of oneself within the whole framework of the author, an apprehension of the 'inner origin' of the composition of a work" (ibid.). Such an "apprehension of the 'inner origin' of the composition of a work" is required because Schleiermacher, in Gadamer's reading, traces the linguistic expression back to individual, aesthetic feeling. Like artistic genius, the individual language-user transcends the constraints of grammatical correctness and semantic conventions. Within this conception, it is "[g]enius itself [which] creates models and rules. It creates new ways of using language, new literary forms" (*TM*, 189; *WM*, 193).

If all symbolic performance displays a rule-transcending originality, then one ought to ask how communication can take place at all. According to Gadamer, Schleiermacher did not explain the possibility of communication in terms of a continuous, integrating tradition or the linguistic mediation of experience. Indeed, in Gadamer's reading,

---

13 Schleiermacher discusses the notion of style in "Über den Stil" (1790–91), defining it as "die Kunst unsre Vorstellungen durch Zeichen deutlich zu machen." See *KGA*, erste Abteilung, vol. 1, 365.

it is Schleiermacher's lack of an adequate notion of (historical) intersubjectivity that made him recast the problem of hermeneutics as a problem of individuality in the first place. In Gadamer's words:

> [i]t is not only the written tradition that is estranged and in need of new and more vital assimilation; everything that is no longer immediately situated in a world – that is, all tradition, whether art or the other spiritual creations of the past: law, religion, philosophy, and so forth – is estranged from its original meaning and depends on the unlocking and mediating spirit that we, like the Greeks, name after Hermes: the messenger of the gods. (*TM*, 165; *WM*, 170)

As recounted by Gadamer, Schleiermacher fails to acknowledge that whatever presents itself to us does so within the framework of a historically and linguistically mediated culture. He assumes that real understanding is immediate, a communication from heart to heart, as it were. This, Gadamer continues, forces him to view understanding as a "re-experience" of the original experience, as *divination*. In Schleiermacher's philosophy, Gadamer claims, "what corresponds to the production of genius is divination, the immediate solution, which ultimately presupposes a kind of con-geniality" (*TM*, 189; *WM*, 193). Hermeneutics is reduced to "an immediate, sympathetic, and con-genial understanding" (*TM*, 191; *WM*, 194).

The question of hermeneutic method

According to Gadamer, Schleiermacher's hermeneutics is geared towards an "individual thought that by its very nature is a free construct and the free expression of an individual being" (*TM*, 188; *WM*, 192). In order to grasp this "free expression of an individual being," Schleiermacher appeals to the idea of a hermeneutic circle, by which he supposedly has in mind a rigid, methodological procedure of interpretation.[14] In developing the notion of the hermeneutic circle, Schleiermacher, unlike Spinoza and Ast, does not focus primarily on the relation between the parts of a text and the text as a whole. Nor does he, as we later find it in Hegel, reflect upon the process of spirit's self-understanding in history. In Schleiermacher's adaptation, the

---

14 In an essay from 1959, Gadamer discusses Schleiermacher's conception of the hermeneutic circle and compares it to Heidegger's ontological retrieval of understanding. See "On the Circle of Understanding," in Connolly and Keutner, *Hermeneutics Versus Science?*, 67–78; "Vom Zirkel des Verstehens," *GW*, vol. II, 57–65.

hermeneutic circle targets the relation between individual language-user and original audience, and its aim is to achieve what Gadamer takes to be the conclusive unlocking of its meaning (*TM*, 191; *WM*, 194). This, Gadamer claims, is made clear by Schleiermacher's insistence that the aim of hermeneutics is to understand a writer better than he or she understood him- or herself. The notion of such a better understanding, Gadamer continues, "is a formula that has been repeated ever since" (*TM*, 192; *WM*, 195), or, stronger still, a formula into which "the whole history of modern hermeneutics can be read" (ibid.).

That said, it is important to stress that Gadamer's interest in this idea is not entirely negative. On the contrary, he acknowledges that it debunks the common view that the author possesses a privileged access to the meaning of the text. As such, the notion of our understanding the author better than he or she understands him- or herself "contains the real [*eigentliche*] problem of hermeneutics" (*TM*, 192, trans. modified; *WM*, 196). The idea that our understanding of a text must be better than the author's understanding of it performs "an important theoretical task, in that it collapses the distinction between interpreter and author" (*TM*, 193; *WM*, 196f.). In Schleiermacher's version, however, the full hermeneutic potential of this dictum has not yet been realized. For, according to Gadamer, the task of understanding a text better than it was understood by its author is not, as it was in Kant,[15] regarded as a matter of moving "beyond the contradictions of a given theory by achieving greater conceptual clarity" (*TM*, 195; *WM*, 198). Rather, it is a question of deploying the critical standards of technical and grammatical analysis in order to retrieve the immediate and spontaneous feeling to which the text lends voice. What counts – what the method is aiming at – is not the truth of the text but the idea of texts as "purely expressive phenomena" (*TM*, 196; *WM*, 200). Any text is regarded as the outcome of free, aesthetic production. Schleiermacher thus "disregards its content as knowledge [*Erkenntnisgehalt*]" (ibid.). It is this disregard – in the name of objective method – for the cognitive claim of the text, hence also for the kind of ontological-historical self-understanding that Gadamer advocates, that allegedly forces later hermeneutics to move beyond the framework of Schleiermacher's romantic theory and proceed towards an ontologically informed reflection on our historical being-in-the-world (*TM*, 197; *WM*, 201).

15 See *CPR*; *KdrV*, B 370.

Individuality reassessed

According to Gadamer, Schleiermacher treats every expression as a quasi-aesthetic object – that is, in terms of its style or unity (expressing the individuality of the writer) and not in terms of its truth. Hence no dialogical encounter can take place between work and interpreter. Interpretation supposedly aims at immediate, aesthetic empathy. If Schleiermacher's hermeneutics emerges in the wake of the *Critique of Judgment,* then it is in other words based on what Gadamer has already criticized as a romantic misunderstanding of Kant's notion of creative genius, and not his more promising discussion of the ideal of beauty.

I have argued that Gadamer's reading of Kant's conception of genius and natural beauty is inadequate. When dealing with this part of the third Critique, Gadamer overlooks the hermeneutic potential of Kant's conception of natural beauty (the experience of nature appearing as if it were created with a view to making us feel at home in the world). Moreover, we have seen that Gadamer's approach to aesthetic consciousness, while helpfully spelling out the problems inherent in a model of aesthetic immediacy, at the same time overlooks the philosophical complexity of the romantic paradigm. This generates an important question with regard to Gadamer's interpretation of Schleiermacher. For if Gadamer, first, fails to do justice to Kant and post-Kantian aesthetics, and if he, second, reads Schleiermacher along the lines of a romanticized Kantianism, then one ought to ask whether perhaps his understanding of Schleiermacher is biased in the same way.

As mentioned at the beginning of this chapter, Gadamer limits his discussion of Schleiermacher's hermeneutics to the technical aspect of interpretation, which he takes to represent an inadequate, aestheticized hermeneutics. This is the critical gist of his reading of early nineteenth-century hermeneutics, what makes him assume, first, that individuality is, by definition, aesthetic individuality, and second, that the only alternative to a Hegelian–Gadamerian model of historical integration is an unhappy combination of aestheticism and strict hermeneutic proceduralism. But, we need to ask, is Gadamer justified in detaching the technical or psychological aspect of interpretation from its grammatical counterpart?

According to Schleiermacher, the critical standards of technical and grammatical interpretation should be treated together. They constitute two inseparable aspects of the hermeneutic practice, neither of which "can be completed by itself" (*HK,* 68; *HKi,* 56). Each "operation presupposes the other," as he puts it (*HK*, 69; *HKi*, 56). Moreover, the double structure of Schleiermacher's hermeneutic standards is not arbitrarily stipulated, but responds to the nature of language itself. Language only exists as a concrete – and individual – application of general linguistic resources.

Schleiermacher's discussion of individuality moves simultaneously on at least two levels. He often refers to the tension between linguistic rules and grammar, on the one hand, and individual applications of these conventional resources, on the other. In other places, however, he considers how a given symbolic convention actualizes itself as an individual; that is, how, say, one linguistic or cultural subgroup relates to the predominant language and culture of its time. There is no need to focus on one of these dimensions at the expense of the other. Rather, the notion of technical interpretation should be viewed as a flexible lens that, on various levels of analysis, centers on the individuality inherent in symbolic performance. Of importance here is the idea that the individual aspect of language – whether conceived in terms of a given individual's use of language or in terms of a given linguistic unity (as compared with other linguistic unities) – cannot be formalized or rendered in the form of subsumptive categories. There can, as Schleiermacher puts it, be no "concept of a style" (*HC*, 96; *HuK*, 172).

The extent to which language is used in an individual way varies with genre and convention. In scientific uses of language, the need for an individualized application of shared linguistic resources is typically minimized. In poetry and literature, however, the situation is different. Here, individual use of language is essential to the genre as such. Nonetheless, even poetic expression depends on linguistic convention. In the same way, no scientific discourse is entirely free of individual elements. The individual and the general aspects of language have no existence on their own, but mutually co-determine one another.[16] The task of the critical interpreter is to figure out to what

---

16 Frank expounds on Schleiermacher's idea of language (and reason) as an individual universal by claiming that "The allegedly universal character of the one rationality reveals itself as an *individual-universal*. That is to say, universal in so far as it still ensures social intercourse and human communication, and thereby the possibility of intersubjectively valid rules of thought, action and speech. But it is also individual as far as this universality is no longer based on a logical a priori, but is founded on synthetic interpretations of the world undertaken by individuals transcending their own identity in future-oriented projections. It is thus the individual who makes possible the intersubjectivity of meanings

extent the text (or utterance) is dominated by individuality or by the general structures of language, and then move onward from there.

Insofar as technical interpretation is oriented towards the style of the text, it being a unique application of the shared linguistic and cultural resources available to the author, it is not, as Gadamer argues, aimed at the subjective intention or unity existing prior to, independent of, or behind language. In Schleiermacher's hermeneutics, this aspect of interpretation investigates the author's way of maneuvering within language and ultimately also within his or her own culture. (This is an aspect of Schleiermacher's philosophy, his expressivism, to which I return in Chapter 6.) According to Schleiermacher, "[t]here is nothing in style but composition and treatment of language" (*HC*, 97; *HuK*, 174).

Schleiermacher's point may be elucidated by means of a few examples. If one is interested in, say, late eighteenth-century German poetry, then an inquiry into the "composition and treatment of language" would deal with the features that set Goethe's poetry apart from that of Hölderlin or Tieck, while also keeping an eye on the shared culture of these and other writers and artists. Turning to twentieth-century Austrian literature, a scholar who is interested in the critical-political thrust of Thomas Bernhard's novels would do well to consult, say, the work of Ingeborg Bachmann, but also texts by Robert Musil, Hermann Broch, Karl Kraus, and Elias Canetti. Or, just to mention an example from philosophy, with regard to the theory of the Scottish Enlightenment, the interpreter would have to reflect on how figures such as Hume, Kames, Hutcheson, Smith, and Ferguson all respond to the same intellectual and historical environment and yet do so in different ways. Hence the explanation of, say, a (for the modern reader) seemingly strange term or apparent contradiction in a text by Smith could be illuminated by referring to the work of contemporary theorists or questions that were debated at the time. Contrary to the view that Gadamer ascribes to Schleiermacher, individuality does not refer to something inner, pre-linguistic, pre-cultural, or pre-cognitive, but is concerned with the way in which ideas

exchanged in communicative acts, while at the same time preventing the given communicative system from becoming truly universal, in the sense that all meaning would become strictly determined and exhaustively definable." Manfred Frank, "Two Centuries of Philosophical Critique of Reason," in *Reason and its Other*, trans. and ed. D. Freundlieb and W. Hudson (Oxford: Berg, 1993), 74f. I return to Frank's reading of Schleiermacher's hermeneutics in Chapter 6.

are historically mediated and modified through the universal media of language and culture.

Method reassessed

Along with the romantic concept of individuality, Gadamer criticizes what he takes to be Schleiermacher's notion of an immediate re-creation (divination) and his reference to a hermeneutic method. Is, then, this criticism more promising than Gadamer's reading of the normative-methodological standards of technical and grammatical interpretation?

In Schleiermacher's work, the concept of divination does not refer to an aestheticizing or quasi-mystical faculty. Divination is best described as a creative hypothesis-making about the meaning of a text or passage. The initial hypothesis is revised or confirmed through a process of comparison with other passages and texts by the same author or with works by other writers from the same culture and period. Divination and comparison are both necessary aspects of interpretation. There is, in Schleiermacher's hermeneutics, no such thing as an understanding based on divination alone. Only by drawing on the potential of comparison, through historical and philological work as well as creative hypothesis-making, can the interpreter succeed. Grammatical and technical interpretation, comparison, and divination are four closely related aspects of interpretation, the marks of a critically reflected, as opposed to an unreflected, lax hermeneutical practice.

To Gadamer, however, this appears as a problematic hermeneutic method, the dream of a totally transparent and identity-positing rationality that, as we have seen, he brushes off as the "Cartesian basis" of enlightenment philosophy (*TM*, 461; *WM*, 465). Nothing of this sort can be attributed to Schleiermacher. The reflected hermeneutic practice does not subsume what is unique under some higher universal; it does not level differences, nor erase distinctions. Quite the contrary, the critical norms of technical and grammatical interpretation are designed to ensure a context-sensitive and detailed reading of the texts of the past, whether artistic or philosophical. From this point of view it is, rather, Gadamer's idea of a continuous, self-mediating classical work, in the face of which the interpreter surrenders his or her critical-reflective capacities, that threatens to reduce historical difference and diversity to an undifferentiated, idealist notion of tradition.

Furthermore, Schleiermacher's notion of universal hermeneutics promises no final interpretation of the text but furnishes the interpreter with a regulative idea, a counterfactual conception of what it would mean to understand a given text or utterance as a unique manifestation of its language and culture. This is not something at which the interpreter can hope to arrive at the end of a successfully conducted interpretation. Rather, it is something that, being situated within a historical life-world that possibly differs from the one of the text and its original audience, we perpetually strive for. Like Gadamer, Schleiermacher studied ancient dialectics, and, for him, hermeneutics is an endless task – a process that, to borrow a point from Gadamer's reading of Plato, unfolds in the mode of a Socratic *docta ignorantia*. Technical as well as grammatical interpretation, Schleiermacher insists, can only "be reached by approximation ['durch Annäherung']" (*HC*, 96; *HuK*, 172). Hence "[t]he hermeneutic rules must be more a method of pre-empting [*zuvorzukommen*] difficulties than observations for dissolving [*aufzulösen*] those difficulties" (*HC*, 14; *HuK*, 84).[17]

Yet again Gadamer's critique is based on untenable assumptions. He reasons that because Schleiermacher does not subscribe to a quasi-Hegelian or Heideggerian paradigm of integration and self-understanding (of the kind that Gadamer recommends), he necessarily falls prey to the most naïve variety of hermeneutic proceduralism. But Schleiermacher's appeal to normative standards in interpretation cannot be placed within such a dualistic schema. Instead, he points out a third way in hermeneutics. Hermeneutics, in his account, is not a formal methodological approach in the sense that it mechanically applies pre-existing rules to a given empirical material. Rather, hermeneutics requires an element of tact and *Fingerspitzengefühl*,

---

17 As emphasized by Thomas Seebohm, Schleiermacher here claims, following Wolf and Boeckh, that a hermeneutic "method can only discover error. It is not a method for discovering the 'true' interpretation once and for all." Thomas Seebohm, *Hermeneutics: Method and Methodology* (Dordrecht: Kluwer Publishers, 2004), 54. Or, also, "[the] idea of methodology is *not* Cartesian. The Cartesian idea, which also dominated the Enlightenment and later empiricist methodologies, was that reflections on the method and limits of reason have to precede all investigations. But in the new science of classical antiquity method is not understood in the same way as method was understood in the Cartesian tradition, i.e., its task is not to discover truth, but to establish a system of rules to avoid error, as well as to determine the limits of method. This conception of method has some affinities with Kant's conception of the method of the empirical sciences. In its essence it is not a search for first, indubitable principles, but is guided by the pragmatic spirit of methodological reflections about the pre-given needs and interests of positive research." Ibid., 51.

which is why it is described as an art (*Kunst*) in the first place.[18]
Furthermore, hermeneutics is not about *Dasein*'s existential self-
appropriation of tradition. From Schleiermacher's point of view,
integrating the understanding of the other into a hermeneutic model
of existential self-understanding would threaten to collapse the distinction between self and other, hence filtering, in Hegel's language,
the voices of the past through the horizon of the present. Schleiermacher insists that only to the extent that the interpreter acknowledges how the past differs from the present can he or she critically
scrutinize the validity of his or her own prejudices. Does this then
mean, as Gadamer claims, that Schleiermacher does not acknowledge
the productivity of tradition and that he proposes, against the thrust
of Gadamer's argument, that understanding is always understanding
of the same (i.e., that it involves no element of application)? To a
certain extent it does. According to Schleiermacher, there is, hypo-
thetically, an interpretation or a set of interpretations that would get
things right. Understanding is not a question of understanding differently, but of understanding correctly. Some interpretations are
better than others. However, because the interpreter is always situated
within his or her own historical culture, he or she does not have direct
access to a conclusive interpretation. This does not imply that the
interpreter should let go of all normativity or the aspiration to reach
an adequate understanding. Nor does it force him or her to ignore
the historicity of his or her own existence or ignore the historical
being of the text as it is passed down to him or her through the
mediating work of tradition. Rather, it is precisely because the interpreter is a historical creature and because the text itself is a historical
expression that the regulative-methodological ideals of technical and
grammatical understanding are called for.

---

18 Schleiermacher discusses the nature of rules with regard to the very activity of interpretation and claims that understanding is an art in the sense that "Art is that for which
there admittedly are rules, but the combinatory application of these rules cannot in turn
be rule-bound" (*HC*, 229; *HV*, 1273). It is hermeneutics' status as an art that makes it a
philosophical discipline: "hermeneutics is to be thought of as connected to art and is
therefore philosophical" (*HC*, 7; *HuK*, 76). The understanding of hermeneutics as an art
(and thus as philosophical) should therefore not be contrasted with the idea of an
argumentatively clear or logical stringent analysis, but with the idea of a mechanical
application of rules. Schleiermacher also speaks of philosophy as an art and, again, links
this up with the problem of rule application: "Doing philosophy is an art [*Kunst*], because
the application of rules cannot in turn be brought under the rules. Rather, such application depends on disposition and talent" (*Di*, 62; *D*, 50; see also *Di*, 3f; *D*, 4).

To summarize the discussion so far, one might say that Gadamer, in analyzing Schleiermacher's idea of a stricter hermeneutic practice, is right in pointing out that early nineteenth-century hermeneutics does not deal with the truth-happening in the encounter with the past. In Schleiermacher's philosophy, dialectics,[19] which he, in alignment with Plato's definition, understands as the art of carrying on a conversation ("als Kunst der Gesprächführung"), is oriented towards the truth of a given claim, but this is not truth in Gadamer's meaning of the term, that is, truth as world-disclosure. (I return to this point in Chapter 6.)[20] Although dialectics is connected with the process of understanding – hermeneutics is a condition of possibility for dialectics[21] – the two do not overlap. Moreover, Gadamer is correct in claiming that Schleiermacher does not consider, as part of his hermeneutics, the significance of historical texts for human self-understanding at large. His hermeneutics does not ask how the eminent texts of tradition are made available to us through a continuous process of historical mediation.[22] It is not directed towards a full account of our historical being-in-the-world and holds no ontological aspirations of the Heideggerian variety. Rather, it is a philosophy that asks how the interpreter may strive to overcome his or her prejudices by means of the methodologically oriented, historical-philological work that hermeneutics, in Schleiermacher's understanding, is all about.

Hence Gadamer is not right in reducing the reference to a standard of validity in interpretation to a quasi-Cartesian, formalist type of rationality. Nor is he right in claiming that the reference to individuality is simply another configuration of aesthetic consciousness.

---

19 Christian Berner explains: "Il est indéniable que l'herméneutique n'établit pas la vérité. Ce qui ne signifie pas qu'elle n'ait aucune prétention à la vérité: la vérité qu'elle vise est celle du sens. Elle veut dégager le sens vrai, le sens objectif, correct et juste d'un discours et c'est par là qu'elle participe au mouvement de la vérité." Christian Berner, La philosophie de Schleiermacher (Paris: Les Éditions du Cerf, 1995), 80f.

20 Friedrich Schleiermacher, Dialektik, ed. Rudolf Odebrecht (Darmstadt: Wissenschaftliche Buchgesellschaft, 1988), 47f.

21 Because it is oriented towards the meaning of an utterance, hermeneutics establishes a "condition de possibilité de la dialectique." Berner, La philosophie de Schleiermacher, 81.

22 This is not to say that such reflections are absent from Schleiermacher's work. According to Gunter Scholtz, "Schleiermacher hatte das Problem der Philosophiegeschichtsschreibung im Zirkel von Philosophie und dem Verstehen ihrer Geschichte gesehen: 'wer die Geschichte der Philosophie vorträgt, muß die Philosophie besizen, . . .und wer die Philosophie besizen will, muß sie historisch verstehen.'" Gunter Scholtz, Ethik und Hermeneutik. Schleiermachers Grundlegung der Geisteswissenschaften (Frankfurt am Main: Suhrkamp Verlag, 1995), 290.

I return to these points in Chapter 6. However, in order to do justice to Gadamer's reading of romantic hermeneutics, it is necessary first to consider how his criticism of Schleiermacher gets modified throughout the late 1960s and 1970s.

Gadamer's modified position

Gadamer's reading of early nineteenth-century hermeneutics in *Truth and Method* is indebted to the late Dilthey's interpretation of Schleiermacher. This interpretation was brought into question by the publication of some earlier manuscripts in which Dilthey emphasizes Schleiermacher's affiliation with the objective idealists, thereby casting doubt on the image of romantic hermeneutics as a psychologist or subjectivist model of interpretation. Informed by this discovery, Gadamer's student Heinz Kimmerle put together a new edition of Schleiermacher's handwritten manuscripts, aiming to show that he initially defended an almost Gadamerian notion of the intertwining of thought and language. However, in Kimmerle's interpretation, this early, almost Gadamerian hermeneutics was later overshadowed by a more problematic orientation towards the inner, emotional states of the writer, i.e., by Schleiermacher as Gadamer knows him.[23] Although Kimmerle's organization of Schleiermacher's manuscripts was later subjected to criticism,[24] the emphasis on the non-psychological aspects of romantic hermeneutics forced Gadamer to reconsider some aspects of his reading.

In the 1972 edition of *Truth and Method*, Gadamer admits that he had reviewed the history of hermeneutics "essentially for the preparatory purpose of filling in the background [of Heidegger's and his

---

23 According to Kimmerle, Schleiermacher's hermeneutics achieves its impact mainly through Dilthey. However, Dilthey's account was not based on Schleiermacher's own manuscripts, but on Lücke's edition, which, as mentioned, also incorporated student annotations. By returning to the handwritten manuscripts, Kimmerle intended to show that "Dilthey's interpretation holds at best for the very latest conception of Schleiermacher, as it is stated in the introduction of the 1819 manuscript and is then carried through in the 1829 Addresses to the Academy and in the final lectures of 1832–33." Heinz Kimmerle, "Introduction," *HK*, 27; "Einleitung," *HKi*, 14.

24 Wolfgang Virmond argues that a part of Schleiermacher's handwritten manuscript that Kimmerle (following Dilthey) places among the later works belongs to the early period, which, in turn, indicates a larger degree of coherence within Schleiermacher's hermeneutics. See Wolfgang Virmond, "Neue Textgrundlagen zu Schleiermachers früher Hermeneutik. Prolegomena zur kritischen Edition," *Schleiermacher-Archiv*, vol. I, 578ff.

own hermeneutics]" (*TM*, 564; *WM*, vol. II, 462). Consequently, his presentation "displays a certain one-sidedness" (ibid.). This one-sidedness, Gadamer continues, led him to overlook Schleiermacher's "discussion of the connection between thought and speaking" (*TM*, 564; *WM*, vol. II, 463). Moreover, while acknowledging the relation between thought and language in Schleiermacher's hermeneutics, Gadamer grants that he may have "overemphasized Schleiermacher's tendency towards psychological (technical) interpretation rather than grammatical-linguistic interpretation" (*TM*, 565; *WM*, vol. II, 464). Yet Gadamer maintains that psychological or technical interpretation is Schleiermacher's "peculiar contribution ['sein eigenster Beitrag']" (ibid.). Failing to specify which notion of technical interpretation he is referring to, Gadamer's claim is not particularly helpful. Is he thinking of the psychological interpretation he had criticized in the 1960 edition of *Truth and Method*? Or does he have in mind a linguistically modified conception of individuality that, along the lines of the 1972 revision of his criticism, traces the individuality of the text back to a particular language-use within a historically mediated culture? Gadamer offers no answer to these questions. In order to illuminate the extent of his revisions, one therefore must consult two earlier essays, "The Problem of Language in Schleiermacher's Hermeneutics" (1968) and "Schleiermacher als Platoniker" (1969).[25] The first of these essays is particularly relevant in this context.

In "The Problem of Language in Schleiermacher's Hermeneutics," Gadamer acknowledges that "for Schleiermacher the problem of language is completely central"[26] and that technical interpretation is oriented towards the specific linguistic style of a given text rather than the subjective intentions of its author. This focus on the individuality of language, Gadamer continues, is balanced by grammatical interpretation, and from the perspective of grammatical interpretation "what is to be understood is something universal and communal."[27] As Gadamer now reads Schleiermacher, his hermeneutics seeks to grasp the

---

25 "The Problem of Language in Schleiermacher's Hermeneutics," trans. David E. Linge, in Robert W. Funk (ed.), *Schleiermacher as Contemporary: Journal for Theology and the Church*, vol. VII (New York: Herder & Herder, 1970), 68–84; "Das Problem der Sprache bei Schleiermacher," *GW*, vol. IV, 361–373. "Schleiermacher als Platoniker" has not been translated into English. The German edition is published in ibid., 374–383.

26 "The Problem of Language in Schleiermacher's Hermeneutics," 68; "Das Problem der Sprache bei Schleiermacher," 361.

27 Ibid., 82; ibid., 372.

particular way in which the text balances "between individual-different production and identical convention."[28] However, even though Gadamer is at this point willing to grant that Schleiermacher's concept of individuality does not depend on the idea of a subjectivist intention or psychological content, but is a matter of meaning understood in light of language-use, he maintains that "grammatical interpretation remains nearer the center of hermeneutics."[29]

Hence we are left with the following picture. If Gadamer, after *Truth and Method*, offers a more plausible reading of Schleiermacher's hermeneutics, the aspects of nineteenth-century hermeneutics that he acknowledges are only those that in his view anticipate his own conception of *Dasein*'s being-in-the-world. Furthermore, he continues to emphasize, depending on the context, *either* technical *or* grammatical interpretation, whereas Schleiermacher would claim that both these aspects of hermeneutics are equally needed. Just as Gadamer fails to engage the hermeneutic potential of Kant's notion of natural beauty, just as he fails to consider the complexity of romantic aesthetics, and just as he fails to take seriously Hegel's reflections on objectivity in historical research, his reading of Schleiermacher systematically omits those aspects of nineteenth-century hermeneutics that would have challenged the orientation of the ontological turn in hermeneutics – such as the emphasis on the possible otherness of the text and the idea of standards of validity in interpretation.

Preparing the grounds for his own ontological turn in hermeneutics, Gadamer's critique of Schleiermacher is at best hyperbolic. At worst, it is plainly wrong. The question I would now like to raise is therefore how we, as readers of early nineteenth-century hermeneutics, should respond to Gadamer's criticism. Should we simply dismiss this critique altogether and follow Gianni Vattimo in arguing that aesthetic consciousness "must be rescued from this [Gadamer's] critique and reevaluated"?[30] In my view, this is not a tenable solution. Rather than leaving behind Gadamer's analysis of the problem of immediacy in aesthetics, which, after all, is one of the convincing aspects of his critique of post-Kantian philosophy, one ought to ask why it is that Gadamer over-generalizes the picture of aesthetic

---

28 Ibid., 72; ibid., 364, trans. modified.   29 Ibid., 83; ibid., 372.
30 Gianni Vattimo, "Hermeneutics and Nihilism: An Apology for Aesthetic Consciousness," in Brice R. Wachterhauser (ed.), *Hermeneutics and Modern Philosophy* (Albany, N.Y.: SUNY Press, 1986), 447.

consciousness and naïve objectivism in early nineteenth-century reflections on the humanities, so that in his reading of Schleiermacher he ends up criticizing a straw-man rather than philosophically engaging the position at stake.

Aesthetic and political humanism

In the 1930s, when Gadamer started working on *Truth and Method*, his aim was not to produce a study of hermeneutics.[31] To the young Gadamer, art was what mattered. At the time when Heidegger addressed the modern predicament of art in his *Ursprung des Kunstwerkes*, Gadamer wished to show that "art can convey truth and therefore form public opinion." Humanism, he claims, has become stifling and irrelevant. It has lost touch with the spirit of the classical tradition and its emphasis on judgment, *sensus communis*, tact, and the relation between taste and morality. We no longer relate to the past as a living and integrated dimension of the present. The past is aestheticized, and the experience of traditional works of art means no more than an occasion for instant, passing pleasure. No self-understanding is involved. No world-disclosive truth is at stake in this experience. Instead, we see a construction of objectivity along the lines of a formalistic methodology. This was a situation in which the humanities were ridden with a harmful combination of romanticism and positivism, and Gadamer, in the 1930s, was prepared to take up the challenge.

When he criticized the aesthetic attitude of the 1930s, Gadamer did not seek to abandon humanism as such. Against the aesthetic humanism of the time he musters a political humanism. Gadamer never offers a definition of political humanism. Yet he makes it clear that a political humanism would take into account the importance of art and tradition, and how our historical being in the world is acted out in our engagement with the classical works of the past. This political humanism, although rarely noted by his commentators, is the driving force of Gadamer's work in the period when the bulk of *Truth and Method* is drafted and also in his later work, especially the essays on art.

---

31 While the term "hermeneutics," not to mention "philosophical hermeneutics," was somewhat unusual at the time, Gadamer initially speaks about his project under the rubric of "Art and History." Grondin, *Hans-Georg Gadamer*, 207ff.

Jürgen Habermas is one of the few to have paid attention to Gadamer's political humanism.[32] In his portrait of Gadamer, in *Political-Philosophical Profiles*, Habermas stages a contrast between Heidegger's allegedly more rural sensitivities and Gadamer's "urbanizing of the Heideggerian province."[33] Although there are obvious differences between the two philosophers – some of them deriving from Gadamer's affinities with the classicist environment in Germany, others from his reading of Hegel – it is important to see that they cannot be explained in light of Gadamer's appeal to a political humanism.[34] Gadamer's political humanism is precisely where he is at his most Heideggerian, even though humanism, as such, is not a term that Heidegger himself would use to describe the project of fundamental ontology.

When addressing Heidegger's importance for the development of twentieth-century hermeneutics, one often rushes to mention his magnum opus of the early years, *Being and Time*. It is in *Being and Time* that Heidegger speaks of hermeneutics as an "interpretation of *Dasein*'s Being" and of the methodology of the human sciences as hermeneutics only in a "derivative sense" (*BT; SZ*, §7, 38). It is here that he notices the circular structure of understanding. Only by presupposing its average self-understanding can *Dasein*'s being be ontologically analyzed (*BT; SZ*, §2, 8), which means that the apparent circle in reality is "a

---

32 Another exception is Robert R. Sullivan, who writes in his introduction to *Philosophical Apprenticeships*, that "Philosophical hermeneutics was first of all a different way of doing politics." "Translator's Introduction," *Philosophical Apprenticeships*, trans. Robert R. Sullivan (Cambridge, Mass.: MIT Press, 1985), xvi.

33 "Hans-Georg Gadamer: Urbanizing the Heideggerian Province," in Habermas, *Philosophical-Political Profiles*, 196f.; "Hans-Georg Gadamer: Urbanisierung der Heideggerschen Provinz," in Habermas, *Philosophisch-politische Profile*, 400f.

34 Habermas claims that Gadamer's hermeneutics "contrasts in the most remarkable way with Heidegger's lordly destruction of Western thought, with the project that devalues the history of philosophy from Plato through Thomas down to Descartes and Hegel as the drama of a mounting forgetfulness of being. Can a more stark contrast be imagined than that between his turn away from every articulate figure of the tradition in the interest of a mysticism of being and Gadamer's quest to renew the humanistic tradition. . .in terms of such key concepts as cultural formation, common sense, judgment, and taste?" "Hans-Georg Gadamer: Urbanizing the Heideggerian Province," 194; "Hans-Georg Gadamer: Urbanisierung der Heideggerschen Provinz," 397. A similar point of view can be found in Robert R. Sullivan's introduction to the English translation of *Philosophical Apprenticeships*, where it is claimed that "Heidegger's contribution to Gadamer's thinking was mainly negative: It helped push the young Gadamer away from the dominant Western philosophical tradition." "Translator's Introduction," *Philosophical Apprenticeships*, x, and in Jean Grondin's proposal that "To put it bluntly, Gadamer is a humanist and Heidegger isn't." Jean Grondin, "Gadamer on Humanism," *LLP*, 157.

remarkable 'relatedness backward or forward' which what we are asking about (Being) bears to the inquiry itself as a mode of Being of an entity" (ibid.). Finally, it is in *Being and Time* that Heidegger delivers his famous critique of Dilthey, claiming that in Dilthey's hermeneutics "everything centers in psychology" (*BT; SZ*, §77, 398), so that he (Dilthey) is almost bound to miss "the authentic disclosedness ('truth') of historical existence ['die eigentliche Erschlossenheit ("Wahrheit") der geschichtlichen Existenz']" (*BT; SZ*, §76, 397).

In *Truth and Method*, Gadamer explicitly claims that Heidegger's philosophy sets up the standards (*Maß*) by which he "desires to be measured" (*TM*, xxv; *WM*, 5), and that the encounter with the young Heidegger came to determine the path of his own thinking. Hence, in order to spell out the hermeneutic import of Heidegger's philosophy, one ought not only to look at *Being and Time*, but also to return to the period before he published this work. Especially relevant in this context is Heidegger's teaching of Aristotle from the early 1920s, which Gadamer himself singles out as the most important intellectual experience of his youth[35] and claims that he was "later to justify in theory and to represent ['theoretisch rechtfertigen und vertreten']."[36]

Throughout the 1920s, Heidegger infuses his reading of Aristotle with a more general criticism of our relation to history and tradition. In the 1921–22 lecture course *Phenomenological Interpretations of Aristotle*, Heidegger worries that we no longer relate to the tradition as something alive and present. The tradition is perceived as dead and irrelevant, an object to be studied at a disinterested distance. Also in his broader teaching from this period, Heidegger criticizes the human sciences for having lost touch with the question of Being. "The fundamental inadequacy of ontology in the tradition and today," he claims, rests with the fact that "it blocks access to that being [*Seienden*] which is decisive within philosophical problems: namely, *Dasein*, from out of which and for the sake of which, philosophy 'is.'"[37] In failing to address *Dasein*'s being, philosophy is nothing but a "great industry of 'problems.'"[38] This also has implications for philosophy's relation to the past. Tradition is now

---

35 See, again, "Selbstdarstellung Hans-Georg Gadamer," *WM*, vol. II, 485.

36 *Philosophical Apprenticeships*, 49; *Philosophische Lehrjahre*, 216.

37 Martin Heidegger, *Ontology: The Hermeneutics of Facticity*, trans. John van Buren (Bloomington: Indiana University Press, 1999), 2; *Ontologie (Hermeneutik der Faktizität)*, *GA*, vol. LXIII, 3.

38 Ibid., 4; ibid., 5.

approached with "industrious curiosity,"[39] and, worse still, it is not only the past, but life itself that is objectified.[40]

We saw at the beginning of Chapter 1 that Heidegger sets out to amend this situation by proposing that the interpreter should salvagingly destroy the tradition in which he or she stands. This is an effort to rescue the works of the past from the conservative, sometimes even petrifying, tendencies of tradition itself. At stake is a return to the (truth of the) works in themselves.[41] Against the tendency towards dreary and pedantic philology, which risks losing sight of the big questions, Heidegger calls for a direct engagement with historical texts. The historical aspect of philosophy, he claims, "is visible only in the very act of philosophizing. It is graspable only as existence."[42] It is a misunderstanding, he further remarks (referring, again, to Dilthey), "to maintain that we would come to an understanding if we do justice to history in. . .calmness and Objectivity."[43] In his scheme of interpretation, calmness and objectivity are not desirable qualities, but the result of "weakness and indolence."[44] Against this, Heidegger advocates "the intention to *confront*."[45] Only such an intention "has its own radical power of disclosing and illuminating."[46] When relating to the works of the past, what matters is not the historical-philological context in which they were written, but their relevance for us here and now.

---

39 Ibid.
40 *The Hermeneutics of Facticity*, 28f.; *Hermeneutik der Faktizität*, 36. See also Heidegger's critique of Dilthey and Harnack in *The Phenomenology of Religious Life*, trans. Matthias Fritsch and Jennifer Anna Gosetti-Ferencei (Bloomington: Indiana University Press, 2004), 120f.; *Phänomenologie des religiösen Lebens*, ed. Matthias Jung, Thomas Regehly, and Claudius Strube, *GA*, vol. LX (Klostermann: Frankfurt am Main, 1995), 166f.
41 The idea of a phenomenological "destruction," or, as Heidegger initially would say, of a phenomenological *Kritik*, is introduced in 1919. At stake is the effort to trace theoretical constructions back to the less abstract context of the life-world. However, the work of destruction is soon expanded to cover the interpreter's relation to the philosophical tradition. What is to be destroyed – and Heidegger makes this clear already in *Being and Time*, §6 – is not really the texts of tradition as such. Rather, under attack is the traditional *understanding* of these texts, the way in which the interpreter tends to take one or several given interpretations of a work for granted. Hence the aim of the phenomenological destruction is to liberate traditional texts from the tradition itself. This is an activity that aims at making classical texts come closer to the interpreter, to awaken them from the dead, as it were. In Heidegger's words, "to bury the past in nullity [*Nichtigkeit*] is not the purpose of this destruction; its aim is *positive*." *BT*; *SZ*, §6, 23. See also Gadamer's "Reflections on my Philosophical Journey," *LLP*, 24f.
42 Heidegger, *Phenomenological Interpretations of Aristotle*, 3; *Phänomenologische Interpretationen zu Aristoteles*, 1.
43 Ibid., 4; Ibid., 2.   44 Ibid.   45 Ibid.   46 Ibid.

This is the context in which Gadamer's philosophy – and his reconstruction of nineteenth-century hermeneutics – must be placed. Gadamer, too, wants to rescue the past from aestheticizing (or objectivizing) attitudes; he, too, wants us to directly confront the words of the great poets and philosophers. Even his 1931 study of *Philebus*, often mistaken for a non-Heideggerian work, is driven by this ambition. In this work he tried, in his own words, "to lay aside all scholarly knowledge for once and take as [his] point of departure the phenomena [i.e., Plato's dialogues] as they show themselves to us" (*PDE*, xxxii; *PdE*, 161). For should it not, he asks rhetorically, "be possible. . .to see Greek philosophy, Aristotle and Plato, with new eyes – just as Heidegger was able in his lectures on Aristotle to present a completely uncustomary Aristotle, one in whom one rediscovered one's own present-day questions in startlingly concrete form?"[47] This kind of thinking not only characterizes Gadamer's own hermeneutic practice in the 1920s and 1930s, but also his general hermeneutic position – his political humanism – in *Truth and Method* and later works. The greatness of the works of the past, their truth, cannot be acknowledged if we turn them into objects of human studies in the narrow sense of the phrase. Instead, we ought to expose ourselves to their sublime, existential bidding – that is, we ought to let them address us with the authority of the classical.

The detour through the phenomenological-existentialist roots of Gadamer's hermeneutics should put us in a better position to see why Gadamer, for systematic, philosophical reasons, misreads Schleiermacher and continues to do so even after the publication of a philologically sounder edition of his theory of interpretation. What Gadamer wants is not so much to get Schleiermacher right or to ask in what way early romantic theory could challenge the hermeneutic framework that develops in the wake of Heidegger's teaching in the 1920s. His aim, rather, is to explain philosophically how it was that aesthetic humanism, coupled with a naïve belief in methodological proceduralism, came about, so that he, having analyzed its historical roots and contemporary symptoms, can prescribe the right cure. Within this project, Schleiermacher, furbishing German Idealism with

47 "Sollte es nicht auch mir möglich sein, die griechische Philosophie, Aristoteles und Plato mit neuen Augen zu sehen – so wie Heidegger in seinen Aristoteles-Vorlesungen einen ganz ungewohnten Aristoteles vorzuführen wußte, in dem man die eigenen Fragen der Gegenwart in überraschender Konkretion wiederfand?" *PDE*, xxxii; *PdE*, 161.

a hermeneutic theory, emerges as a crucial player. There is, in other words, nothing arbitrary about Gadamer's misreading of Schleiermacher. It is not as if Gadamer's misunderstanding of Schleiermacher is just an unfortunate accident, and that he, in this case, happens to be a bad advocate for a hermeneutic theory that is itself in good shape. Rather, in Gadamer's hermeneutics the questions of validity, philological justification, and historical truthfulness are sublated into the understanding of truth in terms of authenticity and self-understanding. It does not really matter to Gadamer whether he gets Schleiermacher right or not. What concerns him is to make us understand the alienation from history that marks our modern predicament and that leaves us with an impoverished, inauthentic existence.

To what extent, then, does Schleiermacher, in his turn to a notion of validity in interpretation, present us with a better hermeneutic model than Gadamer's own, or at least a model in light of which Gadamer's ontological hermeneutics can be amended? This is the question to which I will turn, first, in the final section of this chapter and then in the concluding Chapter 6.

Hermeneutics and the challenge of political humanism

In this chapter, I have argued that Schleiermacher's philosophy cannot be placed within the categories of naïve, aesthetic humanism or an equally naïve methodological proceduralism. This is not to say, however, that he follows Gadamer in conducting an ontological turn in hermeneutics. Instead, the example of Schleiermacher's hermeneutics illustrates that the call for a critique of aesthetic humanism and positivism in hermeneutics does not necessarily lead to a position of the kind that Gadamer is defending. On the contrary, from the point of view of Schleiermacher's theory of interpretation, it would be reasonable to worry that Gadamer's own existential-ontological turn fails to overcome the fallacies of aesthetic humanism. Rather than getting beyond the alleged aesthetic paradigm of early nineteenth-century theories of interpretation, Gadamer's hermeneutics, given the way it locates art at the heart of understanding, risks representing a reinforced, ontologized version of aesthetic humanism – one that is at least as problematic as the one he initially wanted to overcome.

When Gadamer criticizes aesthetic humanism, he is mainly concerned with its reduction of the experience of the truth of art to a question of subjective feeling. Truth and knowledge are not given any role to play within the sphere of art and artistic experience. Against this, Gadamer emphasizes the artwork's capacity for world-disclosure and its ability to present us with the truth about our own being (as finite, historical creatures) and hence trigger a potentially more authentic and fulfilling existence. The truth of art is a momentary flash of self-understanding, an epiphany in which we all of a sudden see the power of the tradition in which we are situated and recollect, in a quasi-Platonic sense, what we already knew but did not reflectively possess.[48] This is what Gadamer has in mind when describing understanding as an "event of being [*Seinsvorgang*]" or simply an event (*Geschehen*) (*TM*, 144; *WM*, 148, see also *TM*, 309; *WM*, 314). The idea of such an event makes up the fabric of Gadamer's so-called political humanism. At stake is an account of the humanities that, while wanting to move beyond the call for a formal method, returns to art's capacity to stage a world-disclosive awakening in which not just the given, historical work, but the entire relationship between the interpreter and the tradition in which he or she is situated is experienced in a new and more truthful manner. When authentic-ally perceived, the interpreter does not stand towards tradition as a subject towards an object. On the contrary, this way of perceiving the hermeneutic situation is the very root of the problem pertaining to the modern philosophy of interpretation. The proper hermeneutic experience allows the interpreter to encounter a totality that is stronger than him- or herself, a totality that he or she cannot reflectively master or objectify, but only deal with to the extent that he or she participates in and subjects him- or herself to the truth of tradition. Gadamer, as we have seen, expands on this experience by exploring the metaphor of games and game-playing, which he retrieves from the Kantian–Schillerian tradition and reformulates in deliberately religious terms.[49] The game-playing involved in our encounter with tradition is not about exercising critical reflection or judgment. It is, rather, about the transformative experience of self-forgetfulness and belonging. This belonging of the interpreter to his or her tradition is so strongly emphasized that Gadamer, even in texts that are written well after the Second World War, is comfortable

---

48 For an elaboration of this point, see "Reflections on my Philosophical Journey," *LLP*, 24.
49 For a discussion of this aspect of Kant's Critique, see Henrich, "Kant's Explanation of Aesthetic Judgment," *Aesthetic Judgment*, 52f. See also Allison, *Kant's Theory of Taste*, 98–119. For Schiller's critique of Kant, see Beiser, *Schiller as Philosopher*, 169–190.

with calling for a rehabilitation of the aesthetic-philosophical relevance of the notion of *Volk*.[50]

Whereas Gadamer accuses the romantics of taking over a Kantian theory of genius (without seeing how genius, for Kant, is closely related to taste), he himself, at least when judged from a perspective like that of Schleiermacher, falls prey to a similar fallacy, except that genius is no longer linked up with the individual's capacity for transcending aesthetic rules and conventions, but with tradition itself. The experience of tradition is all about being played (*TM*, 104, 109; *WM*, 110, 115), "carried away" (*TM*, 125; *WM*, 130), and subject to "ecstatic self-forgetfulness ['ekstatischen Selbstvergessenheit']" (*TM*, 128; *WM*,

---

50 As late as in 1966, Gadamer writes that "we cannot deny that the idea of art being bound to a people ['(die) Rede von der volksverbundenen Kunst'] involves a real insight ['auf etwas Wirkliches hinweist']." "The Universality of the Hermeneutical Problem," *PH*, 5; "Die Universalität des hermeneutischen Problems," *WM*, vol. II, 221. In his previous work, Gadamer had been appealing to the notion of *Volk* in a problematic manner. In 1941, he lectures on Herder for a group of imprisoned French officers in Paris. In the German translation of this lecture, he starts out by claiming that Herder is one of the greatest European voices brought forth by Germany. Gadamer, *Volk und Geschichte im Denken Herders* (Frankfurt am Main: Vittorio Klostermann, 1942), 5. Furthermore, Gadamer emphasizes Herder's critique of French culture. This critique is not explained in light of Herder's questioning of classicist aesthetics. Rather, Gadamer argues that Herder could only develop an adequate notion of the German people and state by breaking with the historical and cultural standards of the French (ibid.). Prescribing a way beyond the twin fallacies of abstract enlightenment and subjectivist romanticism, Herder turns to historical meaning (ibid., 10). However, as Gadamer retrieves this notion of Herder's, historical reality is but the work of powers (*Kräften*) (ibid., 15). Reflecting on how these powers branch off into different cultures and peoples, Herder came to provide the nascent East European nations with a notion of national self-understanding. Yet, Gadamer goes on, these countries did not realize the full potential of Herder's thinking. Hence they missed the way in which the German notion of *Volk* offers a promising alternative to the democratic paroles of the West. (The full quotation goes:"Dies unpolitische Erahnen und Vorbereiten des Kommenden war überhaupt das deutsche Schicksal seiner Epoche, und vielleicht ist das Schicksal solcher politischen Verspätung die Voraussetzung dafür, daß der deutsche Begriff des Volkes im Unterschied zu den demokratischen Parolen des Westens in einer veränderten Gegenwart die Kraft zu neuer politischer und sozialer Ordnung erweist" (ibid., 23).) According to the Gadamer of the early 1940s, the political-philosophical legacy of Herder consists in making us see the contrast between the democratic paroles of the West and the true politics of power, *Volk*, and nation-building. In spite of Gadamer later describing the Herder text as "a purely scholarly study" (*Philosophical Apprenticeships*, 99; *Philosophische Lehrjahre*, 118), he publishes, in 1967, a revised version of this early encounter with Herder. For the edited version of the text, see Gadamer, "Herder und die geschichtliche Welt," *GW*, vol. IV, 318–335. I discuss Gadamer's reading of Herder in "Aesthetic and Political Humanism: Gadamer on Herder, Schleiermacher, and the Origins of Modern Hermeneutics," *History of Philosophy Quarterly*, vol. 24, no. 3 (July 2007), 275–297.

133). A critical-reflective attitude, appealing to standards of validity in interpretation, would be impossible within the political humanism that Gadamer espouses.

Against this, Schleiermacher and the tradition of early nineteenth-century hermeneutics represent a more promising alternative. Unlike what Gadamer claims, their call for critical standards of validity in interpretation is not rooted in a rejection of the interpreter's situatedness in history. Quite the contrary, according to Schleiermacher it is precisely because the interpreter is a historically situated being that he or she needs to be able to appeal to a set of hermeneutic standards and reflective procedures in light of which he or she can critically assess his or her engagement with the past. (I return to this point in the next chapter.) Nor does Schleiermacher appeal to a naïve methodology that culminates in immediate congeniality or divination. Rather, the very point that Schleiermacher keeps reiterating is this: the fact that the interpreter is a historical creature, that he or she cannot, as an individual scholar, plausibly hope to reach the one and sole truth about the meaning of a historical text or event, does not mean that we should let go of the aspiration to question the validity of our prejudices and grasp the meaning of the text in its historical context. Prejudices are not true or authoritative simply because they have shaped the horizon of the present. That is, the attempt to understand the historical conditions of the interpreter's horizon is something Schleiermacher would surely encourage. Moreover, he would claim that, more often than not, self-understanding takes place through an encounter with an other. What he would deny, though – and this is *the* main difference between his position and Gadamer's – is that understanding, on a most fundamental level, is about authentic self-understanding or authentically taking over one's own tradition. Understanding, from his point of view, is all about understanding an other – be it another person's speech, a text, or a culture that is geographically, historically, or culturally distant from the interpreter. Only then, when the object of interpretation is understood in this way, can it aid the interpreter in critically questioning his or her own point of view.

For Gadamer, the term political humanism is related to notions of authenticity and a truthful appropriation of the eminent texts of our own tradition.[51] If Schleiermacher were ever to use such a concept, it

---

51 In the Afterword to *Truth and Method*, Gadamer concedes that "What has occupied me for years. . .are the special problems of eminent texts ['die besonderen hermeneutischen Probleme eminenter Texte']" (*TM*, 576; *WM*, vol. II, 475).

would have to be about the effort, aided by the critical standards of technical and grammatical interpretation, not to reduce that which is other to that which is the interpreter's own. This does not mean that the interpreter has to accept as true or binding whatever the other is saying or doing. What it implies, rather, is that he or she must be prepared to search for the rationality of the acts, claims, or expressions he or she faces, asking how they could plausibly make sense within a context that is no longer his or hers.

This, it seems to me, is a much healthier form of humanism (if that is the word we want to use) than the one promoted by Gadamer. Schleiermacher's hermeneutics emphasizes that understanding others is not simply an event into which the interpreter is passively drawn, but a process that requires hard work, critical skills, reflective standards, and a mix of philological-historical knowledge and sympathetic imagination, which he speaks of as divination. Getting rid of inadequate prejudices is no easy project. A rigid method to guarantee the successful outcome of this process does not exist. Yet Schleiermacher would insist that without philological, historical, and critical-reflective standards our understanding of others potentially lapses into a projection of our own ideals onto the other. This is the hermeneutic legacy of German Idealism – and the reason Schleiermacher's line in hermeneutics is deserving of a renaissance within contemporary philosophy and social thought. And it is, finally, why it is necessary, as I have tried to do so far in this study, to unravel the problematic aspects of Gadamer's engagement with the legacy of German Idealism and investigate the way in which his misunderstanding of this tradition in turn affects his own hermeneutic philosophy. In the sixth and final chapter, I round off the discussion of the hermeneutic legacy of German Idealism by showing in more detail how Schleiermacher's hermeneutics points beyond the philosophical limitations of ontological hermeneutics.

6

NORMATIVITY, CRITIQUE, AND REFLECTION: THE HERMENEUTIC LEGACY OF GERMAN IDEALISM

As part of his attempt to revitalize philosophical humanism – to move from an aesthetic to a political humanism – Gadamer advises that hermeneutics, if conceived in a philosophically adequate way, must move beyond a narrow, scientistic understanding of knowledge and truth. He wishes to rehabilitate, at the very core of his philosophy, the idea of truth as transformative world-disclosure, an existential appropriation of the interpreter's historicity and situatedness within tradition. Only thus, he argues, can hermeneutics overcome the idea of the past as dead and irrelevant to the interpreter's present self-understanding and future projections.

Gadamer's hermeneutics presupposes that a theory of interpretation *either* takes the form of naïve scientism *or* takes as its basis the self-transformative, ontological experience of *Dasein*'s being-in-tradition. This sixth and final chapter argues that early nineteenth-century hermeneutics points a way beyond this *tertium non datur*, as it lies behind and motivates Gadamer's philosophical theory of interpretation. In Schleiermacher's work, the ideals of *Bildung*, understanding the other, and critical self-understanding are not contrary to but, rather, issue from a validity-oriented theory of interpretation. Gadamer's model, we have seen, leaves us with no standard in light of which the interpreter can critically assess his or her work and ask whether the voices of the past, in his or her interpretation, really do emerge as more than a mere echo of the interests of the present. Schleiermacher, by contrast, argues that only by committing to critical norms, such as those of technical and grammatical interpretation, can the interpreter reflectively assess the validity of his or her hypotheses and gradually move towards an adequate reconstruction of the meaning of the other. In this reconstruction, the standpoint of the other may serve as a critical corrective to, or genealogical explanation of, the interpreter's own way of thinking, although this is only possible to the extent that he or she maintains a relative distinction between interpretation and application.

When I conclude the discussion of Gadamer and the legacy of German Idealism with a call for a return to Schleiermacher – not just his hermeneutics, but also the broader context in which the hermeneutics belongs: his ethics, dialectics, and aesthetics – this is not in order to claim that Schleiermacher is the only late eighteenth- or early nineteenth-century thinker who develops a hermeneutic theory deserving of a renaissance. Nor do I propose that Schleiermacher is the first to articulate the hermeneutic concerns of this period. Both at the level of hermeneutic vocabulary and with regard to systematic philosophical insights, the young Johann Gottfried Herder, in the 1760s, anticipates a number of points for which Schleiermacher would later be credited.[1] However, given Gadamer's critique in *Truth and Method*, Schleiermacher's theory has come to serve as an emblematic expression of the general misery of hermeneutics in the period between Kant and Hegel. Hence any retrieval of hermeneutics in the era of German Idealism ought to begin with a rehabilitation of Schleiermacher, even if it should not end here, but give rise to a more comprehensive investigation of the work produced by philosophers since Herder, via Kant, the Schlegels, and all the way to Hegel and the von Humboldt brothers.

A proper treatment of the relationship between Schleiermacher's hermeneutics and his epistemology (dialectics), ethics, and aesthetics would have to involve a detailed discussion of the intellectual development, the systematic gains, as well as the broader philosophical presuppositions of his thinking. Such a project necessarily transcends the framework of this final and concluding chapter. Thus, in rounding off the discussion of Gadamer and the legacy of German Idealism, my ambition is only to provide an initial outline, hopefully to be followed up with a book-length study, of the relevance of early

1 For a survey of the affinities between Herder and Schleiermacher's hermeneutics, see Michael Forster, "Friedrich Daniel Ernst Schleiermacher," *The Stanford Encyclopedia of Philosophy* (Winter 2002 Edition), Edward N. Zalta (ed.), http://plato.stanford.edu/archives/win2002/entries/schleiermacher/. I discuss the relationship between Herder and Schleiermacher in "Aesthetic and Political Humanism: Gadamer on Herder, Schleiermacher, and the Origins of Modern Hermeneutics." For this issue, see also Scholtz, *Ethik und Hermeneutik*, 21ff.

nineteenth-century hermeneutics in the era of post-Heideggerian thought. Furthermore, in advocating a return to nineteenth-century hermeneutics my point is not to claim that Schleiermacher's philosophy, embedded as it is within the intellectual frameworks of idealism and romanticism, provides every piece and detail that is needed in order to develop an alternative to philosophical hermeneutics, but that it is representative of a tradition that, having been sidelined by Gadamer and Heidegger, deserves serious reconsideration.

This chapter begins by asking how Schleiermacher's theory provides an alternative to Gadamer's deconstruction of the distinction between hermeneutics and the experience of art. Next, I review the problem of prejudice and the historical situatedness of reason. Against Gadamer's sweeping claim about the forgetfulness of history in post-enlightenment philosophy, I argue that Schleiermacher's hermeneutics is motivated by a wish to show that the capacity the interpreter possesses for critical reflection is located within history. Schleiermacher's 1813 lecture on translation is then the subject of discussion. In this lecture, Schleiermacher develops the notion of an expansion of horizons, albeit one that differs from Gadamer's more existentially motivated model. In order to realize this, however, we need to turn to Schleiermacher's writings in practical philosophy and see how his hermeneutics is connected to the more comprehensive ideals of *Bildung*, sociability, and the progress of reason in history. Finally, the chapter closes by suggesting that Schleiermacher's philosophy points the way to an overcoming of the ontological turn that has dominated the hermeneutic discourse since Heidegger and Gadamer's work in the late 1920s and early 1930s.

Hermeneutics and aesthetics

Throughout the course of Chapters 1 through 5, we saw how Gadamer's dismantling of the distinction between aesthetics and hermeneutics leads to a number of practical-interpretative as well as systematic-philosophical problems. Hence, in calling for a return to early nineteenth-century theories of interpretation the first question that needs to be asked is how Schleiermacher views the relationship between hermeneutics and the experience of art. Because Schleiermacher takes the area of hermeneutics to be co-extensive with language, this is largely an issue concerning the relationship between hermeneutics and poetry (literature), i.e., linguistic art.

We have already seen that Schleiermacher speaks of applied language as characterized by a dimension of style. According to Schleiermacher, a moment of style or individuality occurs as soon as something is linguistically expressed, that is, as soon as the universal rules of grammar are applied in a concrete context. Considered as a set of grammatical rules, language cannot by itself prescribe rules for the correct application of these rules. Such rules would need new rules for the application of these second-order rules, and so on and so forth ad infinitum. In Schleiermacher's view, the individual language-user grounds his or her linguistic practices in the pre-reflective cultural horizon of which he or she is a part.[2] Yet individual language-use can never be reduced to shared symbolic practices; the individual utterance is never determined all the way through by the linguistic and semantic conventions of the community (*HC*, 8; *HuK*, 78).

Schleiermacher's reflections on style and the individuality of applied language have led a number of interpreters, even those who wish to defend his work against Gadamer's criticism, to claim that he develops an aesthetic or literary hermeneutics and that this is precisely what is so remarkable about his position. An example of such a reading is that of Peter Szondi. According to Szondi, whose 1970 essay on Schleiermacher is dedicated to Paul Celan,[3] whose name has already come up in the discussion of Adorno's anti-hermeneutic sentiments, romantic theory of interpretation represents a hermeneutic modernism *avant la lettre*.[4] Likewise Manfred Frank, in *Das individuelle Allgemeine*, sets out to show that Schleiermacher's work anticipates and points beyond a set of insights later to be associated with the semiological-structuralistic approaches to

2 For example, Schleiermacher writes that "Only those writers are to be seen as One who have treated the object in One period of language" (*HC*, 243; *HV*, 1285). It is worth noting at this point how close Schleiermacher comes to von Humboldt, whose philosophy of language Gadamer explicitly endorses in the third part of *Truth and Method* (*TM*, 439ff.; *WM*, 443ff.).

3 Szondi, at the time, was working on the essays that would later be published in his *Celan Studies*, trans. Susan Bernofsky (Stanford: Stanford University Press, 2003); *Celan-Studien* (Frankfurt am Main: Suhrkamp Verlag, 1972). For Gadamer's reading of Celan, see Gadamer, *Gadamer on Celan; Wer bin Ich und wer bist Du?*

4 See Peter Szondi, "Schleiermacher's Hermeneutics Today," *On Textual Understanding and Other Essays*, trans. Harvey Mendelsohn (Minneapolis: University of Minnesota Press, 1986), 111ff. The essay was originally published in French as "L'herméneutique de Schleiermacher," trans. S. Buguet, *Poetique* 2 (1970), 141–155.

literature.[5] Although Szondi and Frank helpfully re-evaluate the turn towards style and language-use in hermeneutics and constructively reassess the need for a hermeneutic theory that can take into account the complexity of modernist poetry, they fail to question the Hegelian–Gadamerian image of romantic philosophy as being, essentially, a literary or at least aesthetically oriented thinking, rather than contributing to such fields as epistemology, theory of meaning, philosophy of history, and political thinking, *as well as* the theory of art and aesthetic experience.[6] A proper rehabilitation of Schleiermacher's hermeneutics would have to question this assumption.[7] Schleiermacher's notion of individuality – understood as a unique combination of shared linguistic resources and individual application – is not primarily about the aesthetic use of language (although this is certainly an aspect of his contribution), but concerns the rational reconstruction of the meaning of an other, that is, of *thought* as expressed in and through language. This emphasis on thought follows from Schleiermacher's commitment to philosophical expressivism and his postulate about "the identity between thinking and speaking" (*HC*, 83; *HuK*, 160).[8] According to Schleiermacher, the interdependency of thought and language goes both ways. Language is expressive of thought, yet there is no thought without language (*HC*, 8; *HuK*, 77f.). The understanding of hermeneutics as being geared towards thought is in other words given with the definition of it in terms of linguistic expression.[9]

5 *Das individuelle Allgemeine*, 13. See also Manfred Frank, *What is Neostructuralism?*, trans. Sabine Wilke and Richard Gray (Minneapolis: University of Minnesota Press, 1989), 447; *Was ist Neostrukturalismus?* (Frankfurt am Main: Suhrkamp Verlag, 1984), 570f.

6 Frank's more recent research on romanticism has a much broader perspective. Schleiermacher's hermeneutics, however, is not included in this work. See Manfred Frank, *The Philosophical Foundations of Early German Romanticism*, trans. Elizabeth Millán-Zaibert (Albany, N.Y.: SUNY Press, 2004); *Unendliche Annäherung* (Frankfurt am Main: Suhrkamp Verlag, 1997) (the English translation does not cover the entire German text).

7 In his important work on the *Dialectic*, Frank moves beyond the scope of a literary hermeneutics. See "Einleitung des Herausgebers," Friedrich Schleiermacher, *Dialektik*, ed. Manfred Frank, vol. I (Frankfurt am Main: Suhrkamp Verlag, 2001), 10–137. See also Manfred Frank, "Metaphysical Foundations: A Look at Schleiermacher's *Dialectic*," trans. Jacqueline Mariña and Christine Helmer, in Jacqueline Mariña (ed.), *The Cambridge Companion to Schleiermacher* (Cambridge: Cambridge University Press, 2005), 15–34.

8 As Michael Forster has pointed out, Schleiermacher here wavers between the claim that thought is dependent on language and the stronger idea of there being an identity between thought and language. See Forster, "Schleiermacher's Hermeneutics: Some Problems and Solutions," *The Harvard Review of Philosophy*, spring 2005, 101.

9 However, thought is not reduced to propositional thought, but includes the free play of poetry. I return to this point in the next section.

Because of the identity between thought and language, Schleier-macher claims that the interpreter must be at least minimally familiar with the object addressed by the text or utterance he or she is ana-lyzing (*HC*, 5; *HuK*, 75). In the hermeneutic process, the interpreter, taking into account the standards of technical and grammatical analysis, is not intentionally directed towards the feelings of another individual or the merely stylistic features of the text, but towards the object (*Gegenstand*) being addressed by the utterance. Schleiermacher does not deny that, in certain cases, an interpreter may take an interest in the aesthetic features or the feelings that motivate a given text. Yet his argument is designed to show how hermeneutics, aspiring to clarify the conditions of possibility of validity in understanding, must take as its point of departure the kind of understanding that is directed towards thought, as it finds its form in concrete (individual-universal) language. Hence in hermeneutics, style is not regarded primarily as an aesthetic feature, but as an intrinsic part of the way in which thought is expressed.

In Schleiermacher's account, thought is always the thought of someone in particular whose thinking is, in turn, shaped by and con-tributing to a concrete cultural linguistic horizon. Although no language-use is free of the element of individuality, the extent to which a given utterance is expressive of individuality varies, as mentioned, with discipline, genre, rhetorical modus, and individual inclination. In scientific texts, the moment of individuality is typically minimized. In poetry, by contrast, it is present in a more significant way. Poetry and science represent two outer points of language. Yet the particular hermeneutic challenge of poetry does not consist in poetry being deprived of thought, but in its being characterized by a *free movement* or *free play* of thought (*HC*, 64; *HuK*, 139; *HC*, 19; *HuK*, 89, note by Lücke).[10] In poetry, it is therefore difficult, if not impossible, to dis-tinguish thought from "means of presentation" (*HC*, 64; *HuK*, 138).

The example of poetry brings to our attention an important aspect of Schleiermacher's expressivism. While he includes poetry (as art, that is, as free play of thoughts) within the sphere of hermeneutics, Schleiermacher distinguishes between, on the one hand, a broader

---

10 Schleiermacher also speaks of such a free play in his aesthetics, hence evoking the vocabulary of Lessing's *Laokoon*, as well as Kantian aesthetics and Schiller's philosophy of education in culture. As he puts it in the 1819 lectures, "[d]aß die Urbilder der Kunstwerke in dem Gebiet dieses freien Spiels liegen, wird niemand läugnen" (*Ä*, 16).

claim about the linguistic mediation of thinking and, on the other, a narrower claim about propositional or assertoric utterances. Poetry, Schleiermacher argues, is expressive of thought, yet thought, in this case, is not necessarily propositionally structured.[11] Hence his model is not one in which thought is limited to mere assertoric utterance. This is what makes it possible for Schleiermacher to suggest that "Music, painting, poetry are related as arts" (*HC*, 72; *HuK*, 148) and yet include poetry within the scope of hermeneutics. As he explains, "[t]he general hermeneutic difference between poetry and prose is that in the former the particular wishes to have its specific value as such, in the latter the particular has it only in the whole, in relation to the main thought" (*HC*, 65f.; *HuK*, 140). In its free play of thought, poetry maintains the value of particular experience, whereas scientific discourse subsumes the particular under a universal concept. In neither of these cases is the interpreter geared towards an analysis of the text as an expression of individual feeling. At stake, rather, is thought and meaning. Thus understood, individuality is not only a challenge to which the critical interpreter responds, but also a condition of possibility for dialectics, which is defined by Schleiermacher as the process of expanding on one's own point of view through dialogical engagement with another.[12]

In analyzing a given symbolic utterance, the interpreter must take into account the cultural, historical, and linguistic context in which it emerges. Every element of a given language is determined by the linguistic whole of which it is a part. As Schleiermacher puts it, "[l]anguage is infinite because each element is determinable in a particular manner via the rest of the elements" (*HC*, 11; *HuK*, 80). Any word is defined by its relation to other words. This relation is regulated by grammar and convention. Nonetheless, the word's relation to language as a whole is not static. Meaning ultimately resides in use, or, in Schleiermacher's formulation, the individual language-user and his or her expressions are "that in which language reveals itself"

---

11 At this point, Schleiermacher provides a theory of historical variation. He comments on the historical variability and flux of literary genres in the aesthetics lectures (*Ä*, 132f.)

12 "The term ['dialectics'] refers to the art of accomplishing a philosophical construction together with another person. In the Socratic school dialogue took the place of the arbitrary diatribes of the sophists; hence for them the principles for dialogue and for construction of knowledge overall were the same" (*Di*, 6: *D*, 5). Knowledge, in turn, is defined as "the pure coinciding of reason with being ['Das Wissen ist also das reine Aufgehn der Vernunft in dem Sein']" (*Di*, 17; *D*, 13).

(*HC*, 10; *HuK*, 79). As an application of universal grammatical and semantic resources, individual use of language represents an element of spontaneity and potential renewal.

Taking into account this moment of spontaneity in application, Schleiermacher's hermeneutics not only addresses the relationship between a given use of a word and language as a whole, but also encompasses the changing use of a word over time. The historical dimension of language cannot be separated from the way in which a word gains its meaning through its relation to other words in the same language. Not only do we continuously project a given word into ever new contexts, but the realization of that word in those new contexts of application also changes the way we understand its previous occurrences. The combination of its historicity and the infinity of possible grammatical combinations implies that "No language is completely present to us, not even our own mother tongue" (*HC*, 14f.; *HuK*, 84). Even though there is a limit to the possibility of innovation in language – language, Schleiermacher elaborates, "only sustains itself in continual repetition" (*HC*, 13; *HuK*, 82) – it is alive only so long as new expressions are made (*HC*, 32; *HuK*, 103).

The degree to which a language allows for individually generated variation is not only a question of genre but also historically determined. Following Herder, Hölderlin, and Schiller, Schleiermacher distinguishes between the classical, which is dominated by the common, traditional resources of language, and the original, which leaves more room for originality.[13] Genius, however, does not consist in originality alone.[14] Rather, it is expressive of a unique combination of originality and common cultural resources (*HC*, 13; *HuK*, 83). In demonstrating how closely the shared and individual elements are intertwined, literature forms an *Urbild* for language in the production of thought (ibid.).[15]

---

13 Dilthey discusses this point in *Leben Schleiermachers*. Zweiter Band, 55f.

14 This is another point at which it becomes clear what a blatant misunderstanding it is to place Schleiermacher's hermeneutics within the framework of a romantic misreading of Kant's discussion of genius, i.e., a reading of the third Critique that does not take into account Kant's postulate about a necessary relationship between genius and taste (see Chapter 1).

15 The notion of an *Urbild* is spelled out in Schleiermacher's aesthetics. Here he discusses how the *Urbild* combines emotions with a disciplined outer expression. As such, it represents a paradigm of art. Aesthetic expression requires training and education. Rather than a spontaneous outburst of feelings, art is a combination of spontaneity and measure, individuality and tradition, feeling and reason (*Ä*, 10f.). *Urbildung*, in short, requires *Ausbildung*.

Even though the degree to which an expression is characterized by originality is historically relative, it also varies with the expressive modalities of the artist or language-user. Schleiermacher notes in his hermeneutics that one sometimes finds language-use so strongly inclined towards one of the extremes that it may look like it represents it in a pure form. Cicero, he remarks, gets close to presenting the classical without being original (*HC*, 14; *HuK*, 83). Hamann, on the other hand, almost represents the original but without being classical (ibid.). Only the combination of the two makes up an *Urbild* of language (ibid.).

Whereas aesthetics is typically attuned to the problem of expressive originality, the emergence of new meanings is often overlooked in hermeneutics. However, given the intertwinement of thought and language, the occurrence of new meaning not only relates to the history of style and aesthetics, but also concerns the systematic possibilities of thought. New expressive possibilities open up new intellectual vistas. Plato's work is a good example of this, Schleiermacher claims. Plato, we learn, "produced new expressions for the sake of new philosophical ideas" (*HC*, 32; *HuK*, 103). These ideas, however, did not retain their originality, but were soon conventionalized and "passed over into all the Schools" (ibid.). In this way, the interpreter may already be familiar with concepts and ideas that Plato first developed and miss the novelty of his thinking. Taking these linguistic changes into account, hermeneutics is attuned to individuality, although not an aesthetic individuality but one that is geared towards the meaning of the utterance as expressed by a given individual within a given historical culture. According to Schleiermacher, "[e]very utterance can ... only be understood via the knowledge of the whole of the historical life to which it belongs, or via the history which is relevant for it" (*HC*, 8; *HuK*, 77). Or, as he also puts it, in the rhetoric of late eighteenth-century philosophy, "every language-user can only be understood via their nationality and their era" (*HC*, 9; *HuK*, 78).

To summarize the discussion so far, four points must be mentioned, all of which refer to the epistemic debates about individuality and thought, rather than the aesthetic discourse in which Schleiermacher's hermeneutics is frequently situated. First, the area of hermeneutics involves the whole range of linguistic modi, from scientific texts to poetry. Second, Schleiermacher emphasizes that all use of language is marked by an aspect of individuality, even in the case of strictly scientific systematic discourse. Third, Schleiermacher argues that the hermeneutic activity is geared towards the thought expressed by the individual utterance. Fourth, thought is understood in a broad sense so that it includes non-propositional language and the stylistic aspects of the expression.

These four points helpfully indicate a substantial difference between Schleiermacher and Gadamer with regard to the relationship between aesthetics and hermeneutics. As part of his effort to overcome aesthetic consciousness, Gadamer challenges a narrow understanding of truth and knowledge, and claims that the experience of the authority of the classical work of art is paradigmatic for the truth-happening of the hermeneutic experience. It is, he proposes, the merit of his philosophy to point beyond "the narrowness of the concept of knowledge that limited Kant's position" to a hermeneutics "where art and history [are] combined" (*TM*, 489; *WM*, 492). In *Truth and Method*, the experience of a work of art, and in particular a classic or eminent work of literature, is taken to exemplify how tradition discloses a field of meaning that is prior to and constitutive of the critical-reflective capacities of the individual interpreter.[16] In Schleiermacher's work, by contrast, the experience of literature is not seen as paradigmatic for hermeneutics. Rather, poetry, like science, represents a limiting case of linguistic expression. This is not to say that Schleiermacher denies or overlooks the aesthetic experience of literature and poetry. Surely, poetry, drama, and the other linguistic arts should often be approached aesthetically. However, our aesthetic response to art is not the concern of hermeneutics, but is subject to systematic analysis in the lectures on aesthetics, given over the course of three lecture series in the years between 1819 and 1833. Moreover, Schleiermacher's interest in individuality does not mean that he denigrates the cognitive value of scientific texts. His point, rather, is to state that as long as these texts make use of ordinary language, they are part of a hermeneutic discourse. And as far as hermeneutics goes, we deal with the effort to understand the thought expressed in a given linguistic utterance as a more or less unique expression of a given, historical culture.

16 Hence, Gadamer argues, "it is well founded for us to use the same concept of play for the hermeneutical phenomenon as for the experience of the beautiful" (*TM*, 490; *WM*, 494). This is the case because Gadamer defines the very notion of hermeneutic truth in light of this *Spiel*: "What we mean by truth here can best be defined again in terms of our concept of play" (ibid.).

Method, prejudice, and historicity

According to Gadamer, the study of "the significance of history for human knowledge" and the fact that "what we encounter in a tradition says something to us" comprises "the whole value of hermeneutical experience" (*TM*, 489; *WM*, 492). His argument in this context is directed, far too categorically, against the Enlightenment's negative assessment of prejudices. This negative assessment, in turn, gives rise to the call for a scientific method, by virtue of which the critical interpreter can, allegedly, suspend his or her own historical and cultural horizon and so to speak encounter the object under idealized research conditions. With his appeal to critical standards in interpretation, Schleiermacher, Gadamer argues, is guilty of such a misunderstanding. This, however, is wrong.

Schleiermacher includes within the area of hermeneutics "misunderstanding in the mother tongue and in everyday life" (*HC*, 227; *HV*, 1271). The universalization of the hermeneutic problem is but the other side of his turn towards the general epistemic question of how we can speak of validity in interpretation at all, i.e., assume that some interpretations are better or more valid than others (rather than, as Gadamer suggests, all interpretations, due to the element of application, being different).[17] Hence Schleiermacher makes it clear, in the lecture notes from 1809 to 1810, that "The business of hermeneutics should not only begin where understanding is uncertain, but with the first beginning of the enterprise of wanting to understand an utterance" (*HC*, 228; *HV*, 1272). It should include reflection on utterances or texts with whose meaning the interpreter uncritically assumes he or she is familiar.

When formulating the principles of general hermeneutics, which encompass all applied language, including utterances in the interpreter's own language, Schleiermacher's question is not, as in Gadamer's work, "How can hermeneutics best reflect the historical conditionedness of human existence?" As we saw in Chapter 5, Schleiermacher is concerned, rather, with a different problem,

---

17 Schleiermacher defines hermeneutics as "the art of understanding another person's utterance correctly [*richtig*]" (*HC*, 5; *HuK*, 75). Gadamer, by contrast, claims that textual hermeneutics should rather be understood along the lines of legal hermeneutics, which implies that "the text . . . if it is to be understood properly [*angemessen*] – i.e., according to the claim it makes – must be understood at every moment, in every concrete situation, in a new and different way" (*TM*, 309; *WM*, 314).

namely "By what criteria can the interpreter, as a historically situated being, determine whether he or she has misunderstood the utterance of another?" This question does not betray a repression of the historicity of the interpreter, but emerges precisely because not just the text but also the interpreter is situated in a given historical context. And being situated in tradition implies that one's outlook is shaped by reflected as well as unreflected prejudices.

The problem of prejudices presents the critical interpreter with a particular challenge. Typically, the process of interpretation is obstructed by the common mistakes of hastiness and prejudices. Of these mistakes, Schleiermacher explains, prejudice "lies deeper" because it consists in "the one-sided preference for what is close to the individual's circle of ideas and the rejection of what lies outside it" (*HC*, 23; *HuK*, 93). When subjecting him- or herself to prejudices, the interpreter typically "explains in or explains out what is not present in the author" (ibid.). Because the interpreter is situated in history, he or she cannot purge him- or herself of each and every inadequate prejudice at the same time. Instead, the purging of illegitimate prejudices is a gradual, educational project. With regard to "foreign old writings," the interpreter is aided by linguistic and historical knowledge (*HC*, 20; *HuK*, 91). However, such knowledge can never be complete in the sense that it allows the interpreter to stand totally outside his or her own historical situation and gain a full understanding of the context in which the work was originally produced. Understanding, for Schleiermacher, can only be a matter of endless approximation. This is not only due to the pervasiveness of the interpreter's own prejudices, but also to the complexity of the interpretative material. Schleiermacher insists that "Language is infinite because each element is determinable in a particular manner via the rest of the elements" (*HC*, 11; *HuK*, 80). Thus even the native speaker, whose language is a practice he or she masters, is prevented from gaining complete, objective knowledge of it.

In worrying about how prejudices color our understanding of textual material from historically or culturally different environments, Schleiermacher does not propose that misunderstanding is universal or that the interpreter, because he or she does not know whether he or she understands everything, understands nothing at all.[18]

---

18 As Thomas Seebohm puts it, "[w]hat is meant by this elliptical formulation is that a naïve, pre-methodical interpretation has to be treated under the suspicion of possible misunderstanding," *Hermeneutics*, 54.

Understanding is gradual and not, as in Gadamer, a sudden epiphany or happening of truth. This is the case because, for Schleiermacher, understanding is not primarily about the historical self-understanding of *Dasein*, but the correct understanding of the meaning of another language-user. Hence Schleiermacher's hermeneutics is shaped so as to compensate for the way in which prejudices make the interpreter unconsciously project upon a text his or her own ideas, beliefs, or aesthetic priorities, which, in turn, bears with it the risk of reducing the meaning of the other to a meaning that is the interpreter's own.

Schleiermacher would insist that a collapse of the distinction between understanding and application, which Gadamer defends in *Truth and Method* (*TM*, 308f.; *WM*, 313f.), makes it possible for the interpreter freely to project upon the text his or her own pre-reflected or reflected prejudices, thereby breathing, as it were, the interpreter's own meaning into the texts of a past long gone or a culture distant from his or her own. For Gadamer, the cultural expressions of the past present themselves, right away, as partners of a dialogue; they present themselves with an authority, gained in and through their mediation in tradition, which makes the interpreter question his or her own beliefs and prejudices.[19] For Schleiermacher, such a self-presentation of past works is neither possible nor desirable. Instead, he turns to the idea of a historical-philological reconstruction of the meaning of temporally, geographically, or culturally foreign symbolic expressions.

When Schleiermacher speaks about interpretation as the outcome of skepticism (*HC*, 28; *HuK*, 98), it is because he believes that the ubiquity of prejudice makes it necessary for the reflected interpreter to attain a critical attitude, questioning assumptions previously taken for granted. The critical interpreter moves through skepticism by completing it. Unlike Gadamer, Schleiermacher does not argue that a skeptical attitude is based on the repression of the historicity of the interpreter. Furthermore, the skepticism that Schleiermacher advocates is controlled, in the sense that it does not suggest that in the absence of reflected standards, such as the concepts of grammatical and technical interpretation, nothing is understood at all; rather, it expresses the worry that without such standards we do not know what knowledge in the area of hermeneutics amounts to. Hence Gadamer

19 Understanding, as Gadamer puts it, "lets itself be *addressed* [*angesprochen*] by tradition" (*TM*, 282; *WM*, 287).

is wrong in claiming that for Schleiermacher "[u]nintelligibility . . . has a . . . universal significance" (*TM*, 184; *WM*, 188).

According to Schleiermacher, there can be no absolutely certain way to determine whether or not the interpreter has correctly understood the meaning of a given text or literary corpus. Whether the text is close to or distant from the horizon of the interpreter, there is always a risk that the interpreter allows the interpretation to be colored by his or her own prejudices and, as a consequence, hypostatizes thoughts or beliefs that are peripheral to the concerns of the text. By referring to historical context or other works by the same author, the interpreter can point out how a given interpretation of a text misrepresents its meaning or is lacking in justification. Yet a final and indisputable interpretation cannot be provided. As such, the idea of a correct interpretation functions only as a heuristic device that grants direction to the process of understanding.

Again, this approach to hermeneutics follows from Schleiermacher's theory of meaning. Language, on Schleiermacher's model, is expressive of a world, in that it discloses a field of intelligibility and action. Words do not stand for or represent thoughts that are given independently of language. Rather, language opens up a sphere of meaning in which a given object first occurs as such. This does not mean that different linguistic cultures are constitutively cut off from one another. What it does mean, though, is that the limits of a language, or, rather, of human linguisticality, constitute the limits of a world. There is no point of reference outside the sphere of linguistic mediation. All interpersonal or intra-cultural understanding must take place from within the larger horizon of language. This applies not only to the text, but also to the interpreter. The interpreter can never suspend his or her own historical and cultural point of view. Yet he or she can, through critical, hermeneutic work, gradually progress towards a more adequate understanding of the past. In fact, in Schleiermacher, these aspects of interpretation are intrinsically related, in the sense that the critical-reflective interpreter cannot typically cast aside his or her prejudices prior to the interpretative work. Prejudices, rather, are tested out in and through the encounter with the other. I return to this point in my discussion of Schleiermacher's practical philosophy and dialectics.

In Schleiermacher's philosophy, hermeneutics emerges as a key discipline with regard to our study of history, geographically distant cultures, and even the joint, dialogical search for truth in *Dialektik.*[20] In all these cases, the relevance of hermeneutics rests, first, with the acknowledgement of the fundamental historicity of thought and language and, second, with the belief that false prejudices can gradually be overcome through the encounter with the point of view of an other. In this process, however, it is crucial that the interpreter assesses the other's point of view without being blinded by his or her own prejudices, which would prevent him or her from understanding the other, as well as from questioning the validity of his or her own beliefs and approach to the subject matter at stake.

The very idea of a method in understanding does not require a fundamental dismissal of the historicity of thought. Schleiermacher, surely, would agree with Gadamer's claim that "there is undoubtedly no understanding that is free of all prejudices" (*TM*, 490; *WM*, 494). However, the consequence he draws from this is not that we, for this reason, are drawn into truth in understanding, in analogy with the play of art (ibid.). Rather, for Schleiermacher, it is the historical situatedness of thinking that, ultimately, gives the interpreter the capacity to transcend the limitations of his or her own horizon and allows him or her to be critical from within the perspective he or she inhabits. Hence the critical-reflective interpreter is distinguished by the will to take on the task of obtaining correct understanding of a given text in light of the ideals of approximation (*HC*, 91; *HuK*, 168).

In its orientation towards a dimension of normativity in understanding, Schleiermacher's notion of critical-methodological interpretation recognizes the historical situatedness of thought. As opposed to what Gadamer takes to be the case, the orientation towards validity in understanding does not result from a repression of the historicity of the interpreter. Nor does Schleiermacher assert that the idea of a method in understanding can be entirely distinguished from our everyday hermeneutic practices.[21] It is only our practical engagement with others, be they contemporaries or the voices of a past long gone, that can give rise to a reflective discourse

---

20 Schleiermacher, as we have seen, maintains that dialectics depends on hermeneutics (*HuK*, 410).

21 This also applies to dialectics. With regard to dialectics, Schleiermacher writes: "The supreme and most general elements of knowing, therefore, and the principles for doing philosophy themselves, are the same. Thus, transcendental philosophy and formal philosophy are, if they are to contain something real, the same. Contrary to Kant, constitutive and regulative principles do not admit of distinction" (*Di*, 5; *D*, 5).

on what is implied by this understanding. Whereas the process of understanding is laid out more or less schematically in the hermeneutics lectures, Schleiermacher's ethics, to which I return shortly, accounts for the way in which spirit gains self-reflection throughout the course of history. Before proceeding that far, however, we must take a closer look at Schleiermacher's idea of an expansion of horizons, as expounded in his 1813 lecture on the principles of translation.

Translation and the expansion of horizons

According to Gadamer, "[t]he situation of the translator and that of the interpreter [is] fundamentally the same" (*TM*, 387; *WM*, 390). Furthermore, he submits that "[t]he translator's task of recreation differs only in degree, not in kind, from the general hermeneutical task that any text presents" (*TM*, 387; *WM*, 391). In both cases, what is at stake is a familiarizing of the foreign, yet one that concomitantly expands the interpreter's own hermeneutic horizon. Schleiermacher also takes a strong interest in translation. His lecture "On the Different Methods of Translating" is written in the same period as, and addresses topics that are closely related to, the hermeneutics lectures. Yet he does not, like Gadamer, assimilate translation to interpretation. For Schleiermacher, hermeneutics is a matter of understanding a text, translation a matter of re-expressing the meaning of a text in another language. Furthermore, Schleiermacher, in this short yet significant work on translation, tackles the possibility of a comprehensive, dialectical relationship of intercultural understanding, a topic that is largely absent from Gadamer's focus on the integrating force of the interpreter's own tradition.[22]

Schleiermacher's interest in translation feeds off a wide-spanning debate within the German world of books and letters.[23] Around this

---

22 Unfortunately, this point is overlooked by Charles Taylor, who, reading Gadamer through a sympathetic lens, claims that philosophical hermeneutics, with the notion of fluid horizons, presents us with a viable solution to the challenge of understanding others, i.e., "to be able to acknowledge the humanity of their way, while still being able to live ours." In my understanding, Schleiermacher and the tradition of pre-Heideggerian hermeneutics offers a more adequate response to this challenge. See Charles Taylor, "Gadamer on the Human Sciences," in Robert J. Dostal, *The Cambridge Companion to Gadamer* (Cambridge: Cambridge University Press, 2002), 142.

23 Gottsched, for example, criticized the very idea of bringing foreign language texts into a German context: "Die Uebersetzungssucht ist so stark unter uns eingerissen, dass

time translations made up a significant portion of the books available.[24] Moreover, it emerged as an issue worthy of systematic philosophical attention.[25] In Goethe, von Gerstenberg, Herder, and Novalis we find heated discussions of the nature and principles of translation.[26] Rather than being a purely academic debate, the question of translation concerned concrete, historical problems such as whether non-classicist drama like Shakespearean tragedy could find a home in Germany without at the same time being altered with regard to structure, meter, and even content.[27] These questions, in turn, give rise to philosophical reflection on the relationship between the fact of historical situatedness and the issue of normativity in aesthetics and historical research.[28]

man Gutes und Böses in unsere Sprache bringt: gerade als ob alles, was ausländisch ist, schön und vortrefflich wäre, und als ob wir nicht selbst schon bessere Sachen aus den eignen Köpfen unserer Landsleute aufzuweisen hätten." From Gottsched, *Beiträge zur critischen Historie der Deutschen Sprache*, in Roy Pascal, *Shakespeare in Germany 1740–1815* (New York: Octagon Books, 1971), 38f.

24 This is reflected in Schleiermacher's comments about an inner drive that has led the Germans to translation *en masse* (*T*, 62; *MdÜ*, 92).

25 For a discussion of the rise of translation and a critical discussion of the philosophy of translation, see Susan Bernofsky, *Foreign Words: Translation-Authors in the Age of Goethe* (Detroit: Wayne State University Press, 2005), 1–47. For a discussion of the translation of works from the Scottish Enlightenment into the context of German philosophy in particular, see Fania Oz-Salzberger, *Translating the Enlightenment: Scottish Civic Discourse in Eighteenth-Century Germany* (Oxford: Oxford University Press, 1995).

26 Novalis, for example, distinguishes between grammatical, transformatory, and mythical translations and claims that not only books, but everything can be translated in this way. See Novalis, "Miscellaneous Remarks (Excerpts)," in Jay Bernstein (ed.), *Classic and Romantic German Aesthetics*, various translators (Cambridge: Cambridge University Press, 2003), 210f.; "Vermischte Bemerkungen (Blütenstaub) 1797–1798," in *Werke*, ed. Gerhard Schulz (Munich: Verlag C. H. Beck, 1987), 337.

27 At a general level, Schleiermacher rejects the prevailing eighteenth-century idea that one historical expression (such as Homer's epic or Shakespearean drama) can be presented in a form different from or independent of its original manner of expression (*HC*, 33; *HuK*, 104). He discusses Schiller's translation of *Macbeth* in "Rezension von William Shakespeare: Macbeth. Ein Trauerspiel, zur Vorstellung auf dem Hoftheater zu Weimar eingerichtet von Friedrich Schiller (1801)," *KGA*, erste Abteilung, *Schriften und Entwürfe*, vol. III, ed. Günter Meckenstock, 379–398.

28 This becomes particularly clear in Herder's discussion of Shakespeare. The three versions of his Shakespeare essay, written in 1771 and 1773, indirectly respond to von Gerstenberg's discussion of Shakespeare in his *Briefen über Merkwürdigkeiten in der Litteratur* (1766). See Johann Gottfried Herder, "Shakespear," in *Von deutscher Art und Kunst*, in *Schriften zur Ästhetik und Literatur 1767–1781, Johann Gottfried Herder, Werke*, ed. Ulrich Gaier *et al.*, vol. II (Frankfurt am Main: Deutscher Klassiker Verlag, 1993), 498–549; the final version of the essay is translated as "Shakespeare," in Johann Gottfried Herder, *Selected Writings on Aesthetics*, ed. and trans. Gregory Moore

Schleiermacher published his first translation of Plato in 1804. The translation project stayed with him for his entire life. Hence, in the 1813 lecture, Schleiermacher approaches the problems of translation from a practical-pragmatic as well as from a principled-philosophical point of view. He starts out by claiming that in spite of all cultures being linguistically mediated, there are huge discrepancies between the world-views they harbor. In his words, "every language has its own characteristic features, including the rhythms of its prose as well as its poetry" (*T*, 61; *MdÜ*, 90f.). On the basis of his claim about the individuality of applied language, Schleiermacher generalizes the problem of translation. Anticipating a point that will make up the central orientation of his 1819 lecture on hermeneutics, he proposes that even within one's own language, one is often forced to take recourse to a process of translation. "For not only," he explains, "do the dialects of the different clans that make up a people, and the different ways a language or dialect develops in different centuries, already constitute different languages in a stricter sense, between which it is often necessary to translate," but "even contemporaries who share a dialect but belong to different classes that rarely come together in social intercourse and diverge substantially in their education are commonly unable to communicate save through a similar mediation" (*T*, 43; *MdÜ*, 67). Translation is in other words not just about the transference of meaning between different cultures, but also the problem of communication within what at first may seem like a unified linguistic whole. Schleiermacher speaks of the differences in languages, dialects, and socio-economic or cultural linguistic subsets as the *irrationality* (*Irrationalität*) of language (*T*, 48; *MdÜ*, 73).

In the previous chapter, we saw that hermeneutics is divided into a technical and a grammatical side, the former dealing with how an individual expresses him- or herself in and through language, the latter with how all concrete language-use is shaped by the shared grammatical and semantic resources available. Similarly, translation responds to the intermediation of the individual and the universal in language. On the one hand, no human being can think outside of language. Rather, "the form of his ideas, the manner in which he combines them, and the limits of these combinations are all

(Princeton: Princeton University Press, 2006), 291–307. For a more detailed discussion of the philosophical debate about Shakespeare's work, see my "Reading Shakespeare; Reading Modernity."

preordained by the language in which he was born and raised: both his intellect and his imagination are bound by it" (*T*, 46; *MdÜ*, 71). On the other hand, even though the boundaries of language are also the boundaries of thought, "every free-thinking, intellectually independent individual shapes the language in his turn" (ibid.). In Schleiermacher's view, the dialectics between the individual and the universal accounts for the possibility of change within language: "[f]or how else if not by these influences could [language] have gained and grown from its raw beginnings to its present, more perfect state of development in the sciences and arts?" (ibid., see also *T*, 47; *MdÜ*, 72). As in hermeneutics, the dialectic between individual and universal concerns the concrete application of shared linguistic and cultural resources. Furthermore, expressions or ways of combining thoughts that are at first unique and individual are gradually incorporated into the common stock of thinking and language.

The difference between languages makes translation a daunting task. In facing this challenge, the translator encounters two constitutively different possibilities. He or she can decide to make the text familiar to the present-day readers of the translator's own language. Or he or she can try to reproduce the expressive tone and register of the original text so that the audience can sense in the translation "the genius of the language that was native to the writer" (ibid.). This is the choice between a familiarizing and a foreignizing translation.[29] The former involves stretching the text in order to meet the needs of the reader, the latter asks the reader to stretch towards the translated text (*T*, 49; *MdÜ*, 74).[30] These two methods, Schleiermacher observes, "are so very different from one another that one or the other must certainly be followed as strictly as possible, any attempt to

29 I borrow the term "foreignizing" translation from Lawrence Venuti's study *The Translator's Invisibility: A History of Translation* (London: Routledge, 1995).

30 It is worth noting that to some extent this point had already been anticipated by von Gerstenberg in the 1760s. Von Gerstenberg advocates the view that translations geared towards the lay public should be pleasing and easy to read, whereas those undertaken with a view to an educated audience should stay close to the original. See Walter Fränzel, *Geschichte des Übersetzens im 18. Jahrhundert* (Leipzig: Voigtländer, 1914), 126f. In pleading for such a view, von Gerstenberg explicitly breaks with the view, promoted by Gottsched, that the translator should come to the author's aid by improving or even deleting semantically or stylistically difficult passages. For a discussion of translation issues in Schleiermacher's own circle, see Andreas Huyssen, *Die frühromantische Konzeption von Übersetzung und Aneignung: Studien zur frühromantischen Utopie einer deutschen Weltliteratur* (Zurich: Atlantis Verlag, 1969).

combine them being certain to produce a highly unreliable result and to carry with it the danger that the writer and the reader might miss each other completely" (ibid.).

Following the general hermeneutic guidelines sketched out from 1805 onwards – the orientation towards the particular nature of the text or utterance at stake; the effort not to reduce that which is other to that which is the interpreter's own – Schleiermacher recommends the second of the two strategies, that of foreignizing translation. This takes a certain toll on the translator. He or she must for example be familiar with the historical development of the language from which he or she translates: "For just as language is a historical entity, so too is it impossible to appreciate it rightly without an appreciation of its history" (*T*, 51; *MdÜ*, 78). The translator should, in other words, be able to convey not only how a given author was shaped by, but also show how that author contributed to, the development of language:

> for whoever, armed with adequate knowledge, reads a pre-eminent work of this sort in its original tongue will not fail to note the influence this work has had on the language. He will note which words and associations of ideas appear to him there in the first splendor of novelty; he will see how they have insinuated themselves into the language by way of the specific needs of this spirit and its expressive powers; and what he thus notes will largely determine the impression he receives. (*T*, 51; *MdÜ*, 78f.)

It is the task of translation to communicate just these things to the reader; "else he will be missing an often quite significant part of what was intended for him" (*T*, 51; *MdÜ*, 79).

Setting the standards thus high, Schleiermacher comments that the ancients translated very little in this sense. And when extending the focus to France, where the classicist influence was still palpable, he polemically asks: "Who would claim that *anything* has ever been translated, whether from an ancient or a Germanic tongue, into French!" (*T*, 62; *MdÜ*, 92, emphasis added). The Germans, by contrast, are able and willing to translate and discuss the principles of translation at a second-order, reflective level. Promoting a cosmopolitan spirit on behalf of the German-speaking world, Schleiermacher hopes that by pursuing the ideals of a foreignizing translation "everyone will be able to enjoy all the beautiful things that the most different ages have given us as purely and perfectly as possible for one who is foreign to them" (*T*, 62; *MdÜ*, 92).

Schleiermacher's essay on translation promotes the idea that languages are enriched through encounters with other languages. Since language constitutes the limits of thinking, an enrichment of language involves an expansion of the field of symbolic meaning through which the individual realizes and understands him- or herself. This is the point at which translation converges with hermeneutics and dialectics. In Schleiermacher's model, interpretation as well as translation should retain the alien character of symbolic expressions of other cultures or individuals, precisely because this is the only way in which they can challenge the pre-established framework of the interpreter's own horizon of thinking and action. To do the contrary, by making the foreign familiar, and in this way potentially collapsing the distinction between understanding and application, deprives the interpreter of a standpoint in light of which his or her prejudices may be called into question. Only by assessing his or her interpretative efforts in light of the viewpoints, thoughts, or standards of an other, thus also questioning his or her own prejudices and motivations, can the interpreter hope to expand his or her own horizon.

Writing in the spirit of Kant and Fichte's views on the Enlightenment as an ongoing educational commitment, Schleiermacher, as we have seen, presents interpretation as a striving or approximation. No certainty is ever given, only a set of regulative ideals, such as those of technical and grammatical interpretation, against which the interpreter must perpetually measure his or her own practice. In the ongoing hermeneutic activity, the reflective interpreter, like the translator, must take responsibility for the interpretative procedures and principles on which his or her work relies.

Gadamer, too, insists that the interpreter tests his or her own prejudices through hermeneutic practice. However, when assessed from Schleiermacher's point of view, the problem with Gadamer's hermeneutics is that he collapses the distinction between understanding and application (and, concomitantly, rejects the very idea that some interpretations are better or more correct than others).[31] As a consequence of this, the interpreter is left with no way to test, confirm, or question the relevance of his or her hypothesis about the meaning of the work. Given the authority of the classical, an authority

---

31 As Gadamer puts it, "all reading involves application, so that a person reading a text is himself part of the meaning he apprehends. He belongs to the text that he is reading" (*TM*, 340; *WM*, 345).

that escapes the demands of critical-reflective subjectivity, the work is supposed to put forth a claim that is indubitably true and, as such, forces the interpreter to question his or her own prejudices. Because understanding, for Gadamer, is typically oriented towards one's own tradition, this is not primarily a problem about the overcoming of particular prejudices. At stake, rather, is the gradual overcoming of what Gadamer takes to be the arch-prejudice of modernity itself, namely its rejection of or obliviousness to the historicity of reason.

Schleiermacher does not endorse such a project. From his point of view, the critical interpreter would worry that in Gadamer's model, in spite of the authority it grants to the voices of the past, it is nonetheless the interpreter who, in the first place, reads the text so as to make it speak in this way. That is, because the interpreter is caught up with the prejudices of tradition, his or her reading of the very same tradition ends up being an auto-confirmation of, rather than a critical reflection on, the beliefs and assumptions handed down to us throughout history. On the basis of Schleiermacher's theory, the critical interpreter would fear that, as conceived by Gadamer, the conversation with the past could end up a more or less monological exercise.

According to Schleiermacher, the interpreter needs standards of validity by means of which he or she is able to take responsibility for his or her interpretation. Although an interpretation can be right or wrong without an appeal to such standards, the interpreter can only falsify illegitimate interpretations when assessing them in light of the reflected criteria by which we count something to be a valid or adequate interpretation. Only in light of these standards can the interpreter hope to purge him- or herself of inadequate prejudices and gradually get closer to an adequate understanding of the text. Hence the appeal to critical standards in interpretation does not mean that the interpreter thinks of the text or his or her own critical activity as situated outside the realm of historical mediation. Rather, from Schleiermacher's perspective, the critical interpreter would be concerned that the Gadamerian gesture of subjecting oneself to the authority of the text (as it is handed down by tradition) leaves no critical reference by which he or she can possibly ask whether the authority assigned to the text is more than a mere projection – a projection that may well occur as the result of a systematic mis-understanding of the text, utterance, or phenomenon at stake.

Schleiermacher's views on translation and interpretation can be further illuminated by reference to his lectures on the history of philosophy. In this work, Schleiermacher recommends a bottom-up rather than a top-down approach to historical research. The intellectual horizon of the ancient Greeks, for example, is said to be foreign (*fremd*) to that of modern philosophy (*GdaP*, 16), and in order to understand the philosophy of the past the interpreter must approach it with a philological and historical frame of mind. This, however, does not prevent him or her from, but rather stimulates, a systematic-philosophical understanding or discussion of the points of view espoused by the thinkers of the tradition. Schleiermacher regards each period as relatively autonomous, in the sense that it should be understood and discussed in its own right. The ideal is a detailed, historical exposition that, nonetheless, offers a picture of the whole of a given way of reasoning (*GdaP*, 16f.). As such, Schleiermacher allows for no absolute distinction between philosophy and the history of philosophy.

We have seen how Gadamer fails to engage in a proper dialogue with Kant, the romantics, Schleiermacher, and Hegel. He constructs a problematic picture of their positions, which, in turn, establishes the backdrop against which his own ontological shift in hermeneutics gains credence and validity. In his reading of the third Critique, Gadamer takes Kant's notion of the ideal of beauty to point towards a hermeneutic model of art. Kant's account of natural beauty, by contrast, is criticized for representing a bad immediacy that will later funnel into, and provide the premises for, romantic aesthetics. The situation is hardly better when it comes to Gadamer's reading of Hegel. Here, the very notion of absolute knowing is presented as a faulty Cartesian lapse, and the idea of hermeneutic integration is promoted without concern for Hegel's own discussion of the need for a reference to historical context. Finally, when addressing Schleiermacher's hermeneutics, the notion of individuality is never portrayed as more than a questionable subjective aestheticism; the idea of method is never seen as more than the remnant of a problematic epistemic foundationalism.

Schleiermacher insists that the reflective interpreter subjects his or her own practice to an ongoing reflective-methodological scrutiny. In his account, the interpreter is driven by the search for freedom from illegitimate prejudices, but this is obtained through the striving for a correct interpretation, rather than authentic belonging to a tradition that shapes the prejudices of his or her own culture. Hence Schleiermacher does not espouse a problematic aesthetic consciousness or a bad foundationalist quest for method in understanding, but rather seeks to combine a notion of the historicity of reason and the linguistic mediation of thought with a quest for critical self-reflection and interpretative autonomy. This again springs out of his interest in understanding the meaning of the other on his or her own terms. In understanding the texts of the past, what is at stake is not, as in Gadamer, the self-articulation of a living tradition, but the questioning, through hermeneutic-philological work, of the way in which tradition has handed down to us (or, alternatively, failed to pass on) a given text, subject matter, or problem.

Whereas Gadamer's hermeneutics is geared towards overcoming the self-forgetfulness and alienation that follow from the modern repression of historical authority, Schleiermacher's theory of interpretation focuses on questions of normativity. In his view, it would be unreasonable to expect the humanities, as academic disciplines, to take on the burden of overcoming the possible ills of modernity. This, however, does not mean that Schleiermacher's hermeneutics should be interpreted as a narrow, epistemic enterprise. On the contrary, in his work, hermeneutics is closely related to sociality, practical reason, and education (*Bildung*).

Bildung, sociability, and the progress of reason in history

Even though Schleiermacher, in the years between 1805 and 1833, was teaching separate classes in hermeneutics, his theory of interpretation should be related to the larger philosophical framework of his thinking. In this context, the study of translation stands out as relevant but so also does his early theory of free sociality as laid out in the *Speeches* and the essay "Towards a Theory of Social Conduct" from the early Berlin period, as well as his system of ethics.[32] When it is seen in relation to his ethical and social philosophy, it becomes clear how Schleiermacher's reflective turn in hermeneutics and the theory of translation is motivated not only by epistemic concerns alone but also by a larger program of practical philosophy and education (*Bildung*). In fact, in Schleiermacher's philosophy, the appeal to a dimension of

---

32 Scholtz discusses the continuity in Schleiermacher's work on ethics in *Die Philosophie Schleiermachers* (Darmstadt: Wissenschaftliche Buchgesellschaft, 1984), 100–103 and 114–127, viewing it, throughout, as a position that is situated in between Kant and Hegel. Ibid., 121f.

validity in understanding is intrinsically related to his vision of sociality as a genuine intersubjectivity, a unity in manifold.[33]

Both the essay on free sociality and the *Speeches* are published in 1799. In these works Schleiermacher, like other philosophers of his generation, develops a critique of the trend towards institutionalization of religious life. However, unlike, say, the young Hegel, Schleiermacher does not trace the true and original religiosity back to the folk cultures of ancient Greek or early Christian societies, but views it as related to individual subjectivity.[34] In his analysis of religion, Schleiermacher counterbalances the romantic sentiments of the time with a more robust attitude and grants that "[r]eligion never appears in a pure state" (*OR*, 100; *ÜR*, 210). Yet religion, as such, cannot be judged by its *de facto* appearance. The "cultured despisers of religion," who make up the target of Schleiermacher's criticism, have conflated essence and appearance (*OR*, 88; *ÜR*, 198). Contemporary religiosity, Schleiermacher claims, has lost touch with the community of living individuals.[35] It is institutionalized and given muted expression in "the dead letter" (*OR*, 164; *ÜR*, 268, see also *OR*, 108; *ÜR*, 217).[36] A religion that is cut off from its roots in individual subjectivity, however, is no more than "barren uniformity" (*OR*, 108; *ÜR*, 217), hence not a practice worthy of the name religion at all. Religion, he fears, has been eaten up from the inside by a "mania for system," which "does indeed reject what is foreign, even if it is quite conceivable and true, because it could spoil one's well-formed ranks and disturb the beautiful connections by claiming its place" (ibid.). The opposite of

33 For a more detailed discussion of the relationship between hermeneutics and ethics in Schleiermacher's work, see Christian Berner, "Ethische Aspekte der Hermeneutik bei Schleiermacher," *Internationale Zeitschrift für Philosophie*, no. 1, 1992, 68. Berner argues that "Hermeneutik bedeutet bei ihm nicht bloss die Arbeit der Auslegung, sondern auch Verallgemeinerung in einer philosophischen Perspektive." Ibid.

34 For a discussion of the relationship between Hegel and Schleiermacher's interpretation of early Christian religion, see Hans W. Frei, *The Eclipse of Biblical Narrative: A Study in Eighteenth- and Nineteenth-Century Hermeneutics* (New Haven: Yale University Press, 1974), 315ff.

35 Theodore Ziolkowski gives an account of how *On Religion* represents a historicizing of theology. See Ziolkowski, *Clio the Romantic Muse: Historicizing the Faculties in Germany* (Ithaca: Cornell University Press, 2004), 74–88.

36 Schleiermacher here anticipates a number of points that would later be associated with Søren Kierkegaard, whom Schleiermacher possibly influenced through his speeches and his 1833 visit to Denmark. For an account of Schleiermacher's visit, see John Stewart, "Schleiermacher's Visit to Copenhagen in 1833," *Zeitschrift für neuere Theologiegeschichte*, vol. 11, no. 2, 2004, 279–302.

individuality is, in other words, not a shared sociality or intersubjective community, but, rather, an *abstract* universality – the "universal maelstroem ['allgemeinen Strudel']" (*OR*, 142; *ÜR*, 249) that only represents "a schematism of the same" (*OR*, 150; *ÜR*, 256).

Schleiermacher's educated, yet non-religious, acquaintances in Jena and Berlin do not represent such a schematism of the same. Rather, this danger is represented by the "barbarism" of those whose sole aim is acquiring material goods and pleasure (*OR*, 151; *ÜR*, 256) and who leave no room for the *Bildung*, the free unity between the individual and the universal, that Schleiermacher finds decisive for religious conduct in particular and social conduct in general.

The notion of free sociality is built on the claim that a true humanity consists of a plurality of individuals and cultures. The study of this plurality goes beyond the boundaries of the philosophy of religion and involves the larger domain of ethics. For Schleiermacher, though, ethics is not limited to the question of morality but traverses the fields of practical reason, as well as the acquisition of knowledge through "the action of reason on nature."[37] As such, ethics is defined as the aspiration towards total knowledge in the synthesis of the material and the spiritual (*LPE*, 147; *E*, 200), being and knowledge (*LPE*, 141; *E*, 192f.), and the individual and the universal (*LPE*, 37; *E*, 48f.). Schleiermacher's discussion of individuality in the ethics lectures – which he first gave in 1805, i.e., the very year he started teaching hermeneutics – fits well with this picture. "Free sociality," Schleiermacher writes in his ethics, "can only exist inasmuch as personal particularity stands out from the mass" (*LPE*, 97; *E*, 128). Again, standing out from the mass is not the same as being opposed to socializing, but represents, rather, the core of human sociability. This community of individuals encompasses not only the society of the present but also that of tradition. Hence, Schleiermacher claims, it is "the inclination of every great moral person ... to enter into community with the past and the future" (*LPE*, 99; *E*, 131). Such an inclination, he explains, "can admittedly only be realized through works of science and art, but nevertheless proceeds just as often from free sociability and the state as from the scholarly association and the church" (ibid.).[38]

---

37 Quoted from Scholtz, *Die Philosophie Schleiermachers*, 114.
38 It is important to note how such views as these rapidly set Schleiermacher apart from mainstream theology and philosophy at the time. As Ziolkowski notes, "[e]ven

Schleiermacher's theory of free sociability might appear a youthful, rather utopian contribution. However, it is important to keep in mind the historical reality in which this theory was conceived, the short but significant period of the intellectual salon, including the *Mittwochs-gesellschaft* and the famous meetings in the homes of well-educated women such as Rahel Varnhagen and Henriette Herz.[39] The salons cultivated an open and inclusive atmosphere, allowing women and Jews, groups regularly marginalized in public discourse, to play a role that would be unthinkable in the later, more conservative circles of *Die Christlich-Deutsche Tischgesellschaft* that was established in 1811.

Yet Schleiermacher's theory of free, productive sociality, his interest in diversity and cultural manifold, should not be reduced to a theory of the salon as a historical phenomenon; it plays instead an important role in the articulation of the *Ethics* as the culmination of his philosophical system. Just as hermeneutics should be seen as a project of approximation, ethics is an ongoing process of becoming (*LPE*, 6; *E*, 9). This process of becoming (*Werden*), however, is about overcoming the one-sidedness of one's point of view.[40] Such an overcoming takes place through dialogue and intersubjective interaction. This dialogue is not one between interpreter and text – the text, after all, does not speak back – but one that takes place within the community of interpreters. Dialogue proper requires that the interlocutors mutually recognize the individuality or the point of view of the other. As such, the individual appears as the original organ and symbol of reason (*LPE*, 10; *E*, 15). As an organ of reason, the individual stands in a dialectical relation to "the action of reason on nature" (ibid.). This process, in turn, "is only complete when the whole of nature – by means of human nature – has been appropriated organically or symbolically to reason, and the life of individuals is not

his former professor of philosophy, Johann August Eberhard, with whom [Schleiermacher] had studied Kant and the history of philosophy, denounced him as an atheist. While Schleiermacher's views were unacceptable to the rationalists and pietists on the faculty [in Halle], he found friends in his former teacher, the classicist Friedrich August Wolf, with whom he could discuss Plato, and Henrik Steffens, the Norwegian philosopher of nature." *Clio the Romantic Muse*, 89.

39 For a survey of the Berlin salon culture, see Petra Wilhelmy, *Der Berliner Salon im 19. Jahrhundert (1780–1914)* (Berlin: Walter de Gruyter, 1989), in particular 33–114 (see 89–95 for a discussion of Schleiermacher's role within the salon culture).

40 "Die Form der Unvollendung kann sein Einseitigkeit des Gesichtspunktes. Hiebei am meisten falsches Gefühl der Sicherheit und am wenigsten richtige Würdigung der andern" (*LPE*, 6; *E*, 9).

a life lived merely for those individuals, but for the totality of reason and the totality of nature" (ibid.). In Schleiermacher's model, the highest good is nothing but the objective depiction of this process (*LPE*, 11; *E*, 16). At stake is an expression of "the identity of the whole of reason with the whole of nature" (*LPE*, 18; *E*, 24, see also *LPE*, 20; *E*, 27). A crucial role is ascribed to tradition in this process. "The written word," Schleiermacher explains, "is the memory and tradition of language" (*LPE*, 51; *E*, 67). It represents a safekeeping, a communication, and a comprehension of the insights of the past, but also an opportunity of discovery (*LPE*, 48; *E*, 63). In addressing this process of safekeeping, ethics is itself defined as the science of history.[41] It is a science that takes into account the tradition while also pointing forward to the overcoming of intellectual one-sidedness that Schleiermacher, in the translation essay, envisions as a new cosmopolitanism – one that is based not on the erasing of differences between individual languages and the world-views they harbor but on the communication and mutual exchange between them.

Conceived within this framework, as the organ of an intersubjective, historically developing reason, Schleiermacher's notion of individuality has little or nothing to do with the kind of philosophy Gadamer disdains when rejecting the idea of "an intention locked in the impotence of subjective particularity" (*TM*, 489; *WM*, 493).[42] Nor does Schleiermacher's hermeneutics represent the methodological "repetition of the same" that Gadamer also ascribes to him. Rather, in Schleiermacher's philosophy the notion of a critical-reflective hermeneutics works as a corrective to reason's tendency to reduce that which is different to that which is the same, hence undermining the realization of cognitive progress and the aesthetic and ethical (*sittliche*) manifold that he critically elaborates in his ethics, philosophy of religion, and, finally, the lectures in dialectics. This – rather than a model that places the world-disclosive event of art in the midst of

---

41 "The science of history . . . is ethics" (*HC*, 8; *HuK*, 77).

42 That Gadamer here targets Schleiermacher becomes clear from the appeal following this claim: "Let us remember that understanding what someone says is not an achievement of empathy in which one divines the inner life of the speaker" (*TM*, 498; *WM*, 493). Against such a (Schleiermacherian) position, Gadamer points out that "this determination by situation and context, which fills out what is said to a totality of meaning and makes what is said really said, pertains not to the speaker but to what is spoken" (ibid.)

interpretation – is how hermeneutics can aspire towards providing a genuine humanist model.

Overcoming the ontological turn in hermeneutics

Gadamer's philosophical hermeneutics is rooted in an orientation towards ontology. His is the endeavor to overcome the problem of modern nihilism and loss of meaning through the development of hermeneutics as a theory of meaning-constitution in and through tradition. While drawing on the young Heidegger's teaching in the years leading up to the publication of *Being and Time*, Gadamer casts the problem of nihilism as an incapacity to understand ourselves as part of the tradition. This problem spans the entire field of modern society – the museums, the concert halls, as well as the broader understanding of ourselves and our relation to the past – but is given its most poignant articulation in the call for a scientific method in light of which the human sciences can be justified and epistemolog- ically put on a par with the natural sciences. It is only because modern, post-Cartesian, post-enlightenment societies fail to take seriously the meaning-constituting function of tradition that this objectification of the past can take place. Philosophy and science, since Schleiermacher, have approached the past through objectifying epistemic strategies. The result is that our pre-reflective prejudices and intuitions with regard to tradition and historicity, and in particular the notion that they can at all be objectified, remain unquestioned.

According to Gadamer, the very idea that the past can be objectified and turned into a subject of methodological research and scrutiny is based on a misunderstanding whose ramifications tran- scend the boundaries of philosophy as an academic discipline or general intellectual pastime. At risk, Gadamer worries, is human self- understanding as such. By modeling the humanities on the idea that, in order for us to get knowledge about the past, history should be objectified and turned into a subject of methodological procedures we sever the ties to the tradition of which we ourselves are a part. By distancing ourselves from tradition what we really do is distance ourselves from ourselves. No methodological apparatus, no matter how fine-tuned, can help us overcome this alienation. What is required, rather, is a mode of thinking about the past that is suffi- ciently radical to shake up the most fundamental aspects of this paradigm. It is Gadamer's conviction that his political humanism, in placing the work of art at the center of hermeneutics, represents such thinking.

When judged from a perspective like Gadamer's, the problem with Schleiermacher's theory is therefore not that it brings aesthetics into hermeneutics or even aestheticizes philosophy as such. The problem, rather, is that Schleiermacher, in leaning on a misreading of Kant's critique, aestheticizes hermeneutics in the wrong manner, hence providing a philosophical model that contributes to, rather than questions, the nihilism that permeates modern society. By subjectivizing aesthetic experience, the Kantian and romantic traditions exclude us from the very last arena in which tradition was experienced as binding, authoritative, and constitutive for our self-understanding. In emphasizing how the great work of art articulates the most fundamental values, the absolutes, of its community, as well as seeing tradition as a process of integration (rather than a matter of reconstruction), Hegel in part succeeds in repairing the damage of Kantian and romantic philosophy. Yet, in Gadamer's reading, Hegel does not deliver what he promises. At the end of the day, he remains caught up in a quasi-Cartesian model of reflection that, in Gadamer's view, undermines the hermeneutic tenor of his work, in that it, epistemically, places philosophy over art and, closely related to this, caters to a notion of absolute knowing.

This, in short, is Gadamer's critique of the hermeneutic legacy of German Idealism. In the course of this book, I have argued that Gadamer misreads Kant, Hegel, and the romantics. Yet his interpretation of Schleiermacher stands out as particularly faulty. Over the last two chapters, I have argued that Gadamer fails to respond to the philosophical thrust of Schleiermacher's hermeneutics. In Chapter 5 I pursued a mainly negative argument, claiming that Gadamer misconceives the methodological standards of technical and grammatical interpretation. And in this sixth and final chapter, I have sketched a mainly constructive strategy of interpretation, aimed at resituating Schleiermacher's hermeneutics within a more comprehensive theory of meaning, historicity, and intersubjective interaction.

Against this backdrop a number of points can now be made explicit. First, it is evident that Schleiermacher does not deal with the kind of deep-seated problem of existential-ontological meaning that Gadamer inherits from Heidegger. Gadamer, however, presupposes that philosophers in the traditions from Kant and romanticism do indeed, at least indirectly, address the Heideggerian question of the meaning of being, but for lack of insight into twentieth-century ontology they do so in a phenomenologically inadequate way. At no single point throughout *Truth and Method* or the later essays does Gadamer consider Schleiermacher's hermeneutics in relation to the fundamental question it sets out to answer, namely: how can we arrive at a set of standards that makes it possible to speak of validity in interpretation, hence also assisting the critical-reflective interpreter in his or her effort to overcome illegitimate prejudices?

Second, the stark opposition between validity and historicity in interpretation, that is, the very premise on which Gadamer's criticism of German Idealism and romanticism rests, cannot be accepted. In Schleiermacher's work, the turn towards validity in interpretation follows from, rather than represses, the historicity of reason. It is *because* human reason is finite and historical that we need the critical standards of technical and grammatical interpretation in the first place. If reason were ahistorical or transhistorical, if its outlook were not encumbered by its embeddedness within a particular life-form, such standards would not be needed.

Third, Gadamer claims that only an ontologically oriented hermeneutics can account for a notion of *Bildung* through history, the idea of a gradual expansion of the interpreter's horizon. Gadamer presupposes that there is an unbridgeable gap between *Bildung*, on the one hand, and an orientation towards normativity in understanding, on the other. Schleiermacher, I have argued, sees things differently. His is a model in which *Bildung* is only made possible by the existence of critical-reflective standards in interpretation and translation. Only thus can the interpreter, in his or her engagement with the texts of the past, strive to understand the past on its own terms and also, actively and reflectively, take responsibility for his or her new-won knowledge and make it binding on his or her practices and way of understanding him- or herself and the world.

This implies, fourth, that there is no tension or opposition in Schleiermacher's work between hermeneutics and self-reflection. Gadamer, as we have seen, argues that the hermeneutic experience is, ultimately, one in which the critical-reflective capacity of the interpreter is suspended in encountering the authority of tradition. For Schleiermacher, too, human reason is situated within a historical context. Yet the understanding (and assessment) of this historical context, of how we have become the ones that we are, is not a process of fundamental acceptance or subjection, but a critical, reflective, and ultimately discursive activity. In his philosophy, the self-understanding that the interpreter can achieve through the process of the hermeneutic work is epistemic-ethical, rather than existential-ontological by nature.

Finally, the points above undermine the Gadamerian idea of there being an unsurpassable opposition between historicity and autonomy. Because reason is historically situated, it needs to test its most fundamental presumptions by engaging in intersubjective, intercultural, and intertemporal dialogue. This dialogue does not lead it to leave aside the very notion of autonomy as being, itself, a prejudice that derives from the context of post-Cartesian philosophy. Nor is self-understanding reduced to a passive acknowledgement of the authority of tradition. Rather, self-understanding is played out in our active ability to reflect on and take a stance with regard to false or illegitimate prejudices and naïve historical or culturally biased assumptions. Needless to say, this is an intersubjectively mediated process, rather than the achievement of a solitary philosopher.

Whereas Gadamer, in spite of his commitment to a dialogical understanding of rationality, systematically denounces the relevance of critical reflection to the hermeneutic enterprise, Schleiermacher's model is helpful, in that it, at the level of theoretical discussion and concrete textual engagement, shows how critical reflection is itself relative to a historical context. Cultural and temporal distance, in Schleiermacher's understanding, does not make understanding impossible. However, it does turn understanding into a challenge that is in need of ongoing self-reflection and historical work, that is, into an activity that is pursued from a bottom-up, rather than a top-down, perspective.[43]

This is the legacy of early nineteenth-century hermeneutics. Schleiermacher shares with Kant, Fichte, and Hegel a commitment to self-determination and criticism. He combines this with a notion of historical and cultural diversity that challenges hermeneutics in general and philosophy, as a second-order reflection on interpretative practices, in particular. Schleiermacher's contribution therefore does not rest with him offering an alternative response to the questions posed by fundamental ontology – the question of the meaning of being, or, as with Gadamer, the meaning of *Dasein*'s being in tradition – but is

---

43 However, Schleiermacher emphasizes that this should not lead to an "abentheuerliche Sammlung von Einzelheiten" but culminate in an "allgemeines Bild" (*GdaP*, 17).

designed so as to respond to a rather more limited challenge, that of a historically situated reason maintaining a notion of autonomy and self-determination, hence also the ability to gradually purge itself of misinformed prejudices. As such, Schleiermacher's contribution remains relevant if, like some of Gadamer's more recent, Anglophone readers, we wish to retain his *Bildungs*-oriented understanding of historical reason without thereby taking onboard the more problematic consequences that issue from his ontological orientation.

BIBLIOGRAPHY OF WORKS CITED

Adorno, Theodor W. *Aesthetic Theory.* Trans. Robert Hullot-Kentor. Minneapolis: University of Minnesota Press, 1997.
Ästhetische Theorie. Frankfurt am Main: Suhrkamp Verlag, 1970.

Alderman, Harold. "The Work of Art and Other Things." In Ballard and Scott 1973, 157–169.

Alexander, Werner. *Hermeneutica Generalis. Zur Konzeption und Entwicklung der allgemeinen Verstehenslehre im 17. und 18. Jahrhundert.* Stuttgart: M&P Verlag für Wissenschaft und Forschung, 1993.

Allison, Henry E. *Kant's Theory of Taste: A Reading of the "Critique of Aesthetic Judgment."* Cambridge: Cambridge University Press, 2001.
Kant's Theory of Freedom. Cambridge: Cambridge University Press, 1990.

Ambrosio, Francis J. "The Figure of Socrates in Gadamer's Philosophical Hermeneutics." In Hahn 1997, 259–273.

Ameriks, Karl. *Kant and the Historical Turn.* Oxford: Oxford University Press, 2006.
(ed.) *The Cambridge Companion to German Idealism.* Cambridge: Cambridge University Press, 2000.

Apel, Karl-Otto. "Regulative Ideas or Truth-Happening?: An Attempt to Answer the Question of the Conditions of the Possibility of Valid Understanding." Trans. Ralf Sommermeier. In Hahn 1997, 67–94.

Apel, Karl-Otto and Jürgen Habermas (eds.). *Hermeneutik und Ideologiekritik.* Frankfurt am Main: Suhrkamp Verlag, 1971.

Aristotle. *The Works of Aristotle.* 12 vols. Ed. W. D. Ross. Various translators. Oxford: Clarendon Press, 1908–52.

Arndt, Andreas. "Fortschritt im Begriff. Hegels Aufhebung der Hermeneutik in seinen Vorlesungen zur Geschichte der Philosophie." In Arndt *et al.*, 1998, 108–115.

Arndt, Andreas, Karol Bal, and Henning Ottmann (eds.). *Hegel-Jahrbuch 1997. Hegel und die Geschichte der Philosophie.* Berlin: Akademie Verlag, 1998.

Ballard, Edward G. and Charles E. Scott (eds.). *Martin Heidegger in Europe and America.* The Hague: Martinus Nijhoff, 1973.

Baudelaire, Charles. *Art in Paris, 1845–1862.* Ed. and trans. Jonathan Mayne. Oxford: Phaidon, 1981.

Œuvres complètes. Ed. Claude Pichois. Paris: Gallimard, 1976.

Beiser, Frederick. *Schiller as Philosopher: A Re-Examination.* Oxford: Clarendon Press, 2005.

    The Romantic Imperative. Cambridge, Mass.: Harvard University Press, 2003.

    The Cambridge Companion to Hegel. Cambridge: Cambridge University Press, 1993.

    "Hegel's Historicism." In Beiser 1993, 270–300.

    The Fate of Reason. Cambridge, Mass.: Harvard University Press, 1987.

Benjamin, Walter. *Selected Writings.* Vol. I. Ed. Marcus Bullock and Michael W. Jennings. Cambridge, Mass.: Harvard University Press, 1996.

    The Origin of the German Tragic Drama. Trans. J. Osborne. London: NLB, 1977.

    Gesammelte Schriften. Ed. Rolf Tiedemann and Hermann Schweppenhäuser. Frankfurt am Main: Suhrkamp Verlag, 1974.

    Charles Baudelaire: A Lyric Poet in the Era of High Capitalism. Trans. Harry Zohn. London: NLB, 1968.

Bennett, Tony. *The Birth of the Museum: History, Theory, Politics.* London: Routledge, 1995.

Berner, Christian. *La philosophie de Schleiermacher.* Paris: Les Éditions du Cerf, 1995.

    "Ethische Aspekte der Hermeneutik bei Schleiermacher." *Internationale Zeitschrift für Philosophie,* no. 1, 1992, 68–87.

Bernet, Rudolf, Donn Welton, and Gina Zavota (eds.). *Edmund Husserl: Critical Assessments.* 5 vols. London: Routledge, 2005.

Bernofsky, Susan. *Foreign Words: Translation-Authors in the Age of Goethe.* Detroit: Wayne State University Press, 2005.

Bernstein, Jay (ed.). *Classic and Romantic German Aesthetics.* Various translators. Cambridge: Cambridge University Press, 2003.

Bernstein, Richard. "McDowell's Domesticated Hegelianism." In Smith 2002, 9–24.

    Beyond Objectivism and Relativism: Science, Hermeneutics, and Praxis. Philadelphia: University of Pennsylvania Press, 1983.

Bohrer, Karl Heinz. *Die Kritik der Romantik.* Frankfurt am Main: Suhrkamp Verlag, 1989.

Borinski, Karl. *Baltasar Gracian und die Hoflitteratur in Deutschland.* Halle: Max Niemeyer, 1894.

Brandom, Robert. *Tales of the Mighty Dead.* Cambridge, Mass.: Harvard University Press, 2002.

Buchdahl, Gerd. *Metaphysics and the Philosophy of Science.* Oxford: Basil Blackwell, 1969.

Bürger, Peter. *Zur Kritik der idealistischen Ästhetik.* Frankfurt am Main: Suhrkamp Verlag, 1983.

Cambiano, Giuseppe. *Le retour des Anciens.* Trans. Silvia Milanezi. Paris: Éditions Belin, 1994.

Cassirer, Ernst. *The Philosophy of the Enlightenment.* Trans. Fritz C. A. Koelln and James Pettegrove. Princeton: Princeton University Press, 1979.

    Die Philosophie der Aufklärung. Tübingen: J. C. B. Mohr, 1932.

Cavell, Stanley. *In Quest of the Ordinary: Lines of Skepticism and Romanticism.* Chicago: University of Chicago Press, 1988.

Christensen, Darrel L. (ed.). *Contemporary German Philosophy,* vol. I. University Park, Pa.: Pennsylvania State University Press, 1982.

Cohen, Ted and Paul Guyer (eds.). *Essays in Kant's Aesthetics.* Chicago: University of Chicago Press, 1982.

Conolly, J. M. and T. Keutner (eds.). *Hermeneutics versus Science?* Indiana: University of Notre Dame Press, 1988.

Danto, Arthur. *After the End of Art: Contemporary Art and the Pale of History.* Princeton: Princeton University Press, 1997.

Dastur, Françoise. "Esthétique et herméneutique. La critique de la conscience esthétique chez Gadamer." *Phénoménologie et esthétique.* Ed. Renaud Barbaras *et al.* Paris: Encre Marine, 1998.

Davidson, Donald. "Gadamer and Plato's *Philebus.*" In Hahn 1997, 421–432.

de Duve, Thierry. *Clement Greenberg between the Lines.* Trans. Brian Holmes. Paris: Éditions Dis Voir, 1996.

de Mul, Jos. *The Tragedy of Finitude: Dilthey's Hermeneutics of Life.* Trans. Tony Burrett. New Haven: Yale University Press, 2004.

Descartes, René. *The Philosophical Writings.* 2 vols. Trans. John Cottingham, Robert Stoothoff, and Dugald Murdoch. Cambridge: Cambridge University Press, 1985.

Œuvres. Ed. Charles Adam and Paul Tannery. Paris: J. Vrin, 1973.

Dilthey, Wilhelm. *Die Jugendgeschichte Hegels. Die Jugendgeschichte Hegels und andere Abhandlungen zur Geschichte des Deutschen Idealismus.* Ed. Herman Nohl. *Gesammelte Schriften,* vol. IV. Göttingen: Vandenhoeck & Ruprecht, 1990.

Leben Schleiermachers. Erster Band. Ed. Martin Redeker. *Gesammelte Schriften,* vol. XIII. Göttingen: Vandenhoeck & Ruprecht, 1970.

Leben Schleiermachers. Zweiter Band. Ed. Martin Redeker. *Gesammelte Schriften,* vol. XIV. Göttingen: Vandenhoeck & Ruprecht, 1966.

Weltanschauungslehre. Abhandlungen zur Philosophie der Philosophie. Ed. Bernhard Groethuysen. *Gesammelte Schriften,* vol. 8. Berlin: B. G. Teubner, 1931.

Dostal, Robert J. *The Cambridge Companion to Gadamer.* Cambridge: Cambridge University Press, 2002.

"Gadamer's Continuous Challenge: Heidegger's Plato Interpretation." In Hahn 1997, 289–307.

Dutt, Carsten. *Hermeneutik. Ästhetik. Praktische Philosophie. Hans-Georg Gadamer im Gespräch.* Heidelberg: Carl Winter, 1993.

Fichte, Johann G. *Sämtliche Werke.* Ed. Immanuel Hermann Fichte. Berlin: Walter de Gruyter, 1971.

Fischer, Hermann, *et al.* Schleiermacher-Archiv, Band I, Teilband 2. *Internationaler Schleiermacher-Kongreß 1984.* Berlin: Walter de Gruyter, 1985.

Forster, Michael. "Schleiermacher's Hermeneutics: Some Problems and Solutions." *The Harvard Review of Philosophy,* spring 2005, 100–123.

"Friedrich Daniel Ernst Schleiermacher." *The Stanford Encyclopedia of Philosophy (Winter 2002 Edition),* Edward N. Zalta (ed.), http://plato.stanford.edu/archives/win2002/entries/schleiermacher/.

Hegel and Skepticism. Boston: Harvard University Press, 1989.

Frank, Manfred. "Metaphysical Foundations: A Look at Schleiermacher's *Dialectics.*" Trans. Jacqueline Mariña and Christine Helmer. In Mariña 2005, 15–34.

The Philosophical Foundations of Early German Romanticism. Trans. Elizabeth Millán-Zaibert. Albany, N.Y.: SUNY Press, 2004.

"Einleitung des Herausgebers," Friedrich Schleiermacher, *Dialektik,* ed. Manfred Frank, vol. I. Frankfurt am Main: Suhrkamp Verlag, 2001.

Unendliche Annäherung. Frankfurt am Main: Suhrkamp Verlag, 1997.

"Two Centuries of Philosophical Critique of Reason." Trans. D. Freundlieb and W. Hudson. In Freundlieb and Hudson 1993, 67–85.

Einführung in die frühromantische Ästhetik. Frankfurt am Main: Suhrkamp Verlag, 1989.

What is Neostructuralism? Trans. Sabine Wilke and Richard Gray. Minneapolis: University of Minnesota Press, 1989.

Was ist Neostrukturalismus? Frankfurt am Main: Suhrkamp Verlag, 1984.

Das individuelle Allgemeine. Frankfurt am Main: Suhrkamp Verlag, 1977.

Fränzel, Walter. *Geschichte des Übersetzens im 18. Jahrhundert.* Leipzig: Voigtländer, 1914.

Frei, Hans W. *The Eclipse of Biblical Narrative: A Study in Eighteenth- and Nineteenth-Century Hermeneutics.* New Haven: Yale University Press, 1974.

Freundlieb, D. and W. Hudson (eds.). *Reason and its Other.* Oxford: Berg, 1993.

Friedman, Michael. *A Parting of the Ways: Carnap, Cassirer, and Heidegger.* Chicago: Open Court, 2000.

Fruchon, Pierre. *L'Herméneutique de Gadamer. Platonisme et modernité.* Paris: Les Éditions du Cerf, 1994.

Fulda, Hans-Friedrich and Rolf-Peter Horstmann (eds.). *Hegel und die "Kritik der Urteilskraft."* Stuttgart: Klett-Cotta, 1990.

Funk, Robert W. (ed.). *Schleiermacher as Contemporary. Journal for Theology and the Church,* vol. VII. New York: Herder & Herder, 1970.

Gadamer, Hans-Georg. *Gadamer on Celan.* Ed. and trans. Richard Heinemann and Bruce Krajewski. Albany, N.Y.: SUNY Press, 1997.

"Reply to David Detmer." In Hahn 1997, 287.

Gesammelte Werke. Tübingen: J. B. C. Mohr, 1985–1995.

Wer bin Ich und wer bist Du? Frankfurt am Main: Suhrkamp Verlag, 1995.

Heidegger's Ways. Trans. John W. Stanley. Albany, N.Y.: SUNY Press, 1994.

Truth and Method. Trans. Joel Weinsheimer and Donald G. Marshall. New York: Continuum, 1994.

"What is Truth?" Trans. Brice R. Wachterhauser. In Wachterhauser 1994, 33–46.

Hans-Georg Gadamer on Education, Poetry, and History. Ed. Dieter Misgeld and Graeme Nicholson. Trans. Lawrence Schmidt and Monica Reuss. Albany, N.Y.: SUNY Press, 1992.

Plato's Dialectical Ethics. Trans. Robert M. Wallace. New Haven: Yale University Press, 1991.

"Letter to Dallmayr." In Palmer and Michelfelder 1989, 93–101.

"On the Circle of Understanding," Trans. J. M. Connolly and T. Keutner. In Connolly and Keutner 1988, 67–78.

The Relevance of the Beautiful and Other Essays. Ed. Robert Bernasconi. Trans. Nicholas Walker. Cambridge: Cambridge University Press, 1986.

Philosophical Apprenticeships. Trans. Robert R. Sullivan. Cambridge, Mass.: MIT Press, 1985.

"Wilhelm Dilthey nach 150 Jahren (Zwischen Romantik und Positivismus. Ein Diskussionsbeitrag)." In Orth 1985, 157–182.

Heideggers Wege. Tübingen: J. B. C. Mohr, 1983.

Reason in the Age of Science. Trans. Frederick G. Lawrence. Cambridge, Mass.: MIT Press, 1981.

Hegels Dialektik. Sechs hermeneutische Studien. Tübingen: J. C. B. Mohr, 1980.

Dialogue and Dialectic: Eight Hermeneutical Studies of Plato. Trans. and ed. P. Christopher Smith. New Haven: Yale University Press, 1980.

Philosophische Lehrjahre. Eine Rückschau. Frankfurt am Main: Vittorio Klostermann, 1977.

Hegel's Dialectics: Five Hermeneutical Studies. Trans. P. Christopher Smith. New Haven: Yale University Press, 1976.

Philosophical Hermeneutics. Trans. David E. Linge. Berkeley: University of California Press, 1976.

Vernunft im Zeitalter der Wissenschaft. Frankfurt am Main: Suhrkamp Verlag, 1976.

"The Problem of Language in Schleiermacher's Hermeneutics." Trans. David E. Linge. In Funk 1970, 68–84.

Volk und Geschichte im Denken Herders. Frankfurt am Main: Vittorio Klostermann, 1942.

Gjesdal, Kristin. "Between Enlightenment and Romanticism: Some Problems and Challenges in Gadamer's Hermeneutics," *The Journal of the History of Philosophy,* vol. 46, no. 2, 2008, 285–306.

"Aesthetic and Political Humanism: Gadamer on Herder, Schleiermacher, and the Origins of Modern Hermeneutics." *History of Philosophy Quarterly,* vol. 24, no. 3, July 2007, 275–296.

"Reading Shakespeare; Reading Modernity: Hegel and Herder on Art and Modernity." *Angelaki: Journal of the Theoretical Humanities,* vol. 9, no. 3, 2004, 17–31.

Gracián, Baltasar. *A Pocket Mirror for Heroes.* Trans. Christopher Maurer. New York: Doubleday, 1996.

The Art of Worldly Wisdom: A Pocket Oracle. Trans. Christopher Maurer. New York: Doubleday, 1992.

Gray, John Glenn. *Hegel and Greek Thought.* San Francisco: Harper & Row, 1969.

Greenberg, Clement. *The Collected Essays and Criticism.* 4 vols. Ed. John O'Brian. Chicago: University of Chicago Press, 1993.

Grondin, Jean. *Hans-Georg Gadamer: A Biography.* Trans. Joel Weinsheimer. New Haven: Yale University Press, 2003.

"Gadamer on Humanism." In Hahn 1997, 157–170.

Sources of Hermeneutics. Albany, N.Y.: SUNY Press, 1995.

Hermeneutische Wahrheit? Königstein: Forum Academicum, 1982.

Guyer, Paul. "Hegel on Kant's Aesthetics: Necessity and Contingency in Beauty and Art." In Fulda and Horstmann 1990, 81–99.

Habermas, Jürgen. *Truth and Justification*. Trans. Barbara Fultner. Cambridge, Mass.: MIT Press, 2005.

Wahrheit und Rechtfertigung. Philosophische Aufsätze. Frankfurt am Main: Suhrkamp Verlag, 1999.

"A Review of *Truth and Method*." Trans. Fred R. Dallmayr and Thomas McCarthy. In Ormiston and Schrift 1990, 213–244.

"The Hermeneutic Claim to Universality." Trans. Joseph Bleicher. In Ormiston and Schrift, 1990, 245–272.

Philosophical-Political Profiles. Trans. Frederick G. Lawrence. Cambridge, Mass.: MIT Press, 1983.

Zur Logik der Sozialwissenschaften. Frankfurt am Main: Suhrkamp Verlag, 1982.

Philosophisch-politische Profile. Frankfurt am Main: Suhrkamp Verlag, 1981.

Hahn, Lewis E. (ed.). *The Philosophy of Hans-Georg Gadamer.* The Library of Living Philosophers. Vol. XXIV. Chicago: Open Court, 1997.

Hegel, G. W. F. *Introduction to the Lectures on the History of Philosophy,* Trans. T. M. Knox and A. V. Miller. Oxford: Clarendon Press, 1995.

Lectures on the History of Philosophy. 3 vols. Trans. E. S. Haldane and Frances H. Simson. Lincoln: University of Nebraska Press, 1995.

Werke in 20 Bänden. Ed. Eva Moldenhauer and Karl Markus Michel. Frankfurt am Main: Suhrkamp Verlag, 1986.

Lectures on the Philosophy of World History: Introduction. Trans. H. B. Nisbet. Cambridge: Cambridge University Press, 1984.

Phenomenology of Spirit. Trans. A. V. Miller. Oxford: Oxford University Press, 1977.

Aesthetics: Lectures on Fine Art. 2 vols. Trans. T. M. Knox. Oxford: Clarendon Press, 1975.

Die Vernunft in der Geschichte. Ed. Johannes Hoffmeister. Hamburg: Felix Meiner, 1955.

Einleitung in die Geschichte der Philosophie. Ed. Johannes Hoffmeister. Hamburg: Felix Meiner, 1940.

Heidegger, Martin. *Gesamtausgabe.* Frankfurt am Main: Vittorio Klostermann, 1975– .

The Phenomenology of Religious Life. Trans. Matthias Fritsch and Jennifer Anna Gosetti-Ferencei. Bloomington: Indiana University Press, 2004.

Phenomenological Interpretations of Aristotle: Initiation into Phenomenological Research. Trans. Richard Rojcewicz. Bloomington: Indiana University Press, 2001.

Ontology: The Hermeneutics of Facticity. Trans. John van Buren. Bloomington: Indiana University Press, 1999.

"Hegel and the Greeks." Trans. Robert Metcalf. In *Pathmarks.* Ed. William McNeill. Cambridge: Cambridge University Press, 1998, 323–336.

Kant und das Problem der Metaphysik. Frankfurt am Main: Vittorio Klostermann, 1991.

Nietzsche. Trans. David F. Krell. San Francisco: Harper, 1991.

Kant and the Problem of Metaphysics. Trans. Richard Taft. Bloomington: Indiana University Press, 1990.

Hegel's Concept of Experience. Trans. John Glenn Gray. New York: Harper & Row, 1989.

"The Age of the World View." Trans. Marjorie Grene. *Boundary 2*, vol. 4, no. 2, winter 1976, 341–355.

Poetry, Language, Thought. Trans. Albert Hofstadter. San Francisco: Harper, 1975.

Being and Time. Trans. John Macquarrie and Edward Robinson. San Francisco: Harper, 1962.

Der Ursprung des Kunstwerkes. Stuttgart: Reclam, 1960.

Henrich, Dieter. *Aesthetic Judgment and the Moral Image of the World.* Stanford: Stanford University Press, 1992.

"Fichte's Original Insight." Trans. David R. Lacherman. In Christensen 1982, 15–53.

Fichtes ursprüngliche Einsicht. Frankfurt am Main: Vittorio Klostermann, 1967.

Herder, Johann Gottfried. *Selected Writings on Aesthetics.* Ed. and Trans. Gregory Moore. Princeton: Princeton University Press, 2006.

Schriften zur Ästhetik und Literatur 1767–1781, Johann Gottfried Herder. Werke Ed. Ulrich Gaier *et al.*, vol. II. Frankfurt am Main: Deutscher Klassiker Verlag, 1993.

How, Alan. *The Habermas–Gadamer Debate and the Nature of the Social.* Aldershot: Ashgate Publishing Company, 1995.

Huizinga, Johan. *Homo Ludens: A Study of the Play Element in Culture.* Boston: The Beacon Press, 1955.

Husserl, Edmund. *Cartesian Meditations: An Introduction to Phenomenology.* Trans. Dorion Cairns. Dordrecht: Martinus Nijhoff, 1988.

Cartesianische Meditationen und Pariser Vorträge, Husserliana I. The Hague: Martinus Nijhoff, 1973.

The Paris Lectures. Trans. Peter Koestenbaum. Dordrecht: Martinus Nijhoff, 1964.

Erste Philosophie. 2. Teil, Husserliana VIII. Ed. Rudolf Boehm. The Hague: Martinus Nijhoff, 1959.

Erste Philosophie. 1. Teil, Husserliana VII. Ed. Rudolf Boehm. The Hague: Martinus Nijhoff, 1956.

Huyssen, Andreas. *Die frühromantische Konzeption von Übersetzung und Aneignung: Studien zur frühromantischen Utopie einer deutschen Weltliteratur.* Zurich: Atlantis Verlag, 1969.

Hyppolite, Jean. *Genesis and Structure of Hegel's "Phenomenology of Spirit."* Trans. Samuel Cherniak and John Heckman. Evanston: Northwestern University Press, 1974.

Genèse et structure de la Phénoménologie de l'esprit de Hegel. Paris: Aubier, 1946.

Jaeger, Werner. *Humanistische Reden und Vorträge.* Berlin: Walter de Gruyter, 1960.

Jaeschke, Walter. "Paralipomena Hegeliana zur Wirkungsgeschichte Schleiermachers." In Fischer *et al.*, 1985, 1157–1171.

"World History and the History of the Absolute Spirit." In Perkins 1984, 101–117.

Kant, Immanuel. *Critique of Judgment.* Trans. Werner S. Pluhar. Indianapolis: Hackett, 1987.

Critique of Pure Reason. Trans. Norman Kemp Smith. London: Macmillan, 1986.

Was ist Aufklärung? Aufsätze zur Geschichte und Philosophie. Göttingen: Vandenhoeck & Ruprecht, 1985.

On History. Ed. and trans. Lewis White Beck. London: Macmillan, 1963.

Gesammelte Schriften. Preussische Akademie der Wissenschaften. Berlin: Georg Reimer, 1913–42.

Kern, Iso. *Husserl und Kant. Eine Untersuchung über Husserls Verhältnis zu Kant und zum Neukantianismus.* The Hague: Martinus Nijhoff, 1964.

Kimmerle, Heinz. "Das Verhältnis Schleiermachers zum transzendentalen Idealismus." *Kant-Studien,* vol. 51, nos. 1–4, 1959–60, 410–426.

Kisiel, Theodore. *The Genesis of Heidegger's "Being and Time."* Berkeley: University of California Press, 1993.

Kompridis, Nikolas (ed.). *Philosophical Romanticisms.* London: Routledge, 2006.

Lafont, Cristina. *Heidegger, Language, and World-Disclosure.* Trans. Graham Harman. Cambridge: Cambridge University Press, 2000.

The Linguistic Turn in Hermeneutic Philosophy. Trans. José Medina. Cambridge, Mass.: MIT Press, 1999.

Larmore, Charles. *The Romantic Legacy.* New York: Columbia University Press, 1996.

Macann, Christopher (ed.). *Martin Heidegger: Critical Assessments.* 4 vols. London: Routledge, 1992.

Makkreel, Rudolf A. *Imagination and Interpretation in Kant: The Hermeneutical Import of the "Critique of Judgment."* Chicago: University of Chicago Press, 1990.

Dilthey: Philosopher of the Human Studies. Princeton: Princeton University Press, 1975.

Malpas, Jeff, Ulrich Arnswald, and Jens Kertscher (eds.). *Gadamer's Century: Essays in Honor of Hans-Georg Gadamer.* Cambridge, Mass.: MIT Press, 2002.

Margolis, Joseph. "Schleiermacher among the Theorists of Language and Interpretation." *The Journal of Aesthetics and Art Criticism,* summer 1987, 361–368.

Mariña, Jacqueline (ed.). *The Cambridge Companion to Schleiermacher.* Cambridge: Cambridge University Press, 2005.

Matthews, Gareth B. *Thought's Ego in Augustine and Descartes.* Ithaca: Cornell University Press, 1992.

McDowell, John. "Response to Rüdiger Bubner." In Smith 2002, 296–297.

Mind and World. Cambridge, Mass.: Harvard University Press, 1994.

Menn, Stephen. *Descartes and Augustine.* Cambridge: Cambridge University Press, 1998.

Mulhall, Stephen. *Inheritance and Originality: Wittgenstein, Heidegger, Kierkegaard.* Oxford: Clarendon Press, 2001.

On Being in the World: Wittgenstein and Heidegger on Seeing Aspects. London: Routledge, 1990.

Norton, Robert E. *Secret Germany: Stefan George and his Circle.* Ithaca: Cornell University Press, 2002.

The Beautiful Soul: Aesthetic Morality in the Eighteenth Century. Ithaca: Cornell University Press, 1995.
Herder's Aesthetics and the European Enlightenment. Ithaca: Cornell University Press, 1991.
Novalis (Friedrich von Hardenberg). "Miscellaneous Remarks (Excerpts)." In J. Bernstein 2003, 203–213.
Werke. Ed. Gerhard Schulz. Munich: Verlag C.H. Beck, 1987.
Nowak, Kurt. *Schleiermacher. Leben, Werk und Wirkung.* Göttingen: Vandenhoeck & Ruprecht, 2001.
Schleiermacher und die Frühromantik. Eine literaturgeschichtliche Studie zum romantischen Religionsverständnis und Menschenbild am Ende des 18. Jahrhunderts in Deutschland. Göttingen: Vandenhoeck & Ruprecht, 1986.
Ormiston, Gayle L. and Alan D. Schrift (eds.). *The Hermeneutic Tradition: From Ast to Ricoeur.* Albany, N.Y.: SUNY Press, 1990.
Orth, Ernst Wolfgang (ed.). *Dilthey und die Philosophie der Gegenwart.* Freiburg: Karl Alber, 1985.
Oz-Salzberger, Fania. *Translating the Enlightenment: Scottish Civic Discourse in Eighteenth-Century Germany.* Oxford: Oxford University Press, 1995.
Palmer, Richard E. and Diane Michelfelder (eds.). *Dialogue and Deconstruction.* Albany, N.Y.: SUNY Press, 1989.
Pascal, Roy. *Shakespeare in Germany 1740–1815.* New York: Octagon Books, 1971.
Patsch, Hermann. *Alle Menschen sind Künstler. Friedrich Schleiermachers poetische Versuche.* Schleiermacher-Archiv, vol. II. Ed. H. Fischer, H.-J. Birkner, G. Ebeling, and K.-V. Selge. Berlin: Walter de Gruyter, 1986.
Perkins, Robert L. (ed.). *History and System: Hegel's Philosophy of History.* Albany, N.Y.: SUNY Press, 1984.
Pinkard, Terry. *Hegel's Phenomenology: The Sociality of Reason.* Cambridge: Cambridge University Press, 1996.
Pippin, Robert. "Gadamer's Hegel." In Malpas *et al.*, 2002, 217–238.
Hegel's Idealism: The Satisfaction of Self-Consciousness. Cambridge: Cambridge University Press, 1989.
Pöggeler, Otto. "Hegels Kritik der Romantik." Bonn: Friedrich Wilhelms-Universität, 1956. (Dissertation.)
Pöggeler, Otto and Annemarie Gethmann-Siefert (eds.). *Kunsterfahrung und Kulturpolitik im Berlin Hegels. Hegel-Studien*, vol. XXII. Bonn: Bouvier, 1983.
Ricoeur, Paul. "Kant and Husserl." In Bernet *et al.* 2005, vol. I, 320–344.
"Schleiermacher's Hermeneutics." *The Monist*, vol. 60, no. 2, 1977, 181–197.
Rieger, Reinhold. *Interpretation und Wissen. Zur philosophischen Begründung der Hermeneutik bei Friedrich Schleiermacher und ihrem geschichtlichen Hintergrund. Schleiermacher-Archiv*, vol. VI. Ed. H. Fischer H.-J. Birkner, G. Ebeling, H. Kimmerle, and K.-V. Selge. Berlin: Walter de Gruyter, 1988.
Rilke, Rainer Maria. *New Poems.* Ed. and trans. Edward Snow. New York: North Point Press, 2001.
Die Gedichte. Frankfurt am Main: Insel Verlag, 1992.
Rorty, Amélie Oksenberg (ed.). *Essays on Descartes' "Meditations."* Berkeley: University of California Press, 1986.

Rorty, Richard. *Consequences of Pragmatism.* Hertfordshire: Harvester Wheat-
    sheaf, 1991.
    Essays on Heidegger and Others. Philosophical Papers, vol. II. Cambridge:
    Cambridge University Press, 1991.
    Contingency, Irony, and Solidarity. Cambridge: Cambridge University Press, 1989.
    Philosophy and the Mirror of Nature. Oxford: Basil Blackwell, 1980.
Rorty, Richard, J. B. Schneewind, and Quentin Skinner (eds.). *Philosophy in
    History.* Cambridge: Cambridge University Press, 1984.
Scheibler, Ingrid. *Gadamer: Between Heidegger and Habermas.* Lanham: Rowman &
    Littlefield, 2000.
Schiller, Friedrich. *On the Aesthetic Education of Man.* Bilingual edition. Trans.
    Elizabeth M. Wilkinson and L. A. Willoughby. Oxford: Clarendon Press,
    1982.
Schlegel, Friedrich. *Kritische und theoretische Schriften.* Stuttgart: Reclam, 1978.
    Lucinde and the Fragments. Trans. Peter Firchow. Minneapolis: University of
    Minnesota Press, 1971.
Schleiermacher, Friedrich. *Kritische Gesamtausgabe.* Berlin: Walter de Gruyter,
    1984–.
    Lectures on Philosophical Ethics. Ed. Robert B. Louden. Trans. Louise Adey
    Huish. Cambridge: Cambridge University Press, 2002.
    "On the Different Methods of Translating." Trans. Susan Bernofsky. In
    Venuti 2002, 43–64.
    Hermeneutics and Criticism. Ed. and trans. Andrew Bowie. Cambridge: Cam-
    bridge University Press, 1998.
    Dialectic or, the Art of Doing Philosophy: A Study Edition of the 1811 Notes. Ed. and
    trans. Terrence Tice. Atlanta: Scholars Press, 1996.
    Hermeneutik und Kritik. Ed. Manfred Frank. Frankfurt am Main: Suhrkamp
    Verlag, 1993.
    Christmas Eve. Trans. Terrence N. Tice. San Francisco: EM Texts, 1991.
    *Ethik (1812/1813) mit späteren Fassungen der Einleitung, Güterlehre und
    Pflichtenlehre.* Ed. Hans-Joachim Birkner. Hamburg: Felix Meiner, 1990.
    Dialektik. Ed. Rudolf Odebrecht. Darmstadt: Wissenschaftliche Buch-
    gesellschaft, 1988.
    On Religion: Speeches to its Cultured Despisers. Trans. Richard Crouter. Cam-
    bridge: Cambridge University Press, 1988.
    Dialektik (1811). Ed. Andreas Arndt. Hamburg: Felix Meiner, 1986.
    "Die allgemeine Hermeneutik" (1809–1810). Ed. Wolfgang Virmond.
    Schleiermacher-Archiv. Band I, Teilband 2. Ed. H. Fischer, H.-J. Birkner,
    G. Ebeling, H. Kimmerle, and K.-V. Selge. *Internationaler Schleiermacher-
    Kongreß 1984.* Berlin: Walter de Gruyter, 1985, 1271–1310.
    Ästhetik (1819/25). Über den Begriff der Kunst (1831/32). Ed. Thomas Leh-
    nerer. Hamburg: Felix Meiner, 1984.
    Hermeneutics: The Handwritten Manuscripts. Ed. Heinz Kimmerle. Trans. James
    Duke and Jack Forstman. Missoula: Scholars Press, 1977.
    Hermeneutik. Nach den Handschriften. Ed. Heinz Kimmerle. Heidelberg: Carl
    Winter, 1974.
    The Christian Faith. Various translators. New York: Harper & Row, 1963.

Geschichte der alten Philosophie. Ed. Heinrich Ritter. *Sämtliche Werke*, Dritte Abtheilung. Zur Philosophie, zweiten Bandes, erste Abtheilung. Berlin: G. Reimer, 1839.

Sämmtliche Werke. Berlin: G. Reimer, 1835–64.

Scholtz, Gunter. *Ethik und Hermeneutik. Schleiermachers Grundlegung der Geisteswissenschaften.* Frankfurt am Main: Suhrkamp Verlag, 1995.

Die Philosophie Schleiermachers. Darmstadt: Wissenschaftliche Buchgesellschaft, 1984.

"Schleiermachers Theorie der modernen Kultur mit vergleichendem Blick auf Hegel." In Pöggeler and Gethmann-Siefert 1983, 131–151.

Sedlmayr, Hans. *Art in Crisis: The Lost Center.* Trans. Brian Battershaw. Chicago: Henry Regnery, 1958.

Verlust der Mitte. Die bildende Kunst des 19. und 20. Jahrhunderts als Symptom und Symbol der Zeit. Salzburg: Otto Müller Verlag, 1951.

Seebohm, Thomas. *Hermeneutics: Method and Methodology.* Dordrecht: Kluwer Publishers, 2004.

Selge, Kurt-Victor. *Schleiermacher-Archiv.* Ed. Fischer, Hermann *et al.* Band I, Teilband 2, Internationaler Schleiermacher-Kongreß 1984. Berlin: Walter de Gruyter, 1985.

Siep, Ludwig. *Hegels Fichtekritik und die Wissenschaftslehre von 1804.* Freiburg/ Munich: Karl Alber Verlag, 1970.

Smith, Nicholas H. (ed.). *Reading McDowell: On "Mind and World."* London: Routledge, 2002.

Stadler, Ingrid. "The Idea of Art and of its Criticism: A Rational Reconstruction of a Kantian Doctrine." In Cohen and Guyer 1982, 195–218.

Stern, Robert. *Hegel and the "Phenomenology of Spirit".* London: Routledge, 2002.

Stewart, John. "Schleiermacher's Visit to Copenhagen in 1833." *Zeitschrift für neuere Theologiegeschichte,* vol. 11, no. 2, 2004, 279–302.

Szondi, Peter. *Celan-Studies.* Trans. Susan Bernofsky. Stanford: Stanford University Press, 2003.

On Textual Understanding and Other Essays. Trans. Harvey Mendelsohn. Minneapolis: University of Minnesota Press, 1986.

Celan-Studien. Frankfurt am Main: Suhrkamp Verlag, 1972.

"L'herméneutique de Schleiermacher." Trans. S. Buguet. *Poétique* 2, 1970, 141–155.

Taminiaux, Jacques. *Poetics, Speculation, and Judgment.* Ed. and Trans. Michael Gendre. Albany, N.Y.: SUNY Press, 1993.

Heidegger and the Project of Fundamental Ontology. Ed. and trans. Michael Gendre. Albany, N.Y.: SUNY Press, 1991.

Lectures de l'ontologie fondamentale. Essais sur Heidegger. Grenoble: Jérôme Millon, 1989.

Tatarkiewicz, Wladyslaw. *A History of Six Ideas: An Essay in Aesthetics.* Trans. Christopher Kasparek. The Hague: Martinus Nijhoff, 1980.

Taylor, Charles. "Gadamer on the Human Sciences." In Dostal 2002, 126–142.

Sources of the Self: The Making of the Modern Identity. Cambridge: Cambridge University Press, 1989.

Tugendhat, Ernst. "Heidegger's Idea of Truth." Trans. Christopher Macann. In
    Macann 1992, vol. III, 79–92.
Philosophische Aufsätze. Frankfurt am Main: Suhrkamp Verlag, 1992.
Vasari, Giorgio. *The Lives of the Painters, Sculptors and Architects.* 2 vols. Ed.
    William Gaunt. Trans. A. B. Hinds. London: Dent & Sons, 1963.
Vattimo, Gianni. "Hermeneutics and Nihilism: An Apology for Aesthetic Con-
    sciousness." In Wachterhauser 1986, 446–459.
Venuti, Lawrence (ed.). *The Translation Studies Reader.* London: Routledge,
    2002.
The Translator's Invisibility: A History of Translation. London: Routledge, 1995.
Virmond, Wolfgang. "Neue Textgrundlagen zu Schleiermachers früher Her-
    meneutik. Prolegomena zur kritischen Edition." In Selge 1985, 575–590.
Wach, Joachim. *Das Verstehen. Grundzüge einer Geschichte der hermeneutischen
    Theorie im 19. Jahrhundert.* 3 vols. Tübingen: J. C. B. Mohr, 1926–1933.
Wachterhauser, Brice R. *Beyond Being.* Evanston: Northwestern University Press,
    1999.
    (ed.). *Hermeneutics and Truth.* Evanston: Northwestern University Press, 1994.
    (ed.). *Hermeneutics and Modern Philosophy.* Albany, N.Y.: SUNY Press, 1986.
Weinsheimer, Joel C. *Gadamer's Hermeneutics.* New Haven: Yale University Press,
    1985.
Wilhelmy, Petra. *Der Berliner Salon im 19. Jahrhundert (1780–1914).* Berlin:
    Walter de Gruyter, 1989.
Williams, Bernard. *Descartes: The Project of Pure Enquiry.* London: Penguin, 1978.
Wood, Allen. *Hegel's Ethical Thought.* Cambridge: Cambridge University Press,
    1991.
Zammito, John. *The Genesis of Kant's "Critique of Judgment."* Chicago: University
    of Chicago Press, 1992.
Ziolkowski, Theodore. *Clio the Romantic Muse: Historicizing the Faculties in
    Germany.* Ithaca: Cornell University Press, 2004.

INDEX

Note on the index: Proper names such as Gadamer, Heidegger, Kant, Hegel, and Schleiermacher occur too frequently to warrant exhaustive index entries. I have referenced only the main discussions of these philosophers. The same applies to frequently discussed concepts such as understanding, interpretation, judgment, taste, truth, knowledge, reason etc.

CPSIA information can be obtained
at www.ICGtesting.com
Printed in the USA
LVHW081629020522
717705LV00014B/745